athousandtearsfromhome.com

A Thousand Tears *from* Home

A Thousand Tears *from* Home

Gordon Baker

ISBN 978-1-940982-46-5
Library of Congress number: Pending

Publisher:

Media 14:36 Inc.
PO Box 447
Agawam, MA 01001

Website: Media1436.com

Tasman
Sea

N

Tararua
Forest Park

Waikanae

Masterton

Riversdale Beach

Upper Hutt

Wellington

Martinborough

Te Awaite

Pacific
Ocean

Lower North Island, New Zealand,
including Wairarapa District

Dedication.

To my wife Tricia. Her patience, love, and loyalty through many years of marriage have been inestimable, undeserved. Her comments and suggestions for this tale make it a much better book. She is my best critic and encourager.

Acknowledgements.

I am indebted to many friends for helpful comments and suggestions. Among them are: -

Jen Woodring
Pat Butler of OM Arts International
Doris Fleming
Lindsey Jarvi
Scott Tompkins of YWAM
My sister Kathy Thomas
Larry and Linda Gallupe
My brother Stan Baker for various items of research
Dr. Duane Kellogg, formerly Director of Renew
Counseling Associates, Connecticut

The photograph of the Tararua Range on the front cover, was taken from Burnetts Road, west of Masterton. Used by kind permission of Chris Picking, Starry Night Photography.

To my friend Lillian, who also appears on the front cover.

Foreword

This is the story of two women, very different, though joined by a common bond of faith. Tragedy marks both their lives, leaving each of them scarred. Each plays a part in the other's journey towards healing.

The story also represents a point of view on Christian romance. I hope it will contribute to the discussion that continues to swirl around that subject. I note just one factor that seems absent from the discussion, probably because it is less well known, namely the recent neurochemical evidence supporting the view taken in this tale.

Read, ponder, enjoy!

Gordon Baker
Connecticut
September, 2018.

Chapter 1

Te Whiti.

June, 1971.

"Bagley! Just look at you! Your paws are all wet!"
Bagley was Alexi's second-best teddy bear, but he went
everywhere with her. She pulled him up to straddle her hip, as her
mum did with her sister Hannah.

Alexi stood facing the snow-covered Tararua peaks just
west of her home, the early morning sunlight pouring over her
shoulders. The field in which she stood was lush green, though
overlaid just now with white, sparkling frost. The longer stems
especially sent back multi-colored fragments of light.

Along the boundary fence to her right, and also along the
road boundary in front of her, clumps of daffodils and white-gold
jonquils spread their gladness. Two miles away, a band of white
mist crossed her line of vision, marking the rift where, hidden
from view, the Ruamahanga River was joined by the Waingawa,
the two clear streams splashing, mingling, gurgling on their way
south to Lake Wairarapa.

Alexi's mother, Kathy, was inside at the stove, fixing
breakfast for her family. The dread struck her again.

"Alexi! Where is she?" Kathy dropped what she was
doing, and ran to the front bedroom, where the windows
commanded a view of the place Alexi usually stood. There she
was, placidly telling Bagley about the snow, the flowers, the
clouds, the rabbits. Kathy sank back, crumpling onto the bed.

"That stab of fear again?" Her husband Eric had
followed her into the room. He raised her to her feet, arms around

1

her.

"Eric, why do I get these panic feelings? She's perfectly alright!" Eric pushed a strand of hair back from her eyes. "I think it must be because she'll be off to school soon. Maybe I'm afraid of losing her. But that's silly!"

"You said last night that Auntie Aggie is somehow mixed up in these feelings."

Kathy sighed. "Yes, it seems she's connected somehow. But that's silly too. Aggie's a bit strange, but really, she's kind, she's .... oh, you can see her goodness in her eyes. Eric, I'm sorry. It's embarrassing!"

"It's okay Kathy my love. Probably being pregnant is playing havoc with your hormones, making you feel over-protective. Come on, let's finish getting the breakfast on."

*

As the sunlight strengthened, brightening the fields beyond the road, reaching across the dark green of the beech-covered foothills, the mountain peaks stood pure dazzling white against the bright blue of the sky beyond.

Long before she learned the words to describe the scene, its aching beauty was etched on Alexi's heart.

"Oh, the chickens!" she remembered, "I have to feed the chickens before breakfast." She was turning towards the house when a glint of brilliant purple caught her attention, the sunlight splintering from a frosted stalk. "Jesus, thank you for making the pretty colors. I wish they would stay there all day, instead of going away when the ol' sun dries up the frost! And thank you for the mountains!"

She looked again at the mountain peaks, white, strong, almost murmuring with their own life, yet silent, distant, at rest. Her eyes swept the sky for a last glimpse of two hawks poised distantly in the blue reaches above her, then turned and ran to the gate in the garden fence.

Alexi's five-year birthday was not quite three weeks away – she couldn't wait, because that meant she would begin

2

school. School would be a wonderful world of fun, and stories, and writing, and other children to play with. But it meant that she had to attend to the chickens before breakfast. Soon there wouldn't be time to leave them until later.

The gate was on a spring, so it clicked nicely closed again when someone used it. Alexi reached through the hand-opening to find the latch, swung the gate open, then ran on up the path towards the front door of the house, her blue gumboots making satisfying clomping sounds. She ran up the steps onto the wide deck encircling the house, made a right turn, and continued round to the back door. In a farmhouse, you didn't use the front door except on special occasions. Instead you went to the back door, and left your outdoor boots in the porch, before going on into the kitchen.

"You been out with Bagley, feeding grass to Old Joe?" asked her mum. She was back in front of the stove, fixing scrambled eggs and bacon. Old Joe was the aged stallion they kept in the home paddock. "Be quick with the chickens dear! Breakfast is nearly ready!" The fear was receding again for now, but some anxiety still showed in her glance.

"Yes Mum," answered Alexi. She left Bagley beside her stool at the kitchen table, then took the egg basket from its place beside the refrigerator.

"Ol' Joe was down the end, under the willow tree," she called as she went out again. Alexi pushed her feet back into her gumboots, then ran to pick several large silver beet leaves from the garden behind the house. Her dad said chickens like silver beet, and it makes the yolks of their eggs nice and yellow.

Inside the coop, the chickens came cackling, crowding around her. "Polly, you just wait your turn!" admonished Alexi, as one brown-red bird pushed the others aside. When the mornings were warmer, she would wear sandals instead of gumboots, enjoying the feel of smooth plumage against her legs. She lifted the lid of the grain bin, and scattered two scoops of the mixed wheat and barley onto the dirt floor. She watched the scratching, pecking chickens for a few minutes, before dropping the silver beet leaves among them.

"All things bright and beautiful,
All creatures great and small,
All things wise and wonderful,
The Lord God made them all."

As she gathered eggs into her egg basket, Alexi sang the verse she had learned at her Sunday School at Carrington Church. She knew she was one of the "creatures small," and felt herself to be part of a "wise and wonderful" creation.

"The purple-headed mountain,
The river running by."

So, began the next verse. Alexi's experience had not yet imprinted the picture of distant mountains presenting mauve tints, so she imagined mountains with bright purple tops, like the bright purple color in her paint box. She'd never seen such mountains, even in pictures, but she knew they must exist somewhere, because the song talked about them.

She did know about the "river running by". Alexi, along with her mum and dad, and two-year-old sister Hannah, had spent hours playing and splashing at the edge of the river. Sometimes her dad would hold her close, and take her out to the deeper parts, where the current swirled and tugged at them both. Alexi thought the Ruamahunga must be a very big river; she was glad that her dad was there, keeping her safe. And already, she had a real awareness of "the Lord God [who] made them all."

Eric and Kathy Paynter called their home "Shepherd's Rest." Situated at Te Whiti, just south of the Wairarapa District's principal town of Masterton, it was the twenty-acre remnant of an early sheep station. The old woolshed, and several of the early buildings were still in useable condition, and Eric and Kathy had poured cash, time, and hard work into renovating the original homestead. It was now a snug, modern home. Around the buildings, stands of totara, maire, and beech, together with willows along the stream, all made their contribution to the motif of peace and rest.

"Lexi! You finished feeding the chickens? Breakfast is

ready!" This time it was her dad calling. She let herself out of the coop and ran back to the house. Moments later, she was sliding onto her stool beside Hannah. She eyed her plate of scrambled eggs, small rasher of bacon, her toast, and her glass of orange juice.

"Lexi, would you give thanks for our breakfast please?" Peace had descended again on Kathy's heart. She smiled at her daughter.

Alexi bowed her head and brought her hands up over her eyes. "Thank you God, for the new big day, and the sky, and the daff'dils, and for Ol' Joe, and for those two ol' hawks out looking for bunnies." Alexi usually gave a summary of the latest images she had absorbed. She bubbled with gratitude for all the special things that filled her young life, but sometimes forgot that thanks for breakfast was the immediate focus. Just in time she remembered.

"Thank you, God, for our chickens and the nice eggs and the bacon. Thank you that Mum made our breakfast that we can all eat. Amen."

Eric and Kathy exchanged a smiling glance over the bowed heads. Old Joe was often mentioned in Alexi's thanksgiving. Both girls liked to pick fresh, green grass for him, Hannah especially giggling when his lips came down to snuffle up her offering.

During breakfast, Alexi's thought shifted. "Mum, can I go to school now?"

"Lexi, you know you still have nearly three weeks before your birthday. And anyway, your baby brother or sister will be here before then. Mum could be off to the hospital any day now, so that's the next thing to look forward to."

Kathy loved being pregnant, but her delivery was close now, and she was tired of being tired and heavy. Alexi nodded. Yes, she was very excited at the thought of helping Mum with their new baby, and even thoughts of school were eclipsed momentarily.

"Mum, how does baby decide when he wants to be born? Why's he taking so long?"

Alexi had decided that the new baby would be a brother.

5

Privately, Kathy thought she was right, but wasn't making any promises.

"I don't know honey. I guess he just knows. He'll decide to join us any day now."

Kathy's pregnancy was a great time for Alexi to be learning about bodies and babies. Kathy and Eric wanted their children to grow up unembarrassed but respectful about the wonder of their own bodies, and Alexi's vocabulary included correct anatomical names, which she was unabashed about using. The next step was for her to learn that personal references are fine within the family, but needed more restraint elsewhere.

Eric returned to the subject of school. "Lexi, I'm so pleased you're taking charge of the chickens before breakfast. That's helping you to be ready for school. Now you're getting such a big girl."

Alexi's eyes glowed at her dad's praise. "There were seven eggs this morning," she said proudly. When she had as many as six or seven to show, it felt like her own personal achievement.

"Those are fine eggs." Eric glanced at the egg basket. "You're doing a great job!"

He stood up. "Time for me to be away," he said. He walked to the other end of the table and kissed the top of Kathy's head. "Look after yourself precious. Call me the moment anything happens."

"Oh no, I'll just get myself off to delivery!" Kathy teased. "I might remember to call you when it's all over."

"Suit yourself Mumma," he teased back. He looked at his two daughters. "Alright you beautiful ladies, look after your mum while I'm not here. God bless you!" Moments later they could hear his pickup crunching the gravel driveway until it reached the road. Eric's job was in Masterton, as an assistant manager with Wairarapa Transport. He was proud of his company, one of the most modern trucking firms in the nation. The *Times Age* had published his photograph recently, when the company took delivery of two new rigs, each capable of carrying seven hundred and fifty lambs.

Kathy regarded the breakfast remnants on her daughters'

faces and fingers. "Hannah, Alexi, let's get breakfast cleaned up. And you cleaned up! This morning is the Young Mum's group at the church, so we need to get ourselves ready."

"Church," Hannah repeated. "Sandbox. Timmy."

"Yes," Kathy responded, "I expect Timmy will be there. And I expect the two of you will make a splendid mess in the sandbox again."

Alexi was swirling the last of her orange juice in its glass. The mention of church had prompted a new thought in her mind too. "Mum," she asked, "Is Auntie Aggie a witch?"

*

And now gentle reader, we leap back more than twenty years to trace the life of that very same Aggie. We leave Kathy startled, pondering, and Alexi swirling her orange juice. We'll be gone for some time, so let's hope she doesn't spill it before we meet her again.

Chapter 2

Aggie Betteridge.

Post WWII.

Agnes Betteridge ran her fingers over the deep red birthmark on the left side of her face. It began near her earlobe, and ran upwards towards her hairline. Near the top, the skin was roughened, less smooth than the rest of her face. Agnes was small-framed, like her mother, with the same dark brown hair. If it wasn't for the birthmark, people might have thought her pretty, with her clear skin, her grey eyes, and the slight turn-up to her nose. Even as she emerged from babyhood, there was something a little mysterious, out of the ordinary, about Agnes.

She sighed, and thought of her father, whose photograph stood on the mantlepiece. Martin Betteridge joined the Second New Zealand Division late in the Second World War. He departed for the front as First Lieutenant, and was promoted twice in the field to Major, before a shell claimed his life in the Battle of Monte Cassino.

Martin never saw his daughter Agnes. Helen, his widow, grieved terribly for her husband, and poured herself into being the best provider and mother she could be for her precious daughter. Major Betteridge was awarded the Military Cross for his personal supervision of an heroic rearguard action, delaying the enemy while two of his companies made a tactical withdrawal from a hillside under fire. The award was approved, but Major Betteridge did not live to receive his medal.

Early in 1946, just after Agnes' second birthday, Helen received in her mailbox in Pokohiwi Road, Masterton, an official-looking letter, requesting her presence at Government House, Wellington, to receive the medal her husband never saw.

"Oh my! All those important people, all that pomp and

ceremony!" But any hesitation vanished immediately. "Of course, I'll go to receive Martin's medal! My man won that medal! I'm so very proud of him!" Her wardrobe was limited, but she did have the cream-colored suit that would do very well. Helen was a demure twenty-two-year-old, but those who noticed saw strength and courage behind her pretty features.

Hesitation gripped her again when her turn came to walk forward between the files of the honor guard, two rows of men drawn from each of the services, all resplendent in their dress uniforms. But no-one saw that momentary pause, as her head came up, and she stepped confidently forward, Mrs. Major Betteridge! As she reached the front of the room, her heart nearly burst with pride, as Governor General Sir Cyril Newall, Marshal of the Royal Air Force, snapped to attention before her and smartly saluted. Approval leapt into Newall's eyes as he watched her stiffen to attention, the correct form of salute for a non-uniformed person. "The young major had a worthy wife" - the thought flickered through his mind as he reached to shake her hand.

The Military Cross, in its little wooden case, occupied pride of place on Helen's mantelpiece, along with her husband's photograph. One of her regrets was that she did not have a photograph of him in his major's uniform. Photographers were in short supply in the mountains of Italy, probably at the best of times, but certainly during those last bitter months of World War Two. But she did have a fine picture of him, taken three days before he embarked for Europe, looking strong and handsome as First Lieutenant.

Agnes grew up knowing that her father had been a brave man. She thought he looked very nice in the photograph. From the stories she heard from her mother, her ideas of strength and leadership, kindness, integrity, and courage formed around the face that looked out from their mantelpiece. She knew that the medal had been given to her father because he had risked his own life to save the men under his command. She knew that if he were here, he would protect her. As she learned to read, she knew that the word "first" was spelled "1st", because that was how it appeared beneath her father's photograph. She did not discover

9

the equivalence of "first" for at least a year after she could read the inscriptions on the medal case and the photograph.

*

No-one quite knew how or when "Agnes" changed to "Aggie". Helen never called her daughter anything but Agnes. But to everyone else, she was Aggie for about as long as anyone could remember. Perhaps it was because the teasing over her appearance started very early. Toddlers looked at her birthmark with unabashed curiosity.

"Mummy, why does she have that funny mark on her face?"

"Hush dear! She is a very nice little girl!"

But surprisingly early, ingenuous curiosity became tinged with mockery. "Ooh. You have a nasty patch on your face!"

Even the adults, trying to cover for the juvenile rudeness of their children, often seemed a little repulsed themselves. Parents moved quickly to disengage their children from any game or activity in which there could be body contact, with their child's face touching Aggie's.

Aggie grew up experiencing many, many hugs from her mother, and very few from anyone else. If she had been born about fifty years later, some plastic surgery could have been an option. But at that time, children usually just learned to cope.

*

Helen's day began with prayer – she thought of it as her chat time with Jesus – and with reading systematically through her battered old Bible. An equally battered hymn book sat beside her Bible, and Helen could be heard each day softly singing the hymns that lifted her heart above her daily round of concerns.

How she missed Martin at those times! His spiritual leadership had matured her own faith. Strangely though, her devotional times helped to heal the acid ache of knowing he wasn't coming back.

Helen's spiritual depth was strengthened too by her commitment to her church. Carrington Church of God, located on the east side of Masterton, and backing onto the Ruamahunga River, had proved to be a lifeline of friendship, support, and comfort to her. Helen was not especially a social person, and did not visit widely among the church folk, but the friends she did know were valued indeed.

Sunday morning, and Helen's phone jangled. It was her friend Cassie.

"Helen! It's another beautiful day! I have a picnic prepared. Can you and Aggie come with us after church, and we'll have an afternoon relaxing over on Third Creek."

Jon and Cassie Sanders raised sheep and dairy cattle on their property north east of Masterton, out towards Bideford. The property included some deep valleys that had never been cleared of the original bush, and were now havens of shade and rest on hot summer days, with bell birds, tuis, and the soft tinkle of the stream at the bottom of the valley. Jon and Cassie had many times invited Helen and Aggie home from church with them to enjoy a picnic and quiet afternoon in one of these havens. Third Creek was the name they gave to their favorite spot, a valley wide enough to include a narrow strip of grass alongside the stream, where they would set out their picnic lunch.

"Love to Cassie. And Agnes will love being among the trees and birds again. Thank you so much. I'll bring a couple of bottles of the ginger beer Agnes and I made. It's matured just right."

It would be an afternoon of conversation with Cassie, always a refreshing time. Jon would join in the conversation while they ate their lunch, and then would usually retire a little distance away, becoming immersed in a book. He was close enough to contribute an opinion on some point of discussion between Cassie and Helen if asked.

Aggie would make her way up the valley a little, and

11

then stand stock still as she took in the trees, the moss, the birds, even occasionally a deer cautiously picking its way up between the trees. She could stand that way for half an hour or more, absorbing wonders that most people never notice. Occasionally Jon would put down his book, and quietly move through the trees to find her. Then they would stand together, softly murmuring over the names, songs and flight patterns of the birds, or the appearance and foliage of the different trees.

One day, Aggie looked up at Jon. "Thank you for coming and sharing the forest with me. It's almost like having my Daddy here."

A tear started to Jon's eye. From then on, he tried to spend more time being a friend to her.

*

"Mummy!" It was bedtime, but Aggie, not quite eight years old, moved about restlessly.

"What is it Honey? Time you were in bed."

"Mummy, there's a bunny near the back fence. It's hurt. Its back leg is bleeding."

Helen stared at her daughter. "What do you mean? You haven't been down there all day. What are you talking about?"

"Mummy! There is! I …. I just kind of know there is. Can't we go help it please? Please?"

Helen stood for a moment puzzled. It wasn't like Agnes to stall with a story like this. "Get your parka on, and we'll take a quick look. Come on now!"

Aggie's eyes leapt with gratitude. She ran for her parka, slipped her feet into her yard shoes, and opened the back door, with Helen right behind her. There was just enough light left in the evening for them to see clearly. Aggie ran directly down the lawn, past the garden, to the fuchsia bush in the back right-hand corner of the property. Sure enough, a small furry form sat crouched and whimpering on the grass.

"Agnes! How …." Deep, wondering astonishment filled

Helen's heart. Even more amazingly, the frightened animal let Aggie bend down to touch it.

"Look Mummy! See the bleeding down here!" Blood matted the fur round a long gaping wound on the animal's left haunch.

"Stay with him Honey. I'll get a box we can put him in." Helen hurried to the house, and returned with a cardboard box, the bottom covered with an old towel.

Helen lifted the rabbit slowly, carefully into the box, and they both hurried inside. The kitchen table became their examination table. Helen was no vet, but she had an instinctive skill. They couldn't quite tell how the wound had occurred – perhaps some young rabbit shooter had scored a non-fatal hit.

"Give me a hug Sweetheart, and get yourself off to bed, And I'll try to make this guy comfortable. I'll put his box on the floor in the warm cupboard. Say a prayer for our bunny friend!"

So, Hop came to join the Betteridge family. Jon Sanders made a light hutch for him, which could be dragged to different places around the lawn. That way, Hop constantly had a new patch of grass to nibble, and his pellets were left to fertilize the lawn. His leg never mended fully, so Aggie never released him back into the wild. Instead, she brought him treats from the garden, and often sat watching him, admiring his silky softness, and murmuring secret thoughts to him.

From that day on, there were many examples of Aggie "seeing" things. Often it was about an earthquake – Aggie seemed to feel a tremor in the ground that no-one else felt. And sure enough, a report would come of an earthquake that had struck such and such a town. Usually, it was just a minor quake, but Helen would wonder, did the Lord use the prayers of a little girl to calm the energy of the earth?

*

It was about a year after Hop joined them – Aggie was nine. Helen awoke one night just after 11pm to find Aggie

13

standing at her bedside.

"Mummy! Mummy! There's a boat on this big wide river, and it's full of people, and it's raining ever so hard, and the boat is sinking!"

Helen was immediately wide awake, knowing that Aggie was distressed about something. "What is it Honey? What's the matter?"

"The boat's in muddy, brown water, and the people are brown too. Maybe it's in India? And the boat is broke, and it can't get to the shore, and the water's coming up all inside! Mummy we have to help them!"

"Sweetheart, we don't know where they are, and we can't go to them. But we can pray for them!"

"Yes! We need to pray for them!"

Aggie knelt beside her mother's bed, but Helen had slipped out of bed, thrown a dressing gown around her, and gone to her "prayer chair", an old rocker that stood near her bedroom window.

"Come over here Honey, and we'll pray together."

Aggie climbed into her mother's lap, and they joined voices, praying for the people in danger on some unknown river, in some unknown place, perhaps India.

"Mummy! There're babies! Some of the ladies are holding babies! And they're crying and scared! And the babies are crying!"

Mother and child renewed their prayers, crying out for rescue. Helen became aware of Aggie's voice, soft but powerful, speaking words Helen didn't understand.

Gradually Aggie's voice became quieter, until Helen thought she had nodded off to sleep. But then her daughter sat up, looking into her mother's face.

"There's another boat! With a motor. And they put a rope onto the boat with the people, and they pulled it close to the shore! And the people are jumping off, and it's shallow, 'cos they can walk up onto the land."

Aggie gave a sigh and settled her head against Helen's chest. Helen watched her daughter fall into a peaceful sleep again, hearing her breathing settle into a steady rhythm.

"What is this Lord? This precious, precious daughter you have given me ...." She struggled to understand, but could only sigh with wondering gratitude. "Lord, just help me to be the mother that she needs."

Helen was not surprised two days later to see a report in her newspaper about an overloaded ferry on the Ganges in East Pakistan. The ferry had lost power in torrential rain, and was in danger of capsizing. Eventually it had been towed to shore, without the loss of any lives.

*

Three weeks after their midnight prayer time, Helen was grateful when Aggie's gift proved useful in a very practical way. They had just taken their places in their car – Helen would take Aggie to school, before going on to Allied Garments, where she worked as a machinist. As the car backed out of the garage, Aggie said suddenly, "Mum! Stop! You left that saucepan with the meat in it on the stove. And the stove's turned on. It's getting very hot!"

They were running a little late. Helen didn't want to stop and go back just on a whim. She just knew she couldn't have left that pot on the stove with the element still turned on.

"Agnes, really! It's getting late dear! I'm sure I turned that element off and put the saucepan away." She looked at her daughter. Aggie looked frightened, and rather crushed. Helen sighed.

"Alright, I'll go have a look." She still sounded a little irritated, but she was wise enough to know she'd better check.

Two minutes later, Helen slid back into the car. "Thank you so much for telling me Sweetheart. And sorry I sounded cross. We could have had a fire if that had been left there all day."

As they pulled out onto the road and gained speed, Helen looked at Aggie. "Agnes, you are so precious to me. I love you so much."

Aggie gave her a penetrating look. "I love you too Mum." She paused. "Today is going to be a tough day for me."

"The teasing?" Helen asked. She knew Aggie suffered some teasing because of her birthmark.

Aggie nodded.

"How do you know they will tease you today?"

"I just know. Some days I just know that they will be mean to me. Other times it can be bad too, but I don't know before it starts."

Helen's heart ached. What should she do? "Do the other children ever hit you or anything like that? Or do they just use mean words?"

"Usually just silly chants and words," Aggie said. "Sometimes they might push me or bump against me. In the playground or the corridor. But usually they just say mean things." Another pause. Aggie hung her head. "Sometimes they say mean things about you or Daddy."

"What do they say about me or Daddy?" Helen demanded.

"They say that I have red on my face, so my mother and my father must be Red Indians."

Helen tried to control her rage. "Agnes, my treasure, the Red Indians are a dignified people. When those children use a worthy nation to taunt you, that is so disrespectful to them and to you! I need to make a time to talk to Mrs. Nelson."

Aggie considered. Having her Mum talk to her teacher could just make things worse. "No Mum. I can manage it. You pray for me."

In spite of herself, Helen's heart gave a jump. Her daughter's faith and courage amazed her - at nine years old, saying she could manage, but having the maturity to ask for prayer. For the ten thousandth time she looked at her daughter with wonder and gratitude. "Agnes, God bless you today."

But as she let Aggie off at her school, and continued on to Allied, she still wondered. "Lord, I don't want to be an interfering parent. But she needs some protection Lord!"

Helen felt she really did need to do something about this bullying, but she wanted to pray more about it. They surely didn't need for it to backfire on Aggie.

Helen didn't realize it, but some justice for Aggie was

closer than she thought.

Chapter 3

Persecuted.

Pauline McKnight, another friend from Carrington Church, usually picked up Aggie Betteridge from school in the afternoon, along with her own three children. Aggie would spend about an hour at their home while her mother finished her work day. Then she would take the five-minute walk home, to arrive at about the same time as Helen.

"I saw Timothy Bailey and Alex Riley looking for you at lunch time," Chelsea McKnight said to Aggie. "I guess you must have hidden from them."

Chelsea was a year older than Aggie, the oldest of the McKnight children. She had overheard the boys, two of Aggie's tormentors, planning to snatch her lunch, and throw it in the playground. But she had managed to tip Aggie off.

"Yes," replied Aggie. "I got back into the classroom while they weren't looking, and when they came back to find me, I was hiding in the supplies cupboard. It was a bit dark, but I ate my lunch in there."

Aggie liked Chelsea. She wasn't a special friend, but was one of the few who would befriend her in small ways when she could. Most of the children were too afraid of the bullies to take Aggie's side, but being a year older, Chelsea wasn't too concerned for herself.

"I thought they were pretty mad when they couldn't find you!" Chelsea laughed. "They were saying they would get you good when they found you!"

"They paid me out in art class this afternoon. I did this painting of a deer and her baby I saw, up at Third Creek. I thought it looked pretty nice – I wanted to take it home for my Mum. But Timothy and Alex came up and put red splotches all over it."

"They're so mean. I'm sorry about your painting. At least Colin isn't in your art class."

Colin Campbell was in Standard Five, so it would be another year yet before he would go on to high school. It couldn't come quickly enough for pretty much everyone in Aggie's school, including the staff. He was big boned for his age, and overweight. His achievement at the school had been chiefly to throw that weight around, inflicting cruelty on anyone weaker than himself, both children and animals.

"Yes," Aggie replied, her eyes showing the brief burst of fear that rippled through her. "He's the worst."

Pauline McKnight had some shopping to do, so she bundled her children, along with Aggie, into her car.

"I have just a few things to get," she said as they pulled into the supermarket car park. "Let's stay close together, and when we're done here, we'll go over to the ice cream garden." She bought ice cream just often enough that it remained a special treat. She knew that Aggie did not often get such treats, so she tried to spoil them all a little when Aggie was with them.

A few minutes later, they all sat at a rustic outdoor table, comparing their ice cream flavors. Pauline was watching Aggie.

"Lord," she thought, "She really is a strange mixture, this little treasure. So shy, so quiet, so .... what is it? Sad? Yes, sad. Yet there's something else that balances the sadness. No, not quite balances the sadness. A sort of wisdom or strength. Thank you, Lord, that I can treat her. She looked so grateful when she thanked me for the ice cream."

They all licked and nibbled until the last of ice cream and cone had disappeared. "Everyone done?" asked Pauline. "Run over to the tap to wash your sticky hands, and we'll be off. Aggie, it's nearly four o'clock, so we'll drop you off at your house on the way home. Your Mum should be home any minute."

Aggie nodded okay. "Thank you, Mrs. McKnight. It was a lovely ice cream." It was a comfort to her to spend time with the McKnight family. The children didn't seem to fight much among themselves, and they were genuinely friendly to her. Their acceptance, together with the ice cream, helped to sooth her troubled heart. But the ache and hurt of the day still pierced into her spirit as she let herself into the house.

*

Helen felt agitated as she left work. She'd been thinking of Aggie all day, and wondered how she'd managed. Had the day been a tough one, as Aggie had predicted? She wanted to be home as early as she could, but there had been a question about her machine maintenance that had held her up, so that she was late leaving, instead of early.

"Hello, I'm home," Helen called as she came into the kitchen. No response. She skirted round the kitchen table, and into the passageway, intending to walk down to Aggie's bedroom. But as she passed the door of the lounge room, she saw her daughter in the middle of the floor.

Aggie sat with her left knee bent up under her chin. Her right knee was bent a little to the side, the foot tucked in behind her left ankle. In front of her, near her right knee, stood her father's photograph. Beside it lay the Military Cross in its little case.

As Helen came into the room, she could see a single tear in the corner of each of Aggie's eyes. Each tear slowly made its way down her cheek, breaking up over the corners of her mouth. She was unaware of her mother entering the room until she felt Helen's hand on her head. She reached back her hand, and rested it on her mother's foot.

"Mummy, Daddy was a good man wasn't he?"

"Yes dearest. He was a very good man."

"He didn't do mean things to people, did he?"

"No Agnes, he didn't."

"I'm glad he married you. You liked him very much didn't you?"

Helen dropped to her knees beside Aggie, her arm resting round her daughter's shoulders. "Yes Sweetheart, I liked him very much. I loved him!" Her own tears started, but from Aggie there came just the slow march of one tear, followed at an interval by another.

They stayed side by side, Helen giving Aggie's

shoulder a little squeeze every now and again. "What happened today?" she asked at last.

"Aw, it wasn't so bad," Aggie said. "Timothy and Alex tried to take my lunch off me, but I hid from them. I hid in the cupboard in the classroom while I ate my lunch. I liked the tuna sandwich you made! Thank you!"

Helen thought of her daughter sitting in a dark cupboard, isolated from the other children. Yes, she definitely had to do something.

"It's not right that you have to sit in a cupboard to eat your lunch, away from the other children!" She paused. "Anything else Sweetheart?"

"Well, just in art class. I did this painting of a deer with her baby, up at Third Creek. I thought it was pretty, and I was going to bring it home for you. But they came and put splotches of red paint on it."

Helen regarded Aggie gravely. "I'm sorry they spoiled your painting. I would love to have seen it. In fact, I'm sad and angry at the way you're treated."

Aggie looked at her mother. "I was a bit sad too," she said. "But it's okay." She was going to add, "They've done worse before." But she didn't want to recount older trials. She thought her mother might get angrier, and try to get Timothy and Alex into trouble. Aggie would like to see them reined in, but her way was to pull back as much as possible, and let the storm pass over her.

Aggie stood, picked up the photo and medal, and went out to the kitchen to put them back on the mantlepiece.

"I'll go do my homework Mum." She was just beginning to drop "Mummy" in favor of "Mum".

Helen stood at the kitchen counter, preparing dinner, while she planned what hours she could take off work to go over to the school.

*

Two days later Helen sat across the desk from Mr. Bradley, the principal at Aggie's school.

"Mrs.Betteridge, I know that Agnes has suffered some bullying for some time." He transitioned to using Aggie's correct name while talking with her mother. "I didn't know that her lunch was being interfered with. And the incident in the art class is just unacceptable. Thank you for coming to tell me of your concerns. We do have some children in the school who tax our patience. I can see that a tougher line is going to be needed for some of them."

Helen smiled gratefully. "I've mentioned to Agnes several times that I would come talk to her teacher, but she hasn't wanted me to. She just says she can manage it. She doesn't know I'm here now."

"Agnes is a courageous girl," replied Mr. Bradley. "She's a very good student, and her teachers speak highly of her. This school should be a welcoming place for her, and for all our students. I'll talk with Mrs. Nelson to see what else she's noticed in the classroom. And I want to talk with the school board to ensure I have their backing for any measures I may have to take."

Helen almost demurred. It seemed she may be setting in motion something more severe than she had intended. "But Martin would have protected her," she thought. "He would have done whatever was necessary."

"Thank you, Mr. Bradley," she replied. "I just don't want to see Agnes suffer any more through all this."

"I will personally see that she is protected." Mr. Bradley found himself admiring this quiet woman for her strength, hard work, and courage.

*

The school board met on Wednesday evening. Mr. Bradley thanked the members for coming out at short notice.

"Young Colin Campbell is a name you've heard before in regard to bullying in the school. He's still one to be watched carefully, but more recently he's found some lieutenants. Now he's making the bullets, and goading others into firing them. The two Riley boys, Alex and James, and Timothy Bailey are among his recruits. There are a few others, including three or four girls, who need to be confronted. The main target at present is the Betteridge girl, the one with the birthmark on the left side of her face."

The discussion didn't last long. Two board members were concerned about an over-reaction to the problem, but overall, the board agreed that the issue needed to be faced with strength, before it escalated further.

*

It was the next day, Thursday. The school was at morning break, with children running and playing throughout the playground.

Mr. Bradley sometimes made a tour of the grounds during the morning break. As he walked he would note the loners among his students, the exuberant and the aggressive. It was a way of keeping in touch with the heartbeat of the school. On this day, he had walked down the front of a block of classrooms, rounded its end wall, and was about to turn down the back wall of the block. As he reached the corner of the building, his attention was caught by Colin Campbell. Colin was intently watching something still obscured from sight by the corner of the building, his face reflecting malicious delight in whatever it was he saw.

"Yeah, you get her Timmy! Slap her nasty face!" Colin called. "You next Kelly!"

Mr. Bradley took another step forward, and the object of Colin's interest came into view. A small girl was sitting on the ground. Her right knee was bent, pushed a little to the side, her left knee drawn up under her chin. A single tear ran down each of her cheeks. Around her stood a ring of six jeering and chanting children.

"Funny red face! Father's an Injun, mother's a stinkin'

23

squaw!"

Mr. Bradley was just in time to see Kelly Stephenson break from the ring and run past Aggie Betteridge, slapping her head as she went.

Colin saw Mr. Bradley moments before the rest of the group. Immediately his face wore a look of nonchalant unconcern, as though whatever else was going on had nothing to do with him. He made no cry to warn the rest of the tormentors – they could catch whatever was coming to them so far as he cared. Kelly's new position in the ring of children gave her a sight of Mr. Bradley. A cry went up, and the children scattered and ran. Mr. Bradley strode forward to where Aggie sat. He crouched so that his head was only just higher than hers, and reached his hand to tip her face up to look at him.

"Come with me Aggie my dear. These attacks on you have stopped - as from now!" He reached for her hand to help her to her feet. "Come with me please."

He kept hold of her hand as he started walking towards his office. Colin was sauntering off with exaggerated casualness. Mr. Bradley called, "Colin, you come with me too please!"

"Why Sir? I didn't do nothin'."

"We'll talk about that in my office. Come along please."

As they reached the foyer outside the principal's office, Mr. Bradley turned first to Colin.

"Colin, please sit on the bench against the wall here. I'd like to talk with you for a few minutes, but first I need to talk with Aggie."

"Yes sir." Colin had the truculent look of a boy who has had many such interviews with his school principal.

"Aggie, does your mother still work at Allied Garments?" The school had about 350 students enrolled, but there were not many details in their files that their principal was unaware of. Having strings of siblings passing through the school, and the fact that most were enrolled for several years, made it easier.

"Yes sir."

"And she will be there at work today?"

"Yes, she is sir," replied Aggie.

Mr. Bradley turned to face the other side of the foyer where Mrs. Connors, the school receptionist and secretary, subdued all comers with her steely eyes.

"Mrs. Connors, please call Allied Garments and ask if I may speak to Mrs. Betteridge. And please keep an eye on young Mr. Campbell here."

"Of course, Mr. Bradley."

At that moment a loud buzzer sounded outside, signaling the end of the break. Mr. Bradley waited until it ended, then turned back to Mrs. Connors.

"Oh and please notify Mr. Page that I have Colin in my care here. And let Mrs. Nelson know that Aggie is with me."

He entered his office, beckoning Aggie to follow.

"Please sit on this soft chair," he told her. He took a stool and placed it in front of her, about three feet away. Settling himself on the stool, he continued, "Aggie, I know some of the other children have been bullying you, and I have been concerned about it. I was already planning to take some action to protect you, but after what I just saw, the action starts now!"

He paused, regarding the small form in front of him. The tears had ceased their slow march, but she still looked afraid. "Afraid of her persecutors, and probably a little afraid of her school principal," he thought.

"You're safe now my dear," he told her. "I'm going to make sure that things are different for you. I want you to be glad to come to school each day. Not dreading what might happen to you."

The words sounded good to Aggie, and the smile he gave her looked kind and confident. It would take a while for her to believe that she really would be safe, but her eyes softened in gratitude.

Mr. Bradley's telephone rang. He walked to his desk and sat in his swivel chair before picking up the receiver.

"Yes, hello Mrs. Betteridge. I'm so sorry to disturb you. I regret to tell you that there was another incident of bullying this morning, involving Aggie. …. Yes, she's fine, and she's safe here with me now. She's watching me speak with you. It happened during morning break. Some children had her bailed up round the back of a classroom block, and were harassing her. I'm keeping her with me for now. Mrs. Betteridge, I know this is an imposition for you, but I wonder if you could manage to come over to the school during your lunch break. I would like to discuss what is to be done. … Yes, that will be fine. I'm so sorry to trouble you with this. I'm determined to make this school safe for Aggie, and every other student. … Yes, of course. I'll see you at 12.15. Thank you."

Mr. Bradley replaced the phone receiver, sat back in his chair, and smiled again at Aggie.

"How are you feeling now Aggie?"

"I'm alright sir." Her voice was a little firmer.

"I've asked your mum to come over during her lunch hour. I want you to know, and I want her to know, that I will not tolerate any more of the behavior I saw this morning. I'm determined that the school will be a place you can be proud of."

He became thoughtful again, and shifted his gaze to his window. Eventually, he turned back to her. "Do you think you'll be alright to go back to your classroom again now?"

"Yes sir." But her voice was quiet and fearful again.

"Aggie, the bullies know something is up. They won't bother you again today. But, I'll tell you what – I would be honored if you would be our guest in the staff room at lunchtime. Would you like to bring your lunch, and come to Mrs. Connor's desk? She will take you into the staff room to be our guest. I believe there is some lemonade in the refrigerator that you might enjoy.

"Thank you, sir." Again, her eyes showed her gratitude.

Mr. Bradley stood up. "You're a brave girl Aggie. I'll be talking with your mum in my office here, but the rest of the staff will look after you. Ready to go?"

Aggie stood up, and they moved back into the foyer.

"Mrs. Connors, Aggie will be a guest of the staff at lunchtime today. I've asked her to come to your desk. Would you take her into the staffroom at lunchtime please, and make her welcome? She would probably like some lemonade."

Mrs. Connors gave Aggie one of her rare smiles. "My pleasure Mr. Bradley."

"Alright Aggie. Come back here as soon as lunchtime begins."

He turned back to Colin. "Now Mr. Campbell. Step this way please."

Mr. Bradley sat in his chair, and looked across his desk to where Colin stood waiting. He felt some compassion for this lonely boy. Zoe Campbell, Colin's mother, worked at Allied Garments, where Aggie's mother also worked. Zoe had enjoyed a short friendship with a handsome Maori, who moved on as soon as he knew she was pregnant. Life was not easy for her as a single mother, but Zoe did not help matters with many of the choices she made. It was well known that Colin would often be home by himself, or roaming the streets and countryside, until late at night, while Zoe was taking the edge off her sorrows at a bar.

Colin had received few of the benefits and encouragements other children took for granted. He had very little sense of self-worth, and compensated with aggression and cruelty to anyone weaker than himself. He had one redeeming feature that Mr. Bradley admired – a fascination with the Maori heritage he received from the father he never knew. Colin had sought out a few Maori elders at Te Ore Ore Pa, from whom he absorbed Maori lore, and passing fluency as a Maori language speaker. His most prized possession was a stylized fish hook carved from genuine whale bone, which he wore on a leather thong round his neck. His Maori heritage seemed a good starting point.

"Colin, you come from a proud heritage."

"Sir?" Colin had expected something different. He wasn't sure where this was going.

"Your Maori ancestors were fine people. You have many fine traditions."

Colin listened warily.

"May I see the whale bone carving you have please?"

Colin pulled his precious fish hook carving from inside his shirt. He held it up. He was reluctant to pull the leather thong over his head, and actually hand it over. Mr. Bradley made no attempt to take it.

"That's a beautiful carving Colin. You must be proud of it!" He paused, and looked down at his hands. Colin put the

27

carving back behind his shirt. "Colin, your ancestors were warriors! They were strong men! They were fit, and quick, and skillful. They were men of courage!"

He paused again, looking now at the boy's face. "Colin, when those warriors fought, they fought real enemies. They would have been ashamed to use their strength to harm women, or children or anyone weaker than themselves. They used their strength in good ways. You need to use your strength in good ways too, instead of cowardly ways. Do you understand what I'm saying?"

Colin was catching the drift, but he said nothing.

"If you want to throw your weight around, choose an opponent who makes some demands on your courage! There's nothing very honorable about tormenting someone who is not as strong as you are. That's the way of a coward, not a Maori warrior!"

The idea of using his strength in noble ways had some appeal, but Colin also felt some resentment at the suggestion of cowardliness. His thoughts competed with each other.

Mr. Bradley knew of Colin's friendship with elders at the Te Ore Ore Pa. He was just now realizing what a positive influence these wise men could have. One of them was a personal friend from Rotary. Yes, this evening he would make a phone call, mention the ideas he had put to Colin, and leave it to these mentors to take the next steps.

He did not mention his decision to Colin, but said, "You may hear more of this. In the meantime, you will start using your strength to protect Aggie Betteridge, instead of abusing her. Is that understood?"

"Yes sir." Colin had expected something much more severe than this conversation had turned up so far. He was a little off guard, and his response was much less surly than usual. In fact, he really was softened by Mr. Bradley's interest in his carving. The idea that his ancestors had been men of honor, who used their strength to protect, and who showed courage when it was demanded of them, had not had much place in his thinking before. The idea danced around the edge of his consciousness.

Mr. Bradley looked at him thoughtfully for a few more

moments. "Alright Colin. You, along with the rest of the school, will hear more about this tomorrow morning. You may return to your class now."

"Yes sir!" Colin needed no second telling.

Mr. Bradley continued formulating his thoughts, some of which concerned his upcoming conversation with Aggie's mother. Finally, he busied himself with other matters until Mrs. Betteridge was ushered into his office.

Chapter 4

An Unexpected Bonus.

"Mrs. Betteridge! Thank you for giving up your lunch hour to come over to the school. Obviously, you would want to know what's happening, and be reassured of Agnes' safety. I'm deeply grieved by what has happened. I'm even more grieved to tell you that there was some physical assault on this occasion."

Mr. Bradley briefly described the events of the morning. "Agnes is guest of honor in the staffroom during this lunch hour. At the end of the school day, I'll have a staff member stay with her until she's picked up. Mrs. McKnight will be picking her up as usual?"

"Yes, that's right. Thank you for taking care of her. But ….. but what of tomorrow? And the next day ...?"

"Let me tell you what I have in mind. For Standards Three through Six, tomorrow morning will begin with an assembly of all classes and their staff......"

As she listened, Helen could see that Mr. Bradley was serious about stamping out aggressive behavior. She thought about the plan he was outlining.

"This school assembly. It may be difficult for Agnes being there. I'm sure she'd be embarrassed, and maybe a little fearful."

"I would like to give Agnes a day off school tomorrow. Partly for the reason you mentioned, so that she is removed from the scene while this assembly of the school takes place. And partly ..." He paused and looked at her. "Mrs. Betteridge, I think Agnes would benefit from a recovery day, just spending time with her mother. This is a little presumptuous of me, but is there any chance you may be able to take the day off work, to have a day, just the two of you, doing something reassuring and refreshing together?"

Helen sat up straighter in her chair. "Mr. Bradley, that is thoughtful of you. That would be a lovely idea." She looked a little wistful. "But, I don't know … I do have some leave owing, but I try to save my leave days in case Agnes is sick and I need to stay home."

"Well Mrs. Betteridge, it's up to you of course. I don't want to suggest anything that would be a difficulty for you. But I wonder if tomorrow is exactly one of those days for which you save your leave."

Helen nodded. "Yes, perhaps that's right. It would be a lovely day. But it's short notice. I'll have to ask about it this afternoon."

"Yes, of course. Please give it some thought, and please telephone to let me know what you decide. And how you get on with obtaining a day's leave, if that is what you decide to do. If this idea is not going to work, I'll need to make other arrangements to look after Aggie … err, Agnes …. here."

*

Back at Allied, Helen went straight to her boss' office. "Mr. Spenlow, I have something I need to speak to you about briefly. May I come by at knock off time please?

Stephen Spenlow looked up. Helen Betteridge. He didn't know her very well, but from the little he did know, he felt kindly disposed towards her.

"Why don't you come in now Helen? Close the door - that's it. Please sit down."

Helen was a little embarrassed. She wasn't used to talking to others about the challenges she faced as a single mother, especially if there was any hint that she was asking special favors at her place of work. She cleared her throat.

"Mr. Spenlow, you know that I've occasionally had to take a day off to look after my daughter Agnes when she's not well. I haven't told you this before, but Agnes has a birthmark on the side of her face. It is rather noticeable, and she's always been teased about it by other children. She's coped with that remarkably well, but recently it's been getting worse. Just this morning some other children were harassing her and slapping her. I just used my lunch hour to go to the school to talk to Mr. Bradley, the school principal. He's taking steps to try to see that it stops. For tomorrow though, he wants for Agnes to take a day off school, and asked if I could also get a day off, so we could spend some time together, helping Agnes to regroup."

Stephen Spenlow paid close attention to her, but as he listened, other thoughts began to stir. He sat pondering without replying. Helen wondered what he was thinking – had her request offended him? She was about to speak again when he smiled at her.

"Helen, you're a valued member of staff here. Your work is of high quality. I'd like you to take the day off tomorrow as a gift from the company. It will not be deducted from your leave."

Helen was startled, pleased, confused. "I ... I wasn't looking for any special favors," she blurted.

"I know you weren't. This isn't a favor so much as an appreciation. I wonder if there's anything else I can do to make your day tomorrow a special one?"

"No! That is ... ah .. thank you! Thank you for your kindness. I really appreciate it!"

Somewhat flustered, Helen rose and made her way back to her workstation. Stephen Spenlow resumed his thoughts. A week ago, Joy Williamson, supervisor of Helen's shift, had brought him her resignation. Her sister in Central Otago had died, and Joy was moving down there to help her brother-in-law look after her nephews and nieces. Stephen regarded her as invaluable, and was very sorry to see her leave. The news had not been shared with the rest of the staff so far, but Stephen and Joy were already discussing who might replace her as supervisor.

"Helen Betteridge!" he mused. "I didn't think of her! She's so quiet, makes so few waves, she just doesn't come to mind very often. As I see her battling for her kid though, I'm admiring her. She needs some strength, just to make it as a single mother." He reached over to buzz Joy on the intercom.

"Joy, do you have a few minutes?"

"I'll be right over Stephen."

*

Mr. Bradley flipped through the Rolodex next to his phone, then picked up the receiver and dialed Hohepa Te Koari.

"Hello Hohepa! Nathan Bradley. Hohepa, I know of the interest you take in Colin Campbell. You know I'm sure of the troubles we've had with him at the school here. …. Yes, it isn't easy for him. He needs all the friends he can get, and you folks over at the Pa have been an amazing help to him. Hohepa, there has been some serious bullying going on recently, and I'm afraid Colin has been at the center of it. …………"

*

Stephen Spenlow was checking through Helen's file as Joy settled herself into the chair opposite his desk.

"Joy, I just had some fresh inspiration on the question of our new shift supervisor. I'm thinking of Helen Betteridge."

Joy frowned doubtfully. "Helen?"

"She does high quality work, and she nearly always exceeds her quotas. I've just been looking at her totals. She's a single mother looking after her nine-year-old, yet she takes less time off than many of the others. Oh, by the way, her daughter has been getting flak from some of the other kids at school, so I gave her a bonus day off tomorrow, to help her sort things out."

"Careful! You'll have everyone clamoring for a bonus day off!" Joy grinned. "It's true that Helen has more experience than just about anyone else. She's familiar with all the systems we use. And her routine maintenance is always up to scratch – we almost never have trouble with any machine she uses. My concern though, is whether she has the personal strength to deal with the others on that shift. She's so quiet – don't you think they may run right over her?"

"Yes, I'm wondering about that. I think it would be quite a challenge for her. But I sense some resilience in her. She may just rise to the challenge. She would have Zoe Campbell to deal with."

Joy sighed. "Yes, Zoe. Very efficient when she isn't hung over. But the clocking in an hour or two late has been increasing again. It looks like she's asking for dismissal this time."

"Do you think Helen could cope with her?"

"Hmm." Joy pondered. "You know, I'm about fifty-fifty on that. I guess we'd soon see, wouldn't we? It's your call Stephen, but I think I'd like to see her given the chance."

"I think so too, Joy. As you said, we'll see what happens won't we?"

*

The school day was over. Students were streaming out the gates, most on their bicycles, some making their way to the waiting cars of adults who had come for them. Mrs. Connors walked with Aggie to Pauline McKnight's car, where she passed on the message about Aggie's day off the next day.

"Have a wonderful day tomorrow Aggie, and a nice weekend."

"Thank you, Mrs. Connors." Aggie was still digesting the information that she had a bonus day off. And that it had to do with significant things happening to protect her from the harm that had been coming to her. She slipped into the back seat of Mrs. McKnight's car.

As Colin Campbell came out the gate, he encountered Hohepa Te Koari waiting for him. Hohepa's pants were baggy, his jacket loose, open, ill-fitting. His sparse white hair was covered by his battered hat, but short white whiskers prickled across his chin, and up the sides of his face.

"Kia ora Colin."

"Kia ora matua keke." Hohepa was not a blood relation, but Colin correctly used the title "uncle" out of respect.

"How would you like to come with me to check out my eel traps?"

"I have to go to Auntie Mere." That was the technical truth. Officially, Colin was supposed to be supervised each day until his mother finished work. In fact, he usually rambled off somewhere else, and made his way home when he was hungry. All concerned knew that the arrangement was rarely honored, but no-one tried to enforce it. But on this occasion Colin was playing safe.

"I've told Mere that you'll be with me." Hohepa smiled, and Colin's face lit up. He knew that there were big eels to be caught along the river banks if you knew what you were doing. This would be his first introduction to the art.

*

Joy Williamson approached Helen's workstation twenty minutes before knock off time.

"Helen, Mr. Spenlow told me you're to have some rest and recreation tomorrow. Hope it will be a real refreshment for you! Besides that, there's another matter he wanted to chat about. Please could you get packed up now, and come over to his office?"

Helen was surprised for the second time that afternoon. What could this be about? Joy's face seemed pleasant and relaxed, so maybe it wasn't anything threatening. She hoped not – her concern for Agnes was quite enough for now.

"Of course, Joy. No problems I hope?"

"Not at all," Joy laughed.

A few minutes later, Joy and Helen were both back in front of Stephen Spenlow's desk.

"Well Helen, I have some news for you. Joy will be leaving us in two weeks. She's going down to Central Otago to be with her family."

Helen's eyes widened. Joy had been a part of Allied for as long as she had been there. She'd always been a fair, considerate supervisor to work with, though Helen knew she could be stern when she needed to be. Some of the other workers had muttered about her from time to time.

"That's a surprise Joy. I wish you all the best."

Stephen resumed. "So we've been talking about who will replace Joy as shift supervisor. We think you have the qualities we're looking for."

It took a moment to sink in. They were asking her to become the new shift supervisor! Now Helen was really surprised.

"Me? I ... I ... this is really unexpected!"

"You've been with us for eight years now, and have gained good experience. Your work sets a high standard, you're conscientious and punctual. You look after the details that keep things running smoothly."

Helen looked from Stephen to Joy and back again. It seemed like a big change. She didn't know quite what to say.

"Helen, if you decide to accept this offer, you know you'll be supervising the people on your shift. They're fine workers overall, but at times some of them need firm authority. That may be the part of this position that will be the most challenging for you. What do you think about that?"

Helen looked at him thoughtfully. "You're right, Mr. Spenlow. That would be the most challenging part. I've really had no experience supervising staff. Do you think I could learn quickly enough?"

"I'd like you to give it your best shot. If you decide to accept, I want you to start working as assistant to Joy next Wednesday. That way you'll have her backup for about a week and a half. Though you'll need to establish your own authority with the staff. You can't rely on anyone else for that."

Helen looked at Joy again. Joy gave her an encouraging smile.

"Mr. Spenlow, it's an honor for me to be asked. Thank you for that. But a very unexpected honor. May I have the weekend to think and pray about this?"

"Of course, Helen." Stephen Spenlow did not share Helen's religious commitment, so he wasn't sure about the praying part. But as Helen left the office, he turned to Joy and said, "I'm glad she asked for time to think it over. If she had jumped at it immediately, I would have had less confidence in her. Whichever way she decides, I think it will be the right choice for her."

Chapter 5

A Day Off.

Aggie was still not back from the McKnight's when Helen arrived home. She headed straight for her prayer chair, and sat down in the old rocker.

"Shift Supervisor Helen Betteridge! What do you think of that Lord?" She thought over the staff she worked with. Nearly all of them impressed her as pleasant and reasonable women – though the thought of herself as the authority among them gave her a strange feeling. "Nancy, did you complete your maintenance yesterday before you left for the day? The record wasn't filled in." Hmm, at a stretch, she could just see herself saying that to Nancy. But to June, or to Sylvia? Now they were tougher. How would she be able to win their respect?

And Zoe Campbell? Ah, Zoe was a different matter again. Her workstation was in the row in front of Helen's, and two positions further to the right. Each year it seemed Zoe became a little more gaunt, the skin of her face and neck pulled ever more tightly over bone and sinew. The effect enlarged her dark eyes, giving her an almost bird-like appearance. Her black hair lightened each year to charcoal grey.

Helen knew Zoe was in danger of being dismissed because of her constant lateness for work. She would inherit Zoe! To make matters worse, Helen knew that Zoe's son Colin was the primary culprit among Agnes' tormentors. She didn't know how well aware Zoe would be of Colin's role with her daughter, but she thought Zoe would have at least some idea. So maybe Zoe would see her as an enemy right from the start.

"Hmm, Lord, do you want me to accept this offer? Would I really be able to manage Zoe?"

Maybe Zoe would just be sacked, and she wouldn't be a problem any more. No, if she was going to take this job on, she knew she would do her best for Zoe.

"Mum! Hey Mum, is it true that you have the day off work tomorrow?" Aggie had come through the back door into the kitchen and was running down the passageway to find her. "Mum, I don't have to go to school, and we can have a holiday together! Is it true?"

"Yes, my dear. Mr. Spenlow was very kind, and he gave me a paid day off! I don't have to take any of my leave!"

"And why don't I have to go to school? Mrs. Connors said they are having a big school assembly, but I'm excused!"

"Yes! When I talked with Mr. Bradley he said he wouldn't put up with any more bullying in the school, like some of the children have been doing to you. He's going to have an assembly of all the school from Standard Three up. Anyone who has punched you or pushed you or anything has to write a letter saying what they did, and apologizing. In fact, all the children will be writing you a letter, even if they haven't been mean to you. Anyway, he thought it would be best if you weren't there while he's talking to them about it. So, we have a day off!"

Aggie didn't know quite how she felt. She was a little afraid that this attention might backfire on her. Her way had always been to avoid provoking her attackers, hoping they would back off. But it felt good that some grownups were taking steps to protect her. Just for now, there was tomorrow to look forward to!

*

Hohepa drove through the gate of the Pa, and pulled up close to the meeting house. Two large eels were still flopping about inside a sack, safely stowed in the boot of the car.

"Colin, come into the wharenui with me. There are some things I want to show you."

They climbed out of the car, and made their way into the building, with its carved fascia panels, surmounted by a carved figure at the front end of the ridge. Inside were more carvings, notably the poupou, or carved panels lining each wall. Each poupou was separated from the next by a panel of woven flax.

Hohepa stopped in front of the first one. "Look at this Colin. Each poupou tells the story of a person from our tribe. Just from looking at the carving, what do you think this person might have been like? Do you think he was admired by those who knew him? Or was he a wicked person? Did he build up the mana, or honor, of his people, or did he destroy it?"

They discussed the panel, and Colin learned the story depicted, and the strengths and weaknesses of the characters of whom it told. Then they moved on to the next poupou. Over the next hour, Colin came to know several of his warrior ancestors, most of them heroic, some less so. Eventually they emerged again, and sat on a bench beside the building.

Hohepa turned to face Colin. "Colin, are you building the mana of your people?"

Colin had an idea where this might be going, but the thought was not yet well-formed.

"Me? What do you mean?"

"Are you using your strength to protect people weaker than you are? Are you growing into a person other people admire?"

They had only about half an hour, but Hohepa started opening Colin's mind to ideals he had considered very little up to that time. The neglect Colin had experienced was not going to be reversed in a single conversation, but when Hohepa dropped him at home, the foundation for a new vision of himself had been laid. Hohepa promised him many more conversations.

*

Helen and Aggie sat down to their dinner.

"Whose turn is it to give thanks today?" Helen asked. "It's my turn? Okay."

"Father, today has contained lots of unexpected happenings. Thank you for bringing us through today, and thank you that we can have a fun day together tomorrow. Please help us to plan well. And thank you for providing good things, so we can share this dinner together. Amen."

Helen picked up her knife and fork. "It's supposed to be cloudy tomorrow. Maybe a little rain. But I don't think it will be too stormy. We should be alright under the trees up at Third Creek. You always enjoy it so much up there."

"Hmm," responded Aggie.

"I'll call Mrs. Sanders right after dinner, and ask if we can spend the day there. I wonder what we can take for our lunch!" She began reviewing the supplies in the refrigerator, and in the cupboard. "Perhaps we could call by the bakery and get some of those neenish tarts you like so much."

Aggie's eyes brightened. This was a rare treat.

"And maybe some bottles of lemonade."

"No Mum, let's take some of our own ginger beer. That's just as nice."

"And what do you want to do during the day? We can take some books, or you could take your paints. Maybe you could start over on that painting that got spoiled. Oh, and I have something else to tell you about!" Helen smiled mysteriously.

"What Mum?" It was unusual for either of them to hold back on anything, but Helen had the impulse to wait until their day together to share her news from work.

"A nice surprise I had today! Something I need to think and pray about, so you can help me with that tomorrow."

Aggie looked wonderingly at her.

Helen pushed her plate back, and stood up. "I'll just go call Mrs. Sanders." She walked towards the telephone.

"Mum!"

"Yes, my dear?"

Aggie was hesitant. "I …. Could we go somewhere different tomorrow? Third Creek is nice – I like it there. But …... I was wondering …. You know that cottage we found in the mountains? You know, the one up that track off the Dalefield Road? It's lovely up there. And I really like that little cottage."

Dalefield Road was west and a little south of their home. It pushed and wound its way up into the Tararua foothills, penetrating some six miles into the bush. Helen and Aggie had explored the road last summer, and discovered a track that led up a narrow side valley on the northern side of the road. The track followed a small tributary stream bubbling and jumping down the valley. It was barely wide enough for a car to pass, but it widened at intervals where occasional small strips of grassy sand and pebbles bordered the stream. At the far end of the last of these miniature beaches, the track climbed steeply up a bank, while the stream to the left tumbled down a waterfall, some fifteen feet high.

Pushing to the top of the bank, the traveler came upon a much wider space, a small plateau, about half a mile long, and a little less than half of that wide. Running along its center, from east to west, was a line where the bush came to an end. On the northern side, the ground became covered with springy, coarse grass running right to the edge of the plateau, where it fell away sharply in a nearly sheer drop, a mass of jumbled rock. On the southern side, the bush continued to where the stream ran; from the far side of the stream the ground rose again, the bush continuing up the slope.

The track kept its westerly direction across the plateau, following the edge of the bush, until, at the western end it disappeared around the back of a disused building. The building was barely more than an old logger's hut, but was just picturesque enough to be called a cottage. It was sited out on the grassy area, midway between the bush and the lip of the plateau, where it could benefit from the rays of the sun.

"The cottage up in the bush?" Helen was a little doubtful. The mountainside was cooler, more dim, more damp than Third Creek. "If the day is at all grey and showery, it will be more so in the mountains."

"Yes ..." Aggie looked wistful. "If it does rain, we could go into the cottage and keep dry."

"Well, I suppose." Helen still looked doubtful. "Why do you want to go into the mountains?"

"It's sort of dim, and ... and in some places there's big huge grey rocks, and the track where you walk goes way up into the mountains and .... I like it there."

That was about the best that nine-year-old Aggie could

do. As she thought of the bush, her feelings were a little different depending on whether she was picturing the dancing, gurgling streams, the cool dampness of the trees and forest floor, or the great, grey outcroppings of rock. It all added up to a slightly scary, inviting, mysterious, listening strength. It suited the mood of the day.

Helen looked at her daughter, wondering slightly, loving much. "Agnes, what a treasure you are! Alright, let's go to the mountains tomorrow! Come give me a hug!"

Aggie ran to her mother, and held her tightly. "Thank you, Mum!"

*

The next morning, Helen and Aggie allowed themselves the luxury of extra time in bed, but they were still heading for the bakery to buy neenish tarts, and a pastie each, by a little before nine o'clock. The sky was bright and cheerful, though a bank of grey cloud warned that the prediction of later showers just might be fulfilled. In less than twenty minutes they were turning off Dalefield Road, up the track into the bush.

"Shall we drive right up to the cottage, or do you want to stop by the waterfall first?" Helen asked.

"Let's stop by the waterfall. We can get out the camp chairs and sit there for a while, maybe until it's time to have our lunch. And you can tell me about your nice surprise!"

Helen smiled. "Sounds good!"

The verge of the track near to the waterfall was wide enough to park the car, and set out the picnic chairs and lunch basket. Aggie would have taken off her sandals and paddled in the stream at this point, but she wanted to hear about her Mum's surprise. So she settled into one of the chairs and looked up expectantly.

Helen adjusted her cushion, and leaned back in the other chair. "Well my dear, you'll never guess what! Mr. Spenlow at work told me yesterday that Miss Williamson – she's my supervisor I've told you about before – well, she's leaving! She's going down to Central Otago to live. So someone else will be made supervisor."

"Yes?" It sounded as though there was more to the surprise than this.

"Guess who's been asked to be the new shift supervisor?"

Aggie's eyes opened wider. "You! You can be a supervisor? Mum! Wow!"

"Yes, I was amazed that they asked me. I never would have thought of that!"

"So, you'll get more pay, and be one of the bosses?"

"Well, yes, it would be a little more pay. But I wouldn't be a boss exactly. Just a supervisor."

"But that's like a boss isn't it? Mum, that sounds wonderful!"

"I haven't said I'll accept it yet. It's a big compliment that they asked me, but I have to think about whether I could do the job well."

"You could do it couldn't you? They've told you lots of times you're really good at your work."

"I think I can do a good job with most of the things I'd need to do. But I would be in charge of the other ladies on my shift. As you said, kind of like being the boss to them."

"Oh." Aggie looked thoughtful. "You're good at being in charge."

Helen smiled at her daughter's confidence. "I haven't had much experience at being in charge of other people. I think I would do alright with most of the ladies – I hope so anyway. But some grownups can be difficult. Just like at school, most of the children get on well with each other, but there are some that cause problems for their teachers. It's a bit the same with grownups."

Aggie looked at her Mum, considering. She knew all about people who could be "difficult". But, as so often before, her thoughts flew to the photo on the mantelpiece.

"Mum, if Daddy were here, he'd be able to deal with them, wouldn't he?"

"Yes Honey, I'm sure he would. But there's another

matter to think about too. I'd need to stay a little later each day than I do now. You'd have to stay with the McKnight's about another half an hour. How would that be for you?"

"I can go home and look after myself! I'm big enough!"

"Honey, I think you could do a good job of looking after yourself. I trust you to be careful. But there are people about in this world I don't trust. It would be safer for you to be with adults until you are a little older yet. I need to ask Mrs. McKnight about this – she'd need to be willing. Perhaps seeing you'd be there longer, we could ask her for a quiet space where you could start your homework."

Aggie liked the McKnight family, but she would rather not stay another half an hour each day. Still, if she could start her homework, that would make it okay.

"The important thing to know is what the Lord thinks about this. If he's behind it, then he'll show me how to manage the people. Would you like to pray with me about it now?"

"Sure Mum."

They settled back into their chairs and were quiet for some time, each thinking through the issues, and silently asking God for his wisdom. Aggie thought about being with the McKnight's, and how much older she would have to be before she could be at home by herself. She thought too of how Mrs. McKnight was kind to her, and often asked how she was getting on. Helen thought mostly of how she would need to combine strength with fairness if she was to supervise the women on her shift.

As their prayer time ended, neither Aggie nor Helen felt they had received a strong answer. Aggie felt more positive about it than Helen, who was still concerned about its challenges. So, they left it unanswered for the present.

*

Aggie ran over to the bank of the stream, and stopped still, peering into the water. As Helen joined her, she whispered, "See if you can see any little trout hiding in the pools!"

They both stood and probed with their eyes, but nothing

could be seen moving beneath the surface of the water. Just a pair of bright blue dragonflies that came to fascinate them, hovering over the water, darting this way and that, until they disappeared downstream.

Aggie discarded her sandals, and paddled up and down the shallow pool. The stream bed was covered with rocks, so her progress was slow. Helen kicked off her sandals as well, the two of them enjoying the coolness of the water over their feet. Aggie slowly made her way upstream to the waterfall. Its miniature cascades and spray fell about her, dampening her hair and shirt. The rocks on each side of the falling water were drier, and Aggie found footholds that invited her to climb about ten feet up the rock face, where she found a wider rock where she could sit and look down at her mother.

"Careful Honey! Stay there, and I'll get my sketch pad!" Helen went back to the car, and soon returned with pad and pencil. Aggie sat, absorbing the sounds and movement of the water, the rustle of the trees, the colors, the secure feeling of the rock beneath her.

Helen had finished her sketch, and her mind had returned to the question of the shift supervisor offer when Aggie stirred, and began climbing down the rocks again. Helen watched her, stifling the urge to give motherly warnings. She knew Aggie was sure-footed, and the climb wasn't difficult.

Aggie reached Helen's side, and they both stood looking at the sketch. Helen was skilled with pencil and pad, and Aggie had inherited her artistic flair. The lines and shading brought to life the girl beside the water, evoking some of the atmosphere they both felt.

"Mum, I look kind of pretty in the sketch. But I don't think I'm pretty really. Kids say I look funny."

"Agnes, you are beautiful! You're growing into a beautiful woman! Don't you let the taunts of those children undermine you!" She caught Aggie in her arms for a long hug. Aggie didn't reply, but held her mother tightly.

"Hey Mum! Let's go have some lunch!" Aggie's voice was light again.

They retrieved their sandals, and made their way back to

the car. As they sat down with pasties and sandwiches, Helen said, "Let's give thanks for our lunch, and while we do, we can pray about the meeting at the school."

"Dear Father, thank you for this special time together, and for this lunch we can enjoy. And Father, thank you for Mr. Bradley, and his determination to make the school a safe place for everyone. Please give him wisdom, and please help all the students to become thoughtful, and kind. Amen."

They had finished their pasties and were starting on sandwiches, when Aggie looked up at her mother, "Mum. I'm so glad we could have this day together. I think I'll remember it for a long time." She paused, "As soon as we've finished lunch, let's walk up the track to the cottage! Let's bring the sketch pad!"

It was a stiff climb to the top of the bank, but after that the walk along the track was easy. Aggie veered off to her right to feel the springy turf underfoot. In ten minutes, they were climbing the steps of the veranda running the width of the cottage. A clematis vine, subtly fragrant, and bright with blue flowers twined through trellis work running along the roof line.

"Mum!" Aggie cried, "it's my turn to sketch you! Come sit on the edge of the veranda here." She indicated the far end of the veranda where the vine grew around the post supporting the roof.

"This clematis is beautiful," commented Helen as she handed over the pad and pencil.

The pencil drawing couldn't do justice to the wild, glowing colors of the vine, but Aggie managed a creditable sketch of her Mum, with the broad flower petals and leaves beside and above her.

"Now I think it's you who is flattering me," Helen smiled as she surveyed Aggie's work. "Is that pretty woman really your mum?"

"Do you think it doesn't look like you?" Aggie asked anxiously.

"Yes, it does Honey. It's a very good sketch. Thank you! Come! Let's go inside!"

They crossed to the door. The interior was grimy, though still in a reasonable state of repair. The window glass was unbroken.

"If we cleaned up a bit, we could have fun here Mum! We could bring our sleeping bags, and camp out here!"

"It doesn't look as though anyone comes here," Helen replied. "I wonder how many people even know it's here?" She looked at the undisturbed dust on floor, walls and table. "I'm not so sure about camping out though. It would take some effort to clean up enough to sleep and eat here."

As they spoke, the cloud bank that had been threatening all day moved overhead, reducing the light inside the cottage. A wind began to stir the trees nearby. The cottage took on the feel of a haven from a storm. Aggie and Helen looked at each other and giggled. Aggie moved to the west-facing window. Before her, the track past the cottage continued on into the bush. But from here it was just a rough walking track, not wide enough for a vehicle.

*

Immediately, something stirred in Aggie's spirit. The sense that she was in a safe, cozy place, protected from the threat of storm outside, increased a hundred-fold. The room was no longer dirty, uncared for. It was clean, cheerful, furnished, enlarged. And other rooms were added, also welcoming and pretty. By contrast, the feeling of threat from outside also grew, more than a hundred-fold. Something terrible was happening, somewhere further along that track. What was it? She couldn't quite see. A policeman was there, walking along the track. Gladness, and deep, searing pain. Safety, and the most terrible threat. The feelings tumbled within her.

The cloud bank above the cottage moved on a little. A ray of sunshine pierced through again. The vision of far off things faded. Aggie's face brightened

*

"I want to check out the rocks over here." Aggie ran outside, towards the lip of the plateau. "Come on Mum!"

Soon she had found a ledge wide enough for them both to sit side by side. They sat absorbing the view out over the valley to the north, while sunlight played cat and mouse through breaks in the cloud.

Gradually their thoughts returned to the prospect of Helen becoming shift supervisor. Silently they each resumed their prayer from earlier in the day. Eventually, Aggie turned to her Mum. "Mum, I think you should accept the supervisor job."

Helen turned to her and smiled. "Do you Honey? Were you just praying about that too?"

"Yes. I didn't get any clear words or pictures. Just the feeling that it's right for you. And I think it would be fine staying a bit longer at the McKnight's."

"That's just the impression I was getting my dear. It's a bit scary for me, but I think God is telling me he is coming with me."

"Good!" said Aggie firmly.

"I'll still need to check with Mrs. McKnight." She took a deep breath. "Apart from that, look out ladies! Here comes Supervisor Helen!"

Chapter 6

A School Chastened.

The Standard Three through Six classes filled the assembly hall to a little over three quarters capacity. The staff sat in a shallow semi-circle on the stage. Monitors from the Standard Six classes lined the walls.

As Mr. Bradley entered, the entire school rose to their feet. He walked up the steps to the stage, and stood behind the podium.

"Thank you, school. Please be seated."

He turned to face the staff behind him. "I apologize for this intrusion into your teaching schedules. Thank you for your understanding."

Turning back to face the assembled students, he began, "I have rarely had to call an assembly such as this. I have done so today because there is a very important matter that we as a school must deal with." He paused, eyes ranging over the hall. "Most of our students are hard-working, kind, thoughtful, helpful people. But there are a few among us who have been showing cruelty to other students. These ones have been behaving like cowards, attacking other students who are smaller and not as strong as they are."

Some murmurs and fidgeting began in isolated pockets around the hall.

"One student especially has been targeted, not just by individual bullies, but by groups of children ganging up on her. I am talking about Aggie Betteridge."

"Let me tell you a little about Aggie. Aggie's father was killed serving his country in the war that ended just a few years ago. His name was Major Martin Betteridge, and he won the

Military Cross for his courage in the field. Perhaps you did not know that? His widow, Mrs. Betteridge has had to work very hard to support herself and her daughter Aggie. She's shown much courage in accepting the death of her husband, whom she loved dearly, and moving on with her life, making a home for herself and her daughter."

The hall was silent now, all attention focused on Mr. Bradley.

"Furthermore, Aggie has shown herself to be a courageous girl. Some of you have taunted her cruelly, thrown away her lunch, spoiled her artwork, have even pushed her, jostled her so that she has fallen and grazed her knees and her legs. I have even seen with my own eyes some of you slapping her. And let me tell you this about her – she has never snitched on any one of you! Not ever! Which of you would have had the courage to endure all that without coming and complaining to a teacher?"

Mr. Bradley's eyes swept the room again, his gaze resting momentarily on those he knew to be culprits.

"I know fairly accurately who the offenders are. But the information I have comes from other sources, none of it from Aggie herself. She has not told tales on any of you. I hope you appreciate that about her. I've asked her to take a day off school today, so that she can spend some time with her mother, and to spare her the embarrassment of this assembly."

"Aggie was born with a birthmark on her face. Many of you have a birthmark somewhere on your body, but it is usually in a place where it's not much noticed. Aggie is no different, except that her birthmark is larger, and it's on her face, where it's easily seen. That's embarrassing for her. So, she needs you to be even more courteous, and considerate to her, showing her you care about her and want to be her friend just as much as you want anyone else to be your friend."

"There is much more I would like to say, but that may be enough for now. Just remember this – in a civilized society, the weak are not abused. They are protected by the strong ones. If you are strong, make sure you protect those who may be weaker than you."

"Finally, your homework over the weekend will be to write a letter to Aggie Betteridge. Every student in the school will do this. Firstly, in your letter, you will tell Aggie the things about her that you appreciate, and you will promise her that you will help her to feel welcome in our school. Your teachers will help you to get started on this. If you have never been mean to Aggie …." He paused for emphasis. "If you can honestly say you have never been mean in any way to Aggie, you may end your letter there. Just sign your name, and bring it to school on Monday. However, if you know of some way or ways you have been nasty to her, you must say what it was you did, and apologize to her. Is that clear?"

"And thirdly, if you have ever touched her in a mean way – pushing or hitting or slapping, you must not only describe what you did and apologize, but you must have your parents sign your letter, to show they have read it. If you fail to do this, you may be suspended from the school. We do not want people in this school who behave that way."

"In a few moments you will be released from this assembly, and return to your classrooms. Your teachers will help you to make a start on your letters."

He turned again to the teachers behind him. "Teachers, please take the next hour to ensure students know what is required of them, and give some guidance on how to write these letters. Morning break will begin an hour from now. Thank you."

*

For the next hour, teachers wrote on blackboards, describing the requirements Mr. Bradley had specified, making sure each child knew what was expected. The consequence of suspension from school was described, and the impact that could have. In short, a somber mood prevailed as the school was released for morning break.

*

Colin Campbell left the school grounds that afternoon deep in thought. He knew that he was expected to write a letter to Aggie Betteridge confessing some offences to her that he did not especially want to confess. He was more than half inclined to shrug the whole thing off, and get himself suspended from school, if that was the outcome. He could imagine himself spending his days roaming free wherever he liked, instead of having to go to school. Besides, he was not exactly the greatest scholar, and the idea of writing any letter to anyone did not appeal.

The afternoon was warm. Some low banks of cloud had moved in, but they served only to increase the humidity. Colin wandered aimlessly for some time, eventually finding himself sitting on a bench beside the lake in Queen Elizabeth Park. His life experiences up to the present had grown in him the sense of being the rebel, the outcast. He would not have used those words, but he did not seem to fit within the rules and expectations most people lived by.

Yet the ideas his friend Hohepa had spoken of yesterday afternoon were competing with his usual way of thinking. Here was a new view of himself and of the attitude he might have towards the world around him. It wasn't well-formed, but it was troubling him. He'd come to respect Hohepa, perhaps the only man he'd known to take a real interest in him. He knew Hohepa would not be pleased by ideas of him just giving up on the world, getting suspended from school, and drifting around.

Colin remained brooding for a further half an hour before he moved. "Alright," he said to himself, "I'll go see what he has to say." He regained a little bravado to keep his courage up, as he made his way the few blocks to Hohepa's house. Hohepa was in the front yard.

"Kia ora Colin! I hoped I might see you sometime soon!"

Colin looked surprised. And pleased. "You hoped to see me?"

"Yes. I'm guessing you have an assignment from school,

and you could probably use some help."

"Oh!" Colin's face slumped a little, but then he brightened again. "Would you really help me?"

"Come inside and tell me about it. I cooked up those eels we caught – there's some in the fridge."

Soon they were sitting at Hohepa's kitchen table with eel steak and homemade ginger beer in front of Colin. Hohepa chatted about how he had cooked the eel, and made the sauce that covered it, while Colin ate, and downed his glass of ginger beer.

"Well," said Hohepa as Colin pushed away his empty plate and glass, "what do you have to do for school?"

"It's about that Aggie girl .... you know, we were talking about her yesterday. We have to write her a letter saying we'll be nice to her. And that she's welcome to be at our school."

"Hmm. Doesn't sound too hard," smiled Hohepa.

Colin looked uncomfortable. "I think I got to say if I ... well if ... if I did any ... well, bad stuff to her."

Hohepa was looking at him seriously now. "We already talked about some of that too, didn't we? And I think there may be more that we haven't talked about?"

"Yeah, well ... I did some things ... but not all the time!" Colin was struggling between honesty and the need to find some defense. Thoughts of his persecution of Aggie raised another concern. "What does it mean if you're suspended from school?"

"It means you can't go back there, at least not for a while, until problems get sorted out. Getting suspended from school is definitely not a good thing to happen. Is there a chance you might be suspended?"

"I ... I think I got to write out a whole list of the things I did to her, and say sorry. And if I don't get it all right, then I'll get suspended from school! And ... I" A look of real worry was clouding Colin's face now. "And I got to get my mum to read it and sign it!" There was no telling how his mother might react when she became involved.

Hohepa was beginning to appreciate Nathan Bradley's wisdom in the way he was handling this. He really had Colin's attention.

"Colin, it sounds like we have quite a job ahead of us.

We'll put this aside for now, and you can come back in the morning, and we'll work on it for as long as it takes. How does that sound?"

Spending a good part of Saturday toiling over school work did not sound great to Colin, but he knew he would probably just give up if it wasn't for Hohepa's help.

"Yeah. Well, thanks." On the other hand, spending a day at Hohepa's house had its attractions, even if he did have to labor over writing a letter. He looked up and smiled. "Thank you!"

"And for now," Hohepa said briskly, "did you tell Mere you were coming over here?"

Colin hung his head. "No," he said.

"Well, I'll phone her. And then I'll drive you back to your house, and ask your mum if you can come over here tomorrow. You could walk over here by .... let's see, we can make an early start. Can you be here by eight in the morning?"

"Yes." An early start at Hohepa's house. That sounded fine to Colin.

"Good. And tonight, I want you to make a note of everything you can think of, that you did to Aggie Betteridge. You need to have a complete list, right? So you better see that you note down everything you can think of! You don't need to write much – just a word or two to remind you of each time you were not kind to her."

*

Colin arrived at Hohepa's door on Saturday morning at about ten minutes before eight, armed with a note pad, on which he had laboriously written six different offences against Aggie. He knew there were more, but other incidents were vague in his memory, and listing six was a creditable effort for Colin. He chatted briefly with Hohepa, and drank a glass of milk, but soon they were at the table, ready to begin the task.

"I need to start by saying something nice to her. What can I say?"

"Is she a nice person? What do you say to a nice person?"

"I dunno. She's got that funny thing on her face. Makes her kind of weird."

"It's a birthmark. Lots of people have birthmarks. Hers is unusual, being up there on her face. But why does that make her weird? Has she ever done anything nasty to you? Has she ever done anything nasty to anyone you know?"

Colin shook his head.

"So maybe she is a nice person. What would you say to a nice person?"

More pondering, then Colin tried, "Maybe I could say, 'Dear Aggie, you are a nice person.'"

Hohepa nodded and sighed inwardly. This could be a long day. Colin slowly and carefully wrote out his first sentence. And then sat staring out the window.

Hohepa was about to try prompting again, when Colin's face brightened. "I just thought of something! What say I write in Maori! She wouldn't have any idea what I'm writing! So it wouldn't really matter what I say!"

He grinned mischievously at Hohepa. Hohepa did not grin back, but regarded him gravely.

"Colin, I think you have a very good idea there. I would love to have you write a letter in Maori. But," he paused, and looked even more gravely into Colin's eyes. "But do not think you can use the language of your people to mislead anyone, or to be cheap, or dishonest. Do you have what it takes to write to this Pakeha woman in Maori?"

Colin sat, staring at his friend. "Will you help me?" he asked at last.

"You bet," answered Hohepa. "Now let's really get down to business."

*

Colin and Hohepa put in a long day. Each hour they took ten minutes off to stretch, walk around a little, and find a snack. By the end of the day, they were both feeling proud of the effort they had put in. Colin wrote a little about the heritage of the Maori people, and acknowledged he had not lived up to this heritage. He undertook to use his strength to protect Aggie instead of harming her. He had some private reservations about that part – he did want to embrace the ideals that Hohepa was describing, but they were new to him, and he wasn't sure how successful he would be. But he was encouraged by Hohepa' support.

"Well now," said Hohepa finally, "it must be time to go talk to your Mum about all this."

Immediately, some of Colin's rebel persona returned, the sullen, fearful undercurrents competing with the very new sense of honor that had been growing during the day. His mother was unpredictable, but if he was in trouble of any kind, he could expect some backlash from her.

"I don't want to talk to her about it," he said.

"She's going to find out about it all sooner or later," replied Hohepa. "Better she hears it from you than anyone else." He looked at Colin. "Besides, we already told her the reason you were coming here today. She already knows at least some about your past behavior towards Aggie. Come on, let's go face the music together!"

Colin still felt uncertain, but he was glad Hohepa would come with him. As it happened, when they arrived back at Colin's house, Zoe Campbell's reaction was confined to criticizing Colin for wasting Hohepa's day.

"What is wrong with you, hopeless boy! Behaving the way you do at school, so that this good man has to waste his day trying to get you out of trouble!"

"Colin has done some good work today," Hohepa assured her. "I think you're going to find he's not nearly such a hopeless boy as you have thought in the past!"

Zoe glowered at him, not sure what to say. She was in the habit of thinking of Colin as a nuisance to her, and a troublemaker to everyone else. She wasn't used to hearing anything that sounded like support for him.

"Well, thanks for trying to help him," she managed as Hohepa departed.

*

Helen and Aggie usually left for church early each Sunday, to attend their respective Sunday School classes before the service at 10.30. On this Sunday, Helen was lost in thought as they drove. She wanted to ask for prayer for her coming assignment as the new supervisor at work. She knew she would need the Lord's wisdom and courage if she was going to succeed, and wanted the support of her friends at church. But she knew also that she needed to have confidence in the wisdom and discretion of anyone she confided in. And there were some in her class that she did not have confidence in.

There was Adele Stephenson for example. She knew that Adele's marriage to Peter was in trouble – Adele often made disparaging comments about Peter in their class. And her daughter Kelly was known to be a handful.

"Agnes, how well do you know Kelly Stephenson?"

"Not very much. She's in Standard Five."

"Do you know if she has many friends? Does she get on well with other children?"

Aggie was silent for a few moments, then, "She was one of the ones hitting me when Mr. Bradley caught them."

"Really! Was she now?" The daughter of one of her Sunday School classmates! Helen did feel compassion for Adele. She wasn't sure who was more to blame for their marital problems, Peter or Adele. But right now, she was feeling more indignation than compassion.

"Did she hit you at other times, before last Thursday?"

"Hmm. A couple of different times she punched me in the chest, and said that I ... well ... I will never need a bra like she does. She kind of brags about wearing a bra."

Helen pulled the car to the side of the road, and turned to look at Aggie. "Sweetheart, I know you don't want to cause trouble, and you're afraid that telling on other children might make them get at you even more. But Agnes, please tell me if things like that happen. I want to be able to protect you!"

58

Helen pulled Aggie to her, and they cuddled for a few moments. Two or three slow-march tears trickled down Aggie's cheek as the memory replayed. Helen was thinking that Kelly's need for a bra just yet was very doubtful, but was not surprised that she had persuaded her mother to buy one.

"Thank you for telling me about that honey. And like I said, you don't need to keep hurts like that stuffed up inside you! Please tell me when things like that happen."

Aggie looked into her Mum's soft, concerned eyes and gave her a kiss on the cheek. "Thank you, Mum. A couple of times Jesus has come and told me to put the hurts in the Hurt Basket. He takes the Hurt Basket away with him. That helped when he did that. One time was at Third Creek, and the other time was up on the mountain."

Helen was pulling the car back onto the road. She looked at Aggie. "Really? Jesus came, and talked to you? Was that in a dream?"

"I'm not sure. It was sort of like a dream, but I didn't think I was asleep. You know, like sometimes when you're praying, it's like Jesus is right there with you?"

"Yes, I know what that's like sweetheart. I'm glad you know what that's like too.

*

As Helen arrived in her Sunday School room, Adele Stephenson bustled up to her. "Hello Helen! Apparently, your Aggie has been in some trouble at school! But now, all the other children have to write a letter to her! Something about making her feel welcome. I really can't understand what it's all about! Such a pretty little thing, your Aggie, I just can't imagine her stirring up trouble!"

Indignation swelled in Helen, and she was about to make a retort uncharacteristic of her. But the compliment to Aggie was so blatantly insincere, making the whole remark so petty, that her indignation dissipated like smoke in the wind.

"Adele, having the children write letters was initiated by Mr. Bradley. If there is anything you don't understand, you need to talk to him."

As the class began, Helen settled into her chair. "Did I need any further assurance to choose carefully who I talk to about my own prayer needs?" she asked herself. But before she and Aggie left for home after the service, she had managed to share her concern about the supervisor position with Cassie Sanders, and Jill Pembroke, the leader of the class. The three of them had often met to pray together at Cassie and Jon's house.

*

Mr. Bradley sat at his desk on Monday morning, facing boxes filled with letters, the efforts of his students during the weekend. There was one box from each class, and each teacher had included a list noting any student who had failed to produce the required letter. He would do some follow up on those, but his chief concern was to check on the handiwork of those he knew to be offenders.

An hour later, he decided that the response to his instructions had been very satisfactory. All except one of the known offenders had conformed, and in nearly every case the letter was at least passable. The apologies were probably not as comprehensive as they needed to be, and did not ring with sincerity, but he thought they were as much as he could expect. He had also sampled the letters of those who claimed not to have offended, and were writing simple affirmations to Aggie – these were for the most part warm and sincere.

Just two letters lay to one side as he finished his survey. One was written in Maori, and the other was signed by Kelly Stephenson. Mr. Bradley picked up Kelly's letter and read it through again. It consisted of some rather sickly-sweet praise of Aggie, and said nothing about Kelly's role in persecuting her. He buzzed Mrs. Connors.

"Would you have Kelly Stephenson come to my office

60

immediately please?"

"Certainly Mr. Bradley."

Two minutes later Kelly was standing before his desk. "Kelly, I've read your letter to Aggie. You wrote some nice things to her, but you did not mention any of the ways you've hurt her. Why is that?"

Kelly did not know quite what to say. Finding a bolt hole was her instinctive strategy, but she didn't know how many of her offenses against Aggie were known, and didn't want to incriminate herself any further than necessary. Mr. Bradley knew of two other incidents beside the slapping he had personally witnessed, but he didn't want to tip his hand too early either.

"Well?" he asked again.

"I ... I did hardly anything to her. I ... I tried to be her friend." She became flustered and her face started to redden.

"I don't think there's much truth in that," Mr. Bradley replied. "Let's try to get a little honesty going here. Suppose you list for me the things you know you did to Aggie, and I'll prompt you for some you may forget."

That did not sound promising to Kelly. Rather reluctantly she listed four incidents, only one of which Mr. Bradley already knew about.

"I'm ... I'm sorry," she stammered, "some of the other kids, like Colin, and ..."

"I don't need you to be telling tales on other children, thank you," Mr. Bradley cut in.

"But, but the others would've done mean things to me if I hadn't done some stuff to Aggie!"

"And you would have done mean things to some others if they hadn't joined in," he observed dryly. "Well Kelly, you had your opportunity to say sorry to Aggie, and you didn't take it. It was perfectly clear what you needed to do, and you didn't do it. I'm going to suspend you from school for now. Please go sit on the bench outside my office while I phone your parents."

As it happened, Kelly's father was out of town on business, so it was her mother, Adele Stephenson, who bustled into Mr. Bradley's office about half an hour later. She took it upon herself to grab Kelly's hand as she came, bringing her child back into the office with her.

"Hello Mrs. Stephenson," Mr. Bradley began, as they took their seats. "I'm sure you know of the task I gave the senior school over the weekend. The students were fully briefed, and each brought home a written notice so parents would be aware of what was required. It concerned the bullying of Aggie Betteridge. Any child who had assaulted Aggie in any way was required to list his or her offenses, and apologize for each incident. There have been at least three such incidents involving Kelly, perhaps more, but she has not apologized for any of them."

"Kelly is a good child Mr. Bradley," Adele Stephenson plunged right in without waiting to hear more. "I'm sure she hasn't done any real harm to the Betteridge child. Besides, that Aggie has a mean streak of her own you know! She can be pretty nasty!" Turning to Kelly, she continued, "She has said some really hurtful things to you, hasn't she dear?"

"Oh yes Mamma! Really, really bad!" A tear of self-pity was starting to Kelly's eye as she found fresh confidence from her mother's attack.

"So there, you see. I really can't blame Kelly for getting a little of her own back!" Adele sat bolt upright, her face flushed.

Mr. Bradley leaned forward over his desk, his hands clasped just under his chin. "Mrs. Stephenson, I have not heard from any other witness of Aggie provoking other children. But I have personally witnessed Kelly, as part of a gang of five other children, attacking Aggie by taking turns in slapping her head. Aggie was not showing any aggression at all towards these children."

"Oh yes, and what has happened to these other children?" Adele demanded to know.

"Each one of them has apologized rather handsomely," Mr. Bradley replied. "Mrs. Stephenson, I made it quite clear that any child who did not take this opportunity to fully apologize, would be risking suspension. I am suspending Kelly from school until such time as she has made an apology that fully satisfies me, the school board, and Mrs. Betteridge. Please come with me now so that we can collect all Kelly's books and belongings."

Adele's rage boiled over. "Come Kelly dear," she cried.

"Let's get out of this school as quickly as we can. I wouldn't have you attending here a minute longer than we can help! Come get your things!"

*

The sight of Mr. Bradley calmly accompanying fuming Mrs. Stephenson, while they cleared Kelly's desk made a deep impression. As word spread through the rest of the school, the lesson of kindness prevailing over bullying was firmly reinforced. None of Kelly's classmates ever forgot that sight.

*

Mr. Bradley sat at his desk again, and picked up the other letter he had put aside. He reached for his phone, and dialed Hohepa Te Koari.

"Hello Hohepa," he began as his friend answered. "I think you spent quite some time with Colin Campbell during the weekend."

"That we did," came the reply. "Pretty much the whole of Saturday."

"Well Hohepa, a response in Maori wasn't quite what I had in mind! But I see that both you and his mother have signed it. You must have translated it for her?"

Hohepa gave a long chuckle. "Nathan, when we began in English, I thought it was a lost cause. I didn't think he would ever finish to your satisfaction. It was his idea to change to Maori – and he did an excellent job."

"Hmm. I'm really grateful to you for taking the time. I'd like to see a translation myself before long. But in the meantime, I can trust you on this."

"Thanks Nathan. If Aggie Betteridge has any trouble finding a Maori speaker to help her know what Colin wrote to her, I'll be happy to help out."

"Hohepa, once again, I appreciate more than I can say the interest you're taking in Colin." As he hung up the phone, he was wondering what the boxes of letters would mean to Aggie when she started reading them this evening. Especially the one in Maori, written by her chief persecutor.

Chapter 7

The Letter.

On Monday morning, before Mr. Bradley arrived at his school office, Helen was already at Allied Garments. Instead of going straight to her workstation as usual, she detoured to Stephen Spenlow's office.

"Morning Mr. Spenlow. May I speak to you about the supervisor job?"

"Come right in Helen. Please take a seat. So, what's your conclusion?"

"Well, Mr. Spenlow, I'd like to accept the position. I'm honored that you've offered me the job, and I will give my best to seeing you are not disappointed."

"Helen, I'm delighted you've accepted. I'll work with Joy on rearranging duties, and have you start assisting her on Wednesday. That will give you a week and a half of overlap with her before she finishes up Friday of next week. Please don't say anything to the rest of the staff in the meantime – I will make an announcement tomorrow afternoon. How are you feeling about the change?"

"A little jittery. It will seem very different for me. But my daughter and I prayed about it, and I'm sure it will work out."

The religion thing again. Oh well, Stephen didn't think she would impose her Christian ideas on the rest of the staff. He didn't think it would be an issue.

"I think you'll do a fine job Helen. Oh, and supervisor's privilege – you get to call me Stephen instead of Mr. Spenlow."

Helen smiled and nodded as she headed to her workstation.

*

Everyone at school was sobered by Kelly Stephenson's suspension, but nobody seemed to regret her absence. Aggie felt a new sense of respect throughout the rest of that Monday. Some of her classmates gave her open smiles and greetings when they saw her around the school; others seemed to feel some uncertainty, not quite knowing how to adjust their thoughts and feelings to this quiet, shy girl. The snippets Mr. Bradley had told them of her father, and his praise of her and her mother, engendered a new respect among many of her peers, but it would take some time for overall attitudes to adjust.

Mrs. Connors surveyed the pile of seven boxes, containing all of Aggie's letters, and decided this was too much for her to carry home. At the end of the school day, she waited with Aggie until Pauline McKnight arrived, and then helped carry the boxes out to the car. Pauline drove to Aggie's house to drop the boxes off, before going on to her own house.

Aggie was feeling the weight of much more attention than she was accustomed to, so she was in no hurry to get home to start checking out her letters. But curiosity was competing with the apprehension, so when she did arrive home from the McKnight's, she went straight to the boxes. Helen came in just at the same time, and they stood together gazing at the small tower on their lounge room floor. They turned to look at each other, each breaking out with the little giggle that often united them at moments like this.

"That's a lot of letters Agnes! It's going to take you a while to get through those!"

"Hmm," Aggie responded. "It feels very strange to have all these letters written to me. I'm not sure how I feel about it."

"Take your time my dear," Helen answered. "I'll go start on our tea." She went through into the kitchen, leaving Aggie confronting her tower.

She started arranging boxes on the floor, in a circle round her. Which one would she open first? She decided to begin with her own class. The first four letters she pulled out were from girls in her class she did not know so very well. They had been

66

neither especially friendly nor unfriendly to her, so she was surprised by the ones from Christie and Sally, and perhaps Alice's as well – the letters struck a really caring note. Each of these girls said how sorry they were that she had been hurt and bullied.

Aggie was touched. She took the letters into the kitchen.

"Listen to this Mum!" She read the first two letters. No tears started to her eyes, but Helen could see how her heart responded to the unlooked-for kindness. Helen's own eyes became moist as she listened to the care being expressed for her daughter.

Aggie returned to the box of letters from her class. She could see that it would take a long time to go through them all, and she was curious about the letters from people in her class who had been unkind to her. So she began searching. Alex Riley, Timothy Bailey, Angela Braggs, …. Who else? Soon she had a pile of six letters, all of which should contain a long list of confessions and apologies. In fact, none included a list of misdemeanors nearly as long as it should have been, And the apologies they did contain didn't sound especially sincere.

Sadness and disappointment began seeping back into Aggie's heart. The first letters she had read had swelled new hope and gratitude, even a kind of gladness within her. And she still did have a cautious hope for new friendship with some of these classmates. But for the mean ones? Aggie wondered if she should complain about the things they had done to her, that were not even mentioned. But that would mean tattling, and she had never done that before. Why didn't they apologize properly? She would have forgiven pretty much anyone who had genuinely asked.

Aggie was quiet the rest of that evening. Helen wondered at her reserve, and as they ate their tea together, she asked, "How are the other letters?"

"They're okay," Aggie responded after a pause. "I looked at some that were supposed to be saying they're sorry. They kind of did, but they only said a few of the things they've done." She frowned. "Do you think I should make them tell about the other things they should say sorry for?"

Helen thought for a few moments. "I'm not sure," she said. "If you go down that path, it might be a long, unsatisfying struggle. You can't make people sorry if they aren't really. Are you thinking of times when you felt really, really hurt, but the person who hurt you hasn't said anything about what they did?"

"Yes .... No .... Not really .... Oh, I don't know. I'll think about it."

*

During her prayer time as she went to bed that night, the sense of gladness at the possibility of new friendships with some of the girls in her class still danced back and forth with her sadness at the very muted apologies of others in her class. It was so confusing – why did they want to be mean to her?

The next day at school, Aggie noticed Christie and Sally together as she come into the classroom.

"Hello Aggie," called Christie. They both smiled at her, a little uncertainly, but warmly enough.

"Hello." Aggie felt a little awkward. "Thank you for writing nice letters to me. They were, ah, nice," she finished lamely. But the two girls didn't seem to notice her embarrassment, and chatted with her while she moved to her desk.

The lightened atmosphere she had noticed on Monday did seem to continue. There were smiles and greetings from some other girls in her class, suggesting that the promise of new friendships might just be real. And the ones who had been her tormentors were much more reserved, tending to ignore her instead of making their usual taunts.

Aggie noticed that Alex Riley kept his distance, though she did intercept some dark glances from him. The Riley family attended her church, and Alex was part of her Sunday School class. He nearly always used Sunday School time to continue his taunts from the week, so she had endured more from him than from most others. Oh well, she was glad that he seemed to have been reined in for now at least.

*

That Tuesday afternoon at Allied Garments, Mr. Spenlow closed the shift fifteen minutes early, and had the staff gather.

"So, we extend our sympathy to Joy at the passing of her sister," he concluded, "but we are pleased that she will be able to help out with her brother-in-law, and care for her nieces and nephews. That is such a worthwhile task. We wish her all the best."

Stephen Spenlow glanced at Helen before continuing. "Joy has been an excellent supervisor, and I'm very sorry to see her go. Never-the-less, I'm delighted to announce that Helen Betteridge has accepted the role as Joy's successor. Helen will be the new shift supervisor."

A gasp of surprise, not quite audible, but clearly felt, swept through the room. It seemed no one had thought of Helen for the role.

"Helen has been at Allied for eight years now, and she knows our company and its systems quite well. I know you've respected her as a co-worker, and I'm sure you will give her respect and support as your new supervisor."

Somewhat bemused as they were, most of the staff joined warmly enough in a round of applause for Helen. Just two or three exchanged disbelieving glances, their applause half-hearted. Only Zoe Campbell abstained from applauding at all, her face showing distain for the woman who was to be assuming authority over her.

"Joy will be with us for the remainder of this week, and for next week," Stephen resumed. "Helen will work as her assistant until the end of next week, while she learns more of her new role. I know you will make the transition as easy for her as possible."

As she drove home from work, Helen was thinking, "Well, the announcement is made, the die is cast. Please come with me on this road Lord!"

*

The rest of that week was easier than Helen had expected. She and Joy went through the daily and weekly procedures demanded by the supervisor role. She needed some reminding every now and again, but on the whole, she absorbed the details quickly. The women on her shift helped to ease her into her responsibilities – most seemed pleased with the choice of Helen as supervisor in spite of their initial surprise. Some privately offered their congratulations, lifting Helen's hopes that she would manage the role well. The few who were more reserved did not present any challenges those first few days – it seemed they were watching her, assessing whether she would have their co-operation or not.

Even Zoe did not openly challenge her during those initial days. Her hostility was barely concealed, and several times she spoke mockingly, with exaggerated politeness, but Helen chose not to react, replying to Zoe with the same courtesy she showed to the rest of the staff. By Friday, some uncertainty began playing around the edge of Zoe's mind. Mousey little Helen was showing more strength than she had expected. Mousey little Helen had not accepted any of her bait, had not broken down sobbing. Zoe still felt herself to be more than a match for Helen, but it might take a little more than she had imagined to break her.

*

Helen and Aggie arrived home at almost the same time that Friday afternoon. Helen was feeling encouraged that her first three days as supervisor had passed without major incidents. Aggie was still preoccupied with her roller-coaster feelings. Most of the children at school continued to treat her nicely, but the smiles and greetings were beginning to wane a little. The possibility that some real new friendships might develop looked more distant. The one exception was Stephanie Davis. Stephanie had been one of the nasty ones, a friend of Kelly Stephenson, and had followed Kelly's lead in tormenting Aggie. But whether she had been jolted by Kelly's suspension from school, or for some other reason, she did seem to be genuinely sorry for her past behavior, and was going out of her way to befriend Aggie.

So, Aggie's thoughts went to and fro. Overall, school felt a safer, more pleasant place, for which she was grateful. But she was still hurt and puzzled by the response of her former tormentors. Apart from Stephanie's apology, all the others were threadbare, and their manner towards her was more sullen than welcoming. Why did they dislike her? She couldn't work it out.

Then it hit her. Colin! She hadn't found his letter yet! She had been so puzzling over all the rest, that she had forgotten about Colin. Come to think of it, he had looked at her strangely when he'd seen her at school this week. At first there seemed to be something odd, even eager in his glance – what had he been expecting? But this afternoon, while she was waiting for Mrs. McKnight, he'd passed her on his way out the school gate – his glance then had been clearly hostile. What could it mean?

Aggie hurried to her array of boxes. The box from Colin's class she had left to last, but now she turned to it, and opened it quickly. Where was the letter from Colin? Ah, here. Colin's handwriting was not finely developed, but here was the envelope. "To Aggie Betteridge, From Colin Campbell." It was unsealed, so she shook the letter out onto the floor. Aggie gave a gasp of surprise. Folded though it was, she could see that the letter was written in Maori!

She picked it up and unfolded it. Was Colin mocking her, sending her a letter she couldn't read? Yet the words and letters were well-formed, and the whole stretched to nearly four pages. Colin had clearly put in some time and effort – that didn't look like mocking.

"Mum!" Aggie ran out to the kitchen. "Look! Colin Campbell has written his letter in Maori!"

Helen took the letter, glancing through its pages.

"Why would he write in Maori? He knows I can't read Maori!"

They looked at each other, wondering. "I'm not sure

what to think my dear. It does seem strange. I know he's been very mean to you. I hoped he would make a very sincere apology. But I don't know what to make of this."

"Hey, I know Mum! That Maori lady at church, Mrs. Taupiri, she speaks Maori. Do you think she could read it for us?"

"Yes," Helen replied, "I'm sure she could."

Suddenly, Aggie had a sense of urgency about knowing what Colin had written to her. "Mum, could we go over to her house right after our tea? Please?"

Helen smiled. "I'd like to solve this mystery too. I'll give Mrs. Taupiri a call."

*

Colin was more sullen and angry than he'd been for a long time. He had really caught some inspiration from Hohepa about the new person he could become. He'd put more effort into that letter than he'd ever put into any kind of writing. He'd anticipated with some uneasiness, but also some eagerness, taking on a new role of protector and friend to the little Pakeha girl. And she had ignored him all week! At first, he'd been disappointed, but realized that maybe she hadn't got to his letter yet. But as the week wore on, his patience evaporated. She was scorning him! He was humiliated and furious. He would teach her to treat him like this!

On Saturday morning, Colin woke early. He found himself some breakfast, ate abstractedly, then sat staring at his plate. He felt lonely and hurt. He'd listened to Hohepa, followed his advice, and this is where it had got him! Colin wandered out onto the street, unsure of where he was going, but starting to scheme about how he would pay out this stuck-up little kid. Hah! That rabbit she kept in her back yard! He would kill it and skin it, and leave the mess all over its little enclosure. That would show her what he thought of her! But he'd have to leave it until after dark. Wouldn't pay to get caught!

But what to do with the rest of the day? He wandered

72

aimlessly on, eventually finding himself beside the Ruamahanga River, right where Hohepa had taken him to one of the eel traps. And there was Hohepa right in front of him, just coming up the bank with a small eel wriggling on the end of a trace! Disillusioned, humiliated as he was, with thoughts of revenge tumbling in the back of his mind, Hohepa was not a person he wanted to meet just now. But it was too late.

*

Helen and Aggie didn't stop to clear their Friday evening tea dishes. Now they sat at Te Pura Taupiri's kitchen table, explaining the situation. Te Pura's eyes were bright and quick, her face wrinkled, the moko tattooed blue on her brown chin showing clearly under the central light above the table.

"So, we're puzzled why Colin would have used Maori to write to Agnes. We thought it might be insulting, writing something she wouldn't understand, but he seems to have taken a lot of trouble if he was just wanting to insult." Helen passed the letter across the table.

Te Pura chuckled. "Young Colin hey? He's a hard case that one. But Hohepa thinks there's some good in the boy. Might turn out alright." She reached for her glasses. "Let's see what he has to say."

Helen and Aggie watched as Te Pura carefully read Colin's letter, tracing the lines with her finger as she went. She muttered words like "Ponga", and "good, yes very good", breaking out into smiles every now and again. Aggie turned to her mother, raising her eyebrows, along with a little grin. Mrs. Taupiri's response looked encouraging so far.

Finally, Te Pura let the pages drop into her lap. She looked up, her eyes twinkling.

"He's written about the story of Ponga and Puhihuia," Helen and Aggie shot an inquiring look at each other. "It's an old

73

Maori tale of a young warrior named Ponga, and the beautiful maiden Puhihuia, who fall deeply in love. The problem is that they're from rival tribes. Ponga is low born, but Puhihuia is the daughter of a famous chief. Of course, their families tell them to part, but Ponga and Puhihuia elope, and are secretly married."

Aggie's eyes were wide. "Did he write all that?"

Te Pura chuckled again. "No, this is a long and complicated tale. It's about the two tribes as well as the two lovers. Colin may have the story a bit jumbled, but he seems to get the idea that Ponga was a strong hero. Strong in his mind and character, as well as his skill as a warrior. The gist of the letter is that he apologizes for using his strength in bad ways, and promises to follow the example of Ponga, being a man of honor towards the Pakeha maiden." She looked up at Aggie. "That's you my dear. He's talking about being a protector to you instead of a tormentor."

Aggie's mind whirled. This was very different. She hadn't really hoped for very much from Colin, so a story about honor and strength, and … and the idea of even protecting her … it was too big a leap for her to grasp right away.

"I don't quite get it. Why did he write to me about this story?"

Te Pura paused, considering how to explain to Aggie. "Do you know what 'mana' means? It's kind of a pool of all that's good and honorable about a person or a family, or a village. When someone does good things, and respects and helps other people, he's building his own mana, and the mana of his whanau – that is, his family and his people. Colin is saying that the way he treated you was not building the mana of his people. He's saying he's sorry for that, and wants to make other Maori proud of him by treating you well."

Aggie was still finding it hard to believe in this reversal from Colin. "He even said he will protect me instead of hurting me?"

"Yes dearie. That's what he said. I hope he can live up to it."

*

Aggie was in her nightie, ready to snuggle down for her night's sleep. She and Helen were sitting on the edge of her bed, chatting and praying. Colin's letter was still the focus of their thoughts. Could it really mean a whole change of heart from him? They were silent for a while as the matter revolved through their prayers. Eventually, Aggie looked up at her Mum.

"Mum, I think Colin means what he says. He was acting strange this week, but Jesus just showed me he was kind of anxious to see what I thought of his letter. And I left it all week without getting to it! Maybe he feels hurt that I haven't said anything to him."

"Agnes my dear, that's just what was coming to me. It's hard to trust him completely after all this time, and I think you need to be careful while you see how this plays out. But I think we need to cautiously give him the benefit of the doubt."

"Mum, it's awful if he feels hurt I didn't say anything. Could we go to his house tomorrow, so I can tell him I liked his letter?"

"Hmm, I don't know about going to his house to talk to him. I think you need to take this slowly. But maybe you could write him a note to thank him for his letter, and we could take the note round to his house. But just go cautiously – don't write anything that might get thrown back at you."

"Thanks Mum!" The furrows in Aggie's brow smoothed out a little as she wriggled into bed and pulled the covers around her.

*

The early morning light was behind Hohepa as he emerged from the riverside track. He caught the startled look on Colin's face.

"What's up Colin?"

"Nothin! Just walkin' along the river."

Hohepa regarded him for a long moment. He guessed that all was not well with the Aggie Betteridge matter – probably something to do with the reception of Colin's letter to her.

"Colin, tomorrow I'm taking my set line out to Riversdale, to see if I can catch some ocean fish. This guy," he swung the eel up higher, "can go in my bait bucket. How would you like to come with me tomorrow? And now we can go to my house to get the gear checked over, so that we're ready to go in the morning."

What would he do? This man talked as though being strong and good and authentic was possible for him, something attainable! But when he tried to go in that direction, it turned to mush. Life was just a round of disappointment and rejection for the likes of him.

But a fishing trip! Besides, something in him still responded to Hohepa. Spending time with him still won the day.

"Okay. Thanks."

*

At about nine o'clock, Helen's car drew up outside the Campbell house. There seemed to be no-one about.

"I'll put my note in the letterbox," said Aggie. But then she noticed, the letterbox was a wreck, perched lop-sided at the top of its post. "Maybe I should run up and slide it in beside the front door."

"Yes, okay Agnes," said Helen uneasily. She didn't want to encounter Zoe on her home turf, so she hoped they could leave Aggie's note, and move on without attracting attention. Aggie ran to the door of the house, slid the note in beside the lock, then scurried back to the car. Helen pulled out onto the road with a sigh of relief.

*

The job of checking out the fishing gear took longer than necessary as Hohepa spent time working and chatting with Colin. Gradually the story came out. He had waited eagerly to see how Aggie would respond to his letter, but she'd just ignored him. She just didn't care about the likes of him.

Hohepa was uneasy too – he thought she would have responded in some way by now. Would she just gloss over the letter, or would she give some affirmation to this boy who so desperately needed it? He tried to be as encouraging as he could to Colin.

"Colin, you did the right thing! You made an honest apology, and you took a stand on being a real man in the future. Even if she ignores you, you will always know you did the right thing!"

*

Hohepa drove Colin down to the fish and chip shop to buy some lunch. They went to the park to eat. When they were done, Colin set out to walk the rest of the way home.

"He really is a good man," he thought as he walked along. "Somehow I hope he may still be right. Shall I sneak out tonight to kill that rabbit?" Even a few weeks ago he could have done this to Aggie's rabbit, and thought nothing of it. But now, the thought of spending the day with Hohepa tomorrow, carrying the memory of a dead rabbit left to taunt Aggie, just didn't seem like a good idea.

As Hohepa drove home from the park, he was praying. He wasn't a man who attended church, or thought very much about God – spending the day tomorrow fishing with Colin instead of bothering about church service was a case in point. But

77

right now, he was telling the Almighty that this was a crucial time for Colin. "He needs some encouragement if he's going to move forward from here. So, please, we need a miracle!"

*

Hohepa had been home from the fish and chip shop only about forty-five minutes, when Colin arrived back at his door. He was flushed and panting.

"She left a note for me!" he gasped, pushing a small envelope across the table.

Hohepa pulled out the note card and read.

"Dear Colin, I just found your letter last night. It was in the last box, so it took me until now to find it.

It is a very nice letter. No-one ever wrote me a letter in Maori before. Mum and I took it to Mrs. Taupiri from our church, so she could read it to us.

I like the story about Ponga and Puhihuia. It is a good story.

Thank you for saying sorry, and for the other nice things you said.

Agnes."

Colin knew only vaguely who Mrs. Taupiri was, but right now he was intensely grateful to her. And "Agnes"! He remembered that he had heard her real name was Agnes, though nobody he knew ever called her that. Somehow it made her note very special that she had signed it with her real name.

Hohepa was silently praying again. "God, you never answered a prayer that quickly before! I'm ever so grateful!"

*

Aggie caught sight of Colin as she arrived at school on Monday morning. She turned toward him uncertainly. Had he received her note? Did he still look angry? She was relieved to see him walk quickly toward her.

"Hello Aggie. Thanks for your note. If you have any more trouble from anyone, you just let me know, okay?" Only rarely did Colin speak to a girl. He couldn't remember speaking to Aggie at all before, unless it was to taunt her in some way. Suddenly he felt embarrassed.

"Thank you, Colin. I liked your letter too."

They stood looking at each other, both uncertain what to say next. Then each turned, and went their separate ways.

Very little passed between Colin and Aggie for the remainder of that school year, but there was a tacit sense of friendship between them. A week after that first short conversation, Alex Riley decided to make another attempt at lording it over Aggie. He was standing at her school bag, rummaging to find her lunch to throw across the playground when he felt a presence behind him. Whirling quickly, he found Colin's nose an inch from his.

"Alex Riley, you mess with Aggie Betteridge, and I'll mess with you!"

Alex' face flushed. He would like to have made a retort about red face little Aggie being Colin's girlfriend, but that would definitely not have been wise, with Colin standing over him. His mind raced, trying on other responses, but nothing seemed suitable. He side-stepped past Colin and beat his retreat. Chelsea McKnight was close by to witness the incident, so Aggie got to hear of it that afternoon. As the next school day was finishing, once again she saw Colin making his way towards the school gate while she waited for Mrs. McKnight to arrive. She ran over to him.

"Colin! Thank you for stopping Alex Riley taking my lunch!"

"S'or right! You tell me if he does anything else!" The sense of awkwardness still hung between them as they turned away. But Aggie was deeply grateful for the reversal in Colin's behavior. The strange, muted friendship that was beginning was a great source of comfort to her. She turned back, and called to him.

"Colin!" He stopped and turned. "In my prayer times I

thank Jesus that you're my friend now! And I pray for you!"

Colin left the school grounds that day with an unfamiliar mix of feelings. Talking to a girl was embarrassing, but sensing her gratitude gave him a glow of pride he didn't remember feeling before. He was her friend now? He hadn't thought of that, but he supposed it was right. Colin Campbell has a friend? And she's a girl? Something new was happening. He knew he was indebted to Hohepa for inspiring him to start on this new track, but he had little idea as yet where it would lead him.

Chapter 8

Supervisor Helen.

It was Wednesday morning, the middle of Helen's third week in sole charge of her shift. Stephen Spenlow met her as she arrived for the day.

"Good morning Helen! Well, how are you feeling about the job so far?"

"Hello Stephen!" She dropped her bag to the floor beside the door to her office. "I think I'm managing. I still feel a little apprehensive as I arrive each day, but then I get to the end of the day thinking it's been quite a good day. That week and a half working with Joy just flew by! It was scary taking over sole charge! But everything seems to be flowing along as it should."

"How about the women on your shift? You feel comfortable managing them?" The shift workers had not arrived yet, so they could talk freely.

"On the whole, yes. Most of them are friendly and encouraging. They're good workers too. But I know there are a few that could be difficult. I think I haven't really been tested in that area yet."

Stephen nodded. "What about Zoe. Is she doing alright?"

"Hmm, yes, I'm concerned about Zoe. She keeps up this mocking, disdainful attitude toward me. But apart from that, she hasn't really crossed any boundaries yet. She works well, keeps her records up to date, and looks after her machine. I'm thinking and praying about how to get in behind the hostile attitude."

In fact, Zoe had another matter occupying her thoughts, distracting her from schemes about taking Helen down. Something had happened to Colin. She wasn't sure what it was, or whether it would last, but it seemed he was being less of a nuisance at school. And he was doing schoolwork at home! Of course, Zoe knew he was supposed to do homework, though he had very rarely done any. But three times in the last two weeks she had found him reading a school book, or writing in one of his exercise books, when she arrived home from a bar. It was all rather confusing and a little unsettling. Colin was not fitting quite so well into the mold she expected of him.

Last night it had all gotten the better of her. She'd stayed at the bar longer than she intended, and the longer she stayed the more incapacitated she became. It was after three in the morning when a taxi finally deposited her at her door. The clock was showing nearly ten when she came to, with her head pounding and her mouth dry. Zoe used a warm washcloth, bringing some comfort to her face and aching forehead. She tried to focus on the day, and what she had to do next. Oh! How will Mrs. Supervisor Helen cope with me turning up with the morning nearly over?

If Joy was still her supervisor, Zoe thought she would probably be without a job by the end of the day. But with Helen? Would she be able to manage Helen, so she didn't get sacked? She didn't want to lose her job. What would she do? And how would she look after Colin? She was feeling a new sense of responsibility for Colin. Zoe gave a defiant toss of her head. She didn't know how the morning would go, but she'd do her best to manage little Mrs. Helen.

At Allied Garments, Zoe's workstation was the focus of Helen's thoughts. Zoe hadn't showed up, and no phone call had been received. It looked as though this might be the test of leadership that all concerned had been expecting. Sure enough, at eleven thirty-five, Zoe walked a little uncertainly through the door, and over to her workstation. She did not look at all well, her face pale. Helen had been praying all morning for wisdom, for composure, for just the right interaction with Zoe. Now she assumed her sunniest smile, and walked to Zoe's workstation.

"Good morning Zoe! You have some problems this morning? It would be more private in my office. Let's go talk there."

Eyebrows were raised around the room, and glances exchanged as Helen walked towards her office. After waiting just long enough to register her defiance, Zoe followed.

Helen sat behind her desk, and motioned Zoe to a chair.

"What happened today Zoe, to make you so late in?" Helen was grateful that her voice sounded natural and sympathetic. "Thank you, Lord," she murmured inwardly.

"Aw Helen, I don't know what it was. These awful stomach cramps, and terrible sick feeling came on last night. I was up nearly all-night vomiting. I only got to sleep about five this morning, so it was nearly ten when I woke up."

"Zoe, that's awful! You must feel really terrible! I wonder what caused it?"

Zoe was startled. Could this woman be swallowing her story so easily? She assumed a forlorn expression, promptly manufacturing pathetic gratitude for Helen's sympathy.

"I don't know what it was Helen. Just some tummy bug I expect."

"How are you feeling now? Will you be okay today?"

"Oh, I'll manage." She gave a wan smile, almost moved by her own heroism. "Thank you, Helen," Zoe was rising to leave, but Helen spoke again.

"Zoe, before you go, I have something to ask of you." Zoe sat down again. "I wonder if you could do this for me?"

Helen paused for a few moments, looking at her office ceiling. Her eyes returned to Zoe.

"Zoe, could we imagine a little story? Let's just suppose.... This is just a story you know." Her expression was still soft, but her glance was penetrating. "Let's suppose you are down at Daniel's one evening, enjoying a few drinks. You start to think it's maybe time to get on home. But then another thought jumps in."

She smiled at Zoe. "You following my make-believe story? So, this other thought jumps in. You think, 'Oh, I'm enjoying myself! I don't want to go home yet! Why should I go home? I can enjoy myself if I want!' Now right there, you're at a choice point. You know that if you stay longer, you might just stay much longer. You might end up with a very sore head in the morning. And not much change in your purse. You know that it's happened before."

Zoe was startled all over again. How did Helen know exactly what had happened to her last night? Helen's gratitude increased, as she sensed the Lord was giving her the right words to say.

Helen smiled at Zoe again. "Is my story a bit far-fetched? Couldn't ever happen, huh? But this is what I want to ask of you. Just supposing …. just if you ever did find yourself at that choice point. You know it would be important for you, right? You know your job would be seriously at risk. So if that situation, that choice, ever happens, I want to ask that you would phone me. I'll give you my home phone number to keep in your purse, so that you'll be able to call me, from right there in the bar. Before you decide either way what to do, call me first. Will you do that?"

Very rarely had Zoe been lost for words. Right now, she was floored by Helen's evident concern. At the same time, she sensed that this would be her last reprieve. Dumbly she reached out to take the slip of paper with Helen's phone number. She rose again to leave. The inner gloating was gone, replaced by a confused swirl of thoughts and feelings. The old antagonistic words that had been her life's staple were part of the mix, but so was a sense that she had been treated firmly, but with real compassion. This was an almost unique experience for Zoe.

As she stepped back into the machine room, furtive glances were cast in her direction. The rest of the women on her shift had been expecting the sounds of angry argument to filter through the door of Helen's office. They couldn't guess whether Zoe would resume her place at her workstation, or whether she would be packing up her belongings and heading for the door. Either way, they expected to see a haughty, scornful face. Instead they saw Zoe subdued, thoughtful, frowning slightly, intent on getting her task under way. Now the glances were being exchanged around the room, eyebrows raising. How had Helen done it? Zoe took no notice, quickly becoming absorbed in her task.

*

During the afternoon of that same day, Mr. Bradley was speaking by phone again with his friend Hohepa Te Koari.

"Hohepa, what have you done with Colin? You've really done a number on him! He's resigned from being the school Tough Guy – he's actually being helpful towards some of the other children instead of threatening. His behavior towards Aggie Betteridge has completely reversed. And Hohepa, get this, he is doing the homework he's set!"

Hohepa gave a pleased chuckle. "Nathan, you set this ball rolling when you gave him that letter to write. That was the opportunity to do some ideal-raising. I just put him in touch with some pride in his ancestry. Colin did the rest."

"Well, I'm amazed, and incredibly grateful to you. I have to say, he is often quite sullen still at the start of the day. But as he settles in, he seems pleased to be at school. He's even made himself useful to the staff. Sees something that needs to be done, and gets in to help. And Hohepa, when he's thanked for his help, he gets so pathetically pleased. Embarrassed at being praised, but clearly so pleased to be appreciated."

"Yes Nathan, I guess you don't see something like this too often, but when you do, it's sure good to watch! Colin's brought school work over to me a couple of times to get some help. I'm guessing his performance to date has left him well behind. I can help him some, but I wonder if there's some way he can get some tutoring to help him catch up?"

"Yes, I thought of that too. I'll see what I can do."

*

As Mr. Bradley finished his phone call with Hohepa, Aggie was at the school gate waiting for Mrs. McKnight. She hadn't seen Colin for a few days, but as she looked across the playground, she saw him coming towards her. That time of day seemed the time when she most often saw him passing.

"Colin!" He turned and came towards her, pleased to

stop and talk to her, but still shy, embarrassed, a little unsure of himself. "Colin, I wanted to ask you if you would come to our Sunday School on Sunday mornings. We sing songs, and hear stories from the Bible. They explain about Jesus, and how he is our friend. A lot of other kids from school come."

This was all rather confusing to Colin. He'd heard a little about Jesus, but only a very little. How could this person called Jesus be a friend? And singing? That part was not an encouragement. On the other hand, if Aggie was asking him, he was interested. He had thought several times about her comment that she was praying for him. What did she pray he wondered? He stood uncertainly.

"I dunno. What time is it? I'll have to ask Mum."

"It's nine o'clock. At Carrington Church of God, just near to your house. I hope you can come."

Colin nodded, and moved on. In previous times he wouldn't have bothered asking his mother, but would have just taken himself off there if he pleased. Even now, he would probably go, whatever his mother said.

When Zoe arrived home later that Wednesday afternoon however, Colin was not prepared for the strength of her reaction. It had been a hard day for Zoe. For one thing, she was not fully recovered from last night's binge. For another, a few hours of self-talk during the afternoon at her workstation had undermined her sense that Helen was trying to be considerate to her. She was not used to being treated kindly, and all her habits of suspicion and mistrust were back on top. She was thinking how condescending Helen had been. "Talking to me as though I'm the town drunk! How dare she!"

And now, here was Colin asking if he could go to Aggie's Sunday School! The very idea! Here was the upstart daughter of that upstart supervisor, trying to paste religion onto her son!

"Don't you dare go near that church, with its crowd of do-gooders! A lot of good they've ever done the likes of us! You keep away, mind!"

Colin thought it would be best for him to keep away from Carrington Church of God, at least for now.

86

*

Through the day on Thursday, Zoe's defiance resurfaced with a vengeance. She didn't give voice to her thoughts, but the glances she sent Helen's way could have sliced through steel.

"Lord," Helen murmured to herself several times that day, "what's going on? I thought we did well yesterday! What's happened?" She sighed. This was not going to be easy.

*

Life for Aggie was different, yet the same. Colin was different. She wondered what life was like for him at home. Was he friends with his mum, the way she was with hers? Probably not. And she thought about his Maori heritage – it would be fun to speak and write another language like Colin did!

She wasn't nearly so harassed by the other children, though Stephanie Davis was still the only one who'd really had a change of heart. But even with Stephanie, no close friendship developed.

Aggie remained hurt and puzzled – why do they not like me? For a little while, the wall around her heart had shivered and tottered. But then those cold, hard stones consolidated as firmly as ever. It was a pattern that would repeat for a long time to come.

On this Thursday, she arrived home from school hot and grumpy. It was May already, and temperatures were beginning to drop in the evenings, but today had been oppressive. At lunchtime she'd seen Christie and Sally talking together, but when she walked over to join them, they turned away. She felt lonely, and angry, and … and tired!

Helen came home to find Aggie sitting hunched up on her bed. She stopped as she passed the bedroom door. "Hello sweetheart! You doing okay?"

Aggie looked back at her without replying. "I'm tired of

87

everything!" she burst out at last. "It was hot today, and no-one is friends with me, and I'm not pretty, and, and … what's the use of anything?"

Helen was feeling drained too. The day had been long and hot for her, she was anxious about Zoe and her moods, and now she came home to a petulant daughter! Her first impulse was to march away and leave Aggie to her mood. With a major effort, she summoned up the energy to listen and comfort.

Gradually, Aggie's troubled spirit quieted. At bedtime, as she knelt beside her bed, her thoughts drifted to Colin's mother. She didn't see Mrs. Campbell very often, but she knew her by sight.

All at once, a picture formed in Aggie's mind. "Mum! We need to pray for Mrs. Campbell!"

Helen appeared at her doorway. "What is it Agnes?"

"I have this picture of Mrs. Campbell, Colin's mum. She's walking on this old graveled road, and there's loose rocks all around. It's steep, going up a steep hill. And she's kind of staggering, as though she can't walk properly. She keeps stopping and starting, and staring around."

Aggie paused, then continued, "She's at the top of the road. It ends in a big cliff! It just drops straight off the edge! Mrs. Campbell is kind of smiling, funny like. She's thinking she can just walk right over the edge, and she won't get hurt. But then she frowns and stops. She's drinking something from a bottle. Mum! Do you think she'll hurt herself?"

Helen knelt beside her daughter. "I don't know Agnes. I hope not. Let's pray for her."

As they prayed, the picture gradually faded. Sleep began to overtake Aggie. Soon, Helen lifted her into her bed, and left her breathing evenly.

*

That evening, Zoe was back in Daniel's bar. Most of her angry thinking had subsided, but she was still angry enough to feel defiant towards Helen. "And anyway," she thought, "life is just too tough! With all that's going on with Colin, and with work, and with that Helen! To hell with it, I just need a drink. Or several."

An hour later, Zoe was beginning to mellow a little. One part of her mind was telling her that if she didn't get herself out of there, she would most likely be out of a job tomorrow. Another part was still saucy, thinking of the choice words she'd like to send Helen's way. Alright, she would just get herself another couple of shots, and then go home. She rose from her table, and set off for the bar.

Zoe could never understand what made her trip. She was sure she wasn't drunk enough to be falling over. It was almost as though there was a loose rock lying on the floor, and down she went. She landed heavily, winded, but not seriously hurt. She grunted in surprise, and lay still for a moment. The barman, and several patrons were promptly at her side looking down at her.

"Come on Zoe old girl, time for you to be off home."

Zoe snorted, shrugging off the proffered hand as she struggled to her feet. Normally she wouldn't have objected to their familiar way of speaking, but she wasn't going to have anyone tell her when it was time for her to go! She did feel a little shaken up though, so she made her way to a cushioned bench along the side of the bar room and sat, watching the patrons, and the barman filling drinks.

She was about to get up and go for those two shots of whisky when it struck her – she was in exactly the position Helen had described. The choice point between leaving and staying. Hmm, did that chit of a woman really think she would call her? But if she went for those two drinks, it would pretty certainly be the end of her for the night. Was that phone number still in her purse? Yes, here it was.

Zoe walked towards the phone, still undecided, still defiant, but still walking. She dialed the number.

It was just after nine thirty when Helen's phone rang.

"Hello Miss Sourpuss Helen. I'm at Daniel's and I'm just going to have some shots of whisky. So what are you going to do about it Miss Sourpuss Helen?" Zoe's voice was slurred.

So here it was. The challenge. "Zoe, what is the number of the phone you're calling from? Can you give me the number?"

Zoe eventually found the number written in the center of the dial, and repeated it to Helen.

"Zoe, can you stay right where you are please? I am going to hang up, but I'll call you back within five minutes. Will you stay by the phone and wait for me to call back?"

"Really? Five minutes? Better not be longer! I'll wait here."

"Thank you, Zoe. I'll call straight back."

Helen hung up the phone, and quickly dialed Pauline McKnight. "Please Lord, may they be home," she prayed. Pauline's husband Bill answered.

"Bill, it's Helen. I have a big favor to ask. I have an urgent errand, so I need someone to mind Agnes for me. Can you or Pauline come over straight away? It could be for over an hour!"

Bill McKnight was surprised, but he didn't hesitate. "Helen, I don't know what this is about, but I know you wouldn't call if it wasn't important. Either Pauline or I will be there in two or three minutes."

"Thank you so much Bill. I'll explain later!"

After hanging up, Helen called Zoe back. "Alright Zoe, I'm on my way. Thank you for calling. I'll see you in about five minutes. Will you stay right where you are, and wait for me?"

"Alright Helen." Zoe was sobering up a little, losing some of her swagger. Helen had really responded, and was coming down to meet her at Daniel's? That was unexpected. Zoe wondered what would happen next.

She didn't have long to wait. Before she knew it, Helen was shepherding her towards a cafe just three stores down from Daniel's. Helen let her choose her food – a large hamburger, with a strawberry Danish, and a large coffee.

"Zoe, would you go save us a table, and I'll bring the food," Helen asked. As soon as Zoe had moved off, she turned and asked, "Would you make the coffees decaf please?" She wanted Zoe to sleep the rest of the night, and felt sure she wouldn't notice the difference tonight. She ordered a doughnut to go with her own decaf.

Zoe started into her hamburger as soon as it arrived. Helen sipped at her coffee.

"Zoe, I'm so pleased you called me tonight. Good for you! You made a good choice!"

Zoe was still not thinking too clearly, but it was getting through to her that her boss cared enough to come out at night, haul her out of a bar, and buy food for her. A thought struck her.

"Who's looking after your kid?"

"A friend came over to stay with her while I'm with you."

Zoe was baffled. No-one had shown her this kindness – not ever, so far as she could remember. Helen had even called on friends to help her in her mission of mercy. Zoe finished her food and coffee in silence. They went back to the car, and Helen drove her home. She went to the front door with Zoe, and told her, "Zoe, it would be a good idea to drink a large glass of water before you get into bed. Can you do that?"

Zoe nodded. "Helen knows what she's talking about," she thought.

"Good. I'll see you in the morning. And thank you again for calling me."

"Thank YOU." Zoe had not imagined she would ever be thanking Helen for anything, certainly not with the kind of sincerity she was feeling right now.

Helen arrived home at nearly eleven. She told Pauline the events of the evening, and thanked her for her help. "Pauline, please pray with me that this experience will help Zoe. Help move her towards a little more responsibility."

*

The next morning, Helen was relieved to see Zoe arrive at her workstation looking about as refreshed and alert as Zoe ever looked. Helen gave her a fleeting smile, but for the rest of the day was careful to treat her as impartially as she treated the rest of the staff. At the end of the day, she asked Zoe to meet briefly in her office.

"Zoe, I wanted to thank you again for calling me last night. I was so pleased you did. I need to let you know though, that I can't always come out to get you out of a spot. If you're ever in that situation again, please call me again. But another time I might just encourage you over the phone, and it will be up to you to solve the problem."

Zoe regarded her gravely. "Thank you, Helen. You've been more than fair to me."

As Zoe drove home, the same battle raged through her mind. Part of her was angry. "How did I let that little Miss Helen rescue me, Zoe Campbell!?" Another part was replying, "Zoe, you still have your job! Zoe Campbell would be without a job right now if little Miss Helen hadn't treated her kindly."

She arrived home, and went to find Colin. "Colin, if you want to go to that Sunday School, you can go."

Chapter 9

Of This and That.

The days were beginning to get longer, the frosts less frequent. The spring flowers were showing their heads, delighting Helen and Aggie each morning as they left for work and school.

Helen had settled into her role as supervisor at Allied Garments – it was four months since she had met Zoe at Daniel's bar. Since then, Zoe had been consistently on time, turning out a good volume of quality work.

One day, Helen overheard a snippet of conversation between June and Sylvia.

"Hey Sylvia, that Lady Helen is quite the surprise. Gets up my nose a little when she's strict about maintenance, but she's all right. Can't imagine what magic she's pulled with Zoe!"

"You never said a truer word June. Old Zoe, why I've caught her looking almost cheerful sometimes. You're right about Helen too. She must have some hidden magic."

Helen smiled to herself as she slipped into her office. Still, the old Zoe was not easily defeated. She could sometimes assume her disdainful, haughty air. But then, back in mid-June came the evening when she made another phone call to Helen from Daniel's bar. The days then were becoming dull and depressing, with frequent rain setting in. Zoe's house had two windows with broken panes, letting in the chill damp air and the rain. Frequently she stared at them, wishing she could afford to have them fixed.

So, her house was damp, the days were dull, and Zoe sat in Daniel's bar, staring morosely at her empty brandy glass. Another brandy was calling, but that slip of paper in her purse also called out to her. That slip of paper had been her lifeline once before. She reached into her purse. Helen picked up her phone a little before eight on a wet, blustery evening.

"Zoe, how glad I am you chose to call me again."
Gradually she drew out some of the woes filling Zoe's thoughts.

"That must be such a big concern for you Zoe, not being
able to get those windows fixed." Privately, Helen thought that a
little more budgeting and planning through the autumn would
have solved the problem, but right now she was more focused on
encouraging Zoe to a more constructive solution than another
night of drinking.

"Zoe, thank you again for calling me. I think I might be
able to help get something done about those windows. Let's get
together tomorrow at work, and see what we can come up with. In
the meantime, what do you need to do to get yourself home
safely, and get a good night's sleep? Do you need to eat
something immediately, to help you sober up?"

"I should be okay Helen. I've got some food at home."

"Good. So, are you going to call a taxi to get home?"

"No. I got my car here. I'll be or' right."

Helen didn't like the idea of her driving, but knew she
had probably driven many times before, more inebriated than she
was now. She was about to suggest Zoe phone again as soon as
she got home, but then realized that she may not have a phone at
home. She didn't want to embarrass her by asking.

"Tell you what Zoe. It's just on eight. What say Agnes
and I call round to your house in about ten minutes? Just to make
sure you get home okay?"

"I'll be okay. You don't have to do that." But Zoe
sounded pleased.

"You get out to your car now. I'll call Agnes, and we'll
see you in ten minutes. Okay?"

Helen had some egg salad in her fridge, so she quickly
made a sandwich. She and Aggie were waiting when Zoe arrived
home. Helen went to the door with her.

"Have something to drink – water or coffee I mean! But
no caffeine, mind! Here's a sandwich for you. Get yourself a good
sleep, and I'll see you in the morning."

As they drove home, Helen was thinking of a men's
ministry at Carrington Church of God. The men had made a small

94

joke at their own expense by naming the ministry "Hammer and Tongues." The "tongues" part was a reference to the spiritual gift of tongues, which was a part of the church's charismatic tradition. The men of Hammer and Tongues gave their time to attend to house maintenance jobs for those in the community lacking the necessary finances and skills.

"Time to get ready for bed Agnes my love," said Helen as they came into the kitchen. "I'm going to phone Mr. McKnight to see if someone can help Mrs. Campbell with those broken windows."

Bill McKnight answered the phone on the second ring. "Hello Bill. This is Helen. I have a Hammer and Tongues project for you. Zoe Campbell has two broken window panes. She's feeling rather miserable with a cold, damp house."

"Sounds like something we could handle Helen. I could probably get it done Saturday morning."

"Thanks Bill. But please wait for her to phone you. I'll give her your number, and she can take responsibility for initiating the contact. And I would prefer you didn't give her a freebee. Make it a bargain price, and work out a payment plan if necessary. But I don't want her getting any handouts that have come via me. Not good for staff morale!"

Bill laughed. "Gotcha Helen. I'll wait for her call."

When Zoe arrived at Allied bright and early the next morning, she went straight to Helen's office.

"Here I am Helen, right on time! I had a good sleep." It was the first time Zoe had come to Helen on her own initiative, and the first real smile Helen had seen from her. And the first hint of friendship between them.

Helen gave a warm smile in return. "Thank you, Jesus," she breathed inwardly.

"You do look well rested Zoe! I'm glad to see you! About your windows – there's a group of men at our church who do odd jobs for people, at just the cost of materials. I asked one of them about your windows, and he said he thought they could handle that. I can give you his name and number if you'd like to try that idea."

Zoe stared. She had wondered what Helen meant by

saying she may be able to get some help with the windows. Had she heard right? Some men from Helen's church would come and fix them for just the cost of the glass? She was feeling recently that she was living in a rather pleasant dream – soon she would wake up and find herself right back in the depressing, no-win circles that had always trapped her.

First there was Helen. Far from being the weak little kitten she could dispose of at will, Helen had twice helped her get past the urge to drown her sorrows at the bar, and instead keep the job she so depended on.

Then there was Colin. Zoe knew her own attitude towards Colin was still moody, not nearly so loving as she should be. Perhaps she still resented getting pregnant, bringing the little bundle that was Colin into the world, obliging her to change her careless ways. Colin was still no saint, but he was definitely different. He didn't seem to bug her nearly so much. He even told her when he went out, where he was going – well sometimes at least. He was paying attention to his school work! That was a wonder!

And now, people from Helen's church would help her get her windows fixed. Zoe was still suspicious of anyone taking any sort of interest in her, and had been mostly scornful of churches and church people. However, a cautious trust in Helen was growing, and having that broken glass replaced was a big incentive. She made the call to Bill McKnight, and was impressed by the friendliness of the men who came to do the job for her.

So, some warmth slowly crept into Zoe's relationship with Helen, at least on the good days. There were still many days when Zoe was more like her cynical, disdainful self, but then she would remember that she still had a job, and would become cautiously grateful again.

*

"Colin Campbell! Mr. Bradley wants to see you in his office immediately." Colin's heart sank. It was months since he had been summoned to the principal's office. What could the trouble be? With a worried frown, he tramped out of the classroom.

"Come in Colin. Please take a seat." Mr. Bradley seemed cheerful enough. He smiled as Colin sat down. "Life has changed for you! You're becoming a very good student! Mr. Page tells me you're enjoying your work, and you've begun reading well. Your two tutors are saying the same. How are you feeling about your school work now?"

Colin's face flushed with pleasure. He was a little tongue-tied. "Thank you, sir," he managed after a pause. "I didn't know I was good at reading, and writing, and ... and all that."

"It's not just your school work, but your behavior as well. You're earning respect and friendship from the other children, and the staff. You're building your mana, and the mana of your people."

Colin blushed again, unsure of what to say.

"I'm proud of you Colin. Thank you for helping to make our school a safe, pleasant place to be. By the way, I heard Aggie asked you to her Sunday School. Did you go?"

"Mum said I could go, but I only went once. You have to get all dressed up, and they do all this singing, and telling stories, and how you're supposed to be good. I didn't understand most of it."

Mr. Bradley nodded thoughtfully. He continued to muse as Colin left to return to his classroom. He wasn't especially religious himself, but he thought that some religious training wouldn't hurt for Colin. "Te Pura Taupiri. She goes to that church. I think I'll give her a call."

Two days later, Te Pura waited for Colin at the end of his school day, and invited him to join her on Sunday mornings for a snack, and a gentler introduction to the mysteries of Sunday School. Gradually Colin became familiar with the Bible Te Pura gave him as his own, with the stories she showed him from it, and with the overall Christian story.

Colin's role as protector to Aggie consolidated slowly. Just a few of the old aggressors at school would occasionally send her some taunts, but no-one dared arouse Colin's wrath. They both grew to appreciate the friendship between them, though it remained on a muted level, with few interactions between them. Both continued to feel a little awkward with anything more than a very brief exchange of words. Aggie knew of Colin's visits with Mrs. Taupiri, and was glad he was learning more of Jesus. She heard too of how he was advancing in his school work, and privately cheered him on in her prayers.

*

Aggie and Helen were with Jon and Cassie Saunders again, sharing a Sunday afternoon at Third Creek. It was early September, but the day felt almost like full summer already. Lunch was over, and Aggie had wandered away down the track, to sit watching the stream flowing under the platform bridge crossing Third Creek.

Cassie sat watching Helen. "Helen, since you became supervisor at work, you've grown so much. You have such a confident, poised air about you."

"Do you think so Cassie? Is that …. good? I hope I'm not becoming a bossy old woman."

"It's good Helen. It's all good."

Helen smiled. "Thank you, Cassie. I guess I do feel stronger. More, um, confident. Yes, I suppose confident is the right word." Her smile faded. "But I'm concerned for Agnes though."

"Yes?"

Helen sighed. "School is much safer, more pleasant for her now. But she still keeps to herself too much. There's the birthmark – I think the kids at school have mostly stopped noticing it, but she's still so self-conscious about it. And her father. I do my best to make up for Martin, but she still pines for him so much."

Cassie nodded sympathetically. "That's tough Helen. You really do such a good job, being both Mum and Dad to her."

98

"I try to Cassie. And most of the time, she's a treasure. The Lord means everything to her, and I know her prayer times are very real to her. But sometimes she gets moody, even snappy. At those times I feel like there's a wall between us, a stone wall keeping us apart. At those times I just don't know what to do.

*

Two weeks later, on Saturday afternoon, Aggie was in her bedroom, working on some sketches. She paused, thinking about the sketch before her. All at once she saw herself standing on the riverbank watching Colin. Colin was swimming and wading in the river close by some machinery. As she watched, some distant operator must have activated the machinery, and she saw it move.

"Colin! Come away!" Something lent power to her voice, carrying it across the water. Colin stopped and looked up. His eyes searched the bank, looking for her.

"Colin!" she cried again, even more urgently. He still couldn't see her, but the urgency of her voice reached him. He let go of the cable he was holding, and swam towards the bank. As he did so, the cable jerked to life, moving round a pulley. As Colin reached the bank he looked back, hearing the noise of the moving cable. He lay a few moments, trembling with shock. Then again, his gaze searched for Aggie. She was nowhere to be seen.

Back in her room, Aggie emerged from her reverie. She wasn't sure what had happened, but she knew God had used her in some way.

Later that evening, Colin's mind was still awhirl. His mother wasn't home, and anyway, what help would she be with this crazy torrent of feelings? He decided he would visit Aggie. It was still only a few months since he had nosed around her yard, as he had in many other back yards, but he had never visited openly, going to the door to knock. Now though, he had to know what this thing at the river meant. Helen answered the door, and invited him in, offering him a seat at the kitchen table.

As Aggie joined him and Helen in the kitchen, he wasted no time in blurting out his question.

"Aggie, were you down at the river today?"

"No, I wasn't .... But I ...." Her voice trailed off. "Colin, why don't you say what happened to you, before I tell you my side."

He paused, looking wonderingly at her. What could this be all about? "Alright. I was splashing around up the river, and I got to the place where that dredge is, that pulls river shingle up for the Te Ore Ore crusher. I could hear the crusher wasn't operating, so I thought it was safe to get right up to the dredge and the cable. Then I heard you – I'm sure it was you, though I couldn't see you anywhere. You sounded really scared, and yelled at me to come away. I looked for you, but then you yelled again, even more scared. So, I swam to the bank, and, and the dredge started up! Right then! And I would've been caught in it if you hadn't yelled out to me! I'm so sure it was you!"

Aggie's eyes were wide. Prickles ran from her head down the back of her neck. "Colin, this afternoon I was working on some sketches. After a bit, I kind of drifted off – I guess I was kind of thinking and praying about my sketches, and then suddenly, it was like I was standing on the river bank, and I saw you. And, and then I just knew the machine thing was going to start up, and you would be caught, so I called out to you as loud as I could. You were looking for me, but you didn't move, so I called out again, just as that rope thing started to move. And you swam to the bank just in time. And, and then, I kind of woke up again, in my bedroom."

Now prickles were running down three spines. They sat in silence. Tears started to Colin's eyes, the first he could remember crying for a very long time. But he was unashamed. Helen's eyes were moist too. Colin had been absorbing spiritual awareness through his times with Hohepa, but now for the first time, the Christian teaching he had been learning with Te Pura became something almost tangible. Aggie, her mother, Te Pura, these other Christians at her church – they were all in touch with something very real. And his life had been saved by it!

At last Helen spoke. "Would it be alright if we all pray?"

Colin and Aggie both nodded. "Father, how grateful we are that you used Agnes' prayers and her love for you to warn Colin this afternoon. Thank you for saving his life. Lord, you clearly have a future for Colin to live for you. Please continue to show him your love for him."

As Helen's eyes opened, Colin's face across the table seemed more stunned than ever.

"What ... what is it Colin? You okay?"

"You talked to God, just like .... just like he's right here, right beside you!" Colin glanced around the room uncertainly. "I never ... I never heard .... You talk to God like that all the time? Just like you're sort of ... friends with him?"

Helen and Aggie were both smiling and nodding at him. Colin thought Te Pura was right - it was time to go back to that Sunday School.

When Colin arrived home from Aggie's, he went straight to find his mother. and told her about his day, and how Aggie had called to him, though she was still at home in her bedroom. Zoe was not ready for a story like this, and scoffed about him hearing ghosts. But Colin was clearly in earnest about his miraculous escape from death – she couldn't deny that. So Zoe shook her head, and continued to wonder. Something was happening. Something bigger than she could fathom.

Chapter 10

A Birthday and a Departure.

"Agnes, what would you like to do for your birthday? It's only five weeks away." Helen and Aggie were sitting at breakfast one warm Saturday morning early in January. "Would you like to ask a few friends to come over, and do something special? You'll be ten this birthday!"

Hollowness invaded Aggie's stomach. She didn't really have friends to invite to a birthday party. She sighed.

"Mum, I don't have that many friends. Couldn't we just do something, you and me?"

"I know sweetheart. I don't want to push you. But I get concerned. You seem like such an alone girl. I would love for you to have fun with some friends."

Yes, a part of Aggie would like friends, but she'd been disappointed many times before. In the end they decided to ask Chelsea McKnight, and another girl from her Sunday School class.

A bold impulse invaded Aggie. "And I'll ask Stephanie Davis. She's been quite nice to me since she wrote me that letter last year. Sometimes she comes over to talk to me at school."

A shimmer of gladness skimmed though Helen. "That's a good idea." She smiled. "What say we go up to the cottage?"

Several times through the summer, they had visited "their" cottage in the Tararuas, sweeping and scrubbing, making the cottage suitable for relaxing, reading, or sitting to enjoy food they brought with them. On two occasions while they were there, a thunder shower had passed over, making the cottage a cozy haven, as they had experienced on their visit last autumn.

Aggie frowned. "Mum, I don't know. I suppose it would

be nice. But … Mum, that seems like our special place." Aggie couldn't quite explain her feeling, but it seemed like just having friends for her birthday already invaded her customary, private aloneness. To take friends to "their" cottage seemed like too big an invasion.

"I don't know," she went on. "I just have a bad feeling about bringing other people there. What about Third Creek? We could go to Third Creek, and I could show them my sketches, and take them to the place where I did the sketch. And I could show them the cave!"

Sunday picnics at Third Creek had also been part of their summer. And they had been there with the Sanders just over a week ago, on New Year's Day, when Aggie had explored right to the top of the valley. It narrowed at that point, the sides becoming rocky and almost vertical, making further progress impossible. For a while she scrambled around the base of the rocky walls, examining the flowers that managed to find a footing in some of the fissures. She was about to turn back when she noticed an opening in the rock, almost hidden behind an outcrop. It was a little higher than where she stood, but some natural steps in the rock below the opening made it easy for her to climb up and peer inside.

Aggie felt excitement rising. A cave! The opening was not large, but it was easy for her to step across the threshold. She was standing in a cavern about ten feet across, but she had no idea how deep it was, as the light from outside penetrated only a few feet. The floor was soft – it seemed to be sandy. Aggie slowly shuffled forward towards the blackness. The toe of her sneaker bumped against a rock she hadn't been able to see in the darkness. Her toe hurt only for a few moments, but it was enough for her to realize she had better not go any further without being able to see where she was going. She turned around and made her way back to the opening.

"Mum!" Aggie burst into the picnic circle where her mother sat with Mr. and Mrs. Sanders. "I went right up to the top of the valley, and I found a cave, and it's quite big and awfully dark! I went inside, and stubbed my toe on a rock 'cos I couldn't see in the dark." Her words tumbled over each other.

103

Jon Sanders sat upright. "I've never found a cave up there. You said it's quite big? You can walk into it?"

"Yes! I went right inside it!"

"Well, my goodness! Can you show me where it is?"

Jon and Aggie walked back up the valley until they stood before the opening Aggie had discovered. Jon had a little more difficulty squeezing through, but soon he stood beside Aggie, looking around the cavern.

"This is a surprise," he exclaimed. "I didn't know there were caves in these hills. I wonder how far it goes?" He put his hand on Aggie's shoulder. "I'm glad you found this. But you were wise not to explore any further without a good light. There could be holes in the floor further in that you can't see in the dark. We'll come back another day with some lights and a good length of rope."

So Third Creek Cave was discovered. Two days later, Jon, Helen and Aggie walked back to the cave, where Jon taught them some caving safety rules. Even so, Helen wouldn't let Aggie explore by herself, until they had firmly established that the cave was just a single cavern, about fifty feet deep, and varying from ten to thirty feet wide.

Now Aggie was suggesting a birthday party at Third Creek, with exploring the new-found cave as a prime activity. Helen thought it sounded a little unusual, but she supposed it might work.

And so it did. The four girls laughed and giggled all day. They squealed especially over the cave. Helen's heart grew progressively lighter as she watched them.

That evening at bedtime, she asked Aggie, "Did you have a nice day?"

"Yes I did Mum. Thank you! I'm glad I asked Stephanie to come. She really is quite nice when you get to know her."

*

Aggie's friendship with Stephanie was like a tender shoot slowly pushing above the ground. Gradually, over the next three years, their paths converged. As ten-year-old's, one interest they shared was their flair for sketching and painting. Their class teacher, Mrs. Rose spoke to them one day.

"Aggie, Stephanie, I've noticed you're both producing some very nice artwork. I want to show you some books that will help develop your skills."

She sat them down, and opened a book filled with fascinating pencil drawings. "You see how this book has lessons on all kinds of drawing skills. I'd like you to work through this together each art class. You can start with the first lesson here." She showed them the opening pages, filled with sketches of leaves and trees. "Each art class, you can take the next section, and practice the drawings. Later, we'll get on to some more books on painting."

Mrs. Rose had a love of learning, and the girls flourished under her encouragement. Her guidance also expanded Aggie's reading and writing horizons, so that her imagination became a lively inner world, peopled with all sorts of characters and realms. Soon she began composing short imaginative stories of her own.

*

"Mum, what's my father like?"

Zoe shifted uneasily on her chair. Colin had never asked about his father before, and Zoe didn't especially want to talk about him. But Zoe had changed. Only a few months ago, she would have said, "Don't bother your head about him." Or something equally angry.

"I met your father at Daniel's bar. He was handsome and funny, we got talking, and I had too much to drink. I invited him home, and he stayed about three months. I'm ashamed to say I was a flighty girl back then. I should've known better."

Zoe was startled. Her mind hummed. "Did I just tell Colin I'm ashamed of something? What's coming over me?" She noticed Colin's eyes, warm and affectionate. That was different too! Some of the warmth invaded Zoe.

"What do you mean, you should've known better?"

"If I'd been sober, I would've known he was a no-hoper, who would never hold down a job. He just wanted to sponge off me, and I was silly enough to let him."

Colin couldn't have explained his feelings, but his mother's honest answers maintained the warm glow in his eyes. Still, he felt troubled too. His father a no-hoper? His thoughts went to the people he knew at Aggie's church. He'd begun attending the Sunday School again last November, so he knew some of the people, and was hearing about a different way of looking at life.

Christmas especially had been mind-bending for Colin. In the past he'd heard vague stories, but this year he heard for the first time about the Creator of the universe entering the world as a baby. Colin was shaken to the core. He had never imagined a story so audacious! A girl, not much older than him, having a baby with no human father, a baby who was also the God of all there is? Could it be true? Just watching Aggie, and Helen, and some of the other folks at the church, told him it was true. For a whole week, the wonder of it kept hitting him all over again, and he would shake his head in amazement.

But now he wondered, is there a place in all that for a boy whose father is a no-hoper?

*

Allied Garments expanded the factory, and the shift Helen supervised grew along with the company. She managed the transition well, and continued to enjoy her job. And Aggie? Aggie and Stephanie now counted each other as friends, though Helen suspected Stephanie would have spent more time with Aggie if Aggie welcomed her more.

"Lord," mused Helen as she rocked in her chair, "Aggie is still so withdrawn, so isolated. Her imagination is flowering with all those books she's reading, but so often she just withdraws into her world of dreams. The abuse at school has pretty much stopped. I'm so grateful for that. But, but she's still bound up by sadness. I wish I knew how to release her."

Helen could not remember her laughing in an uninhibited way. And in the moments when her griefs overflowed, there was no deep sobbing or release of tears – rather it was the slow march, one after another, making their way down her cheeks. Sometimes Helen would find her sitting on the floor with the photograph of her dad, and his Military Cross beside her, her eyes closed, deep in some reverie. Helen would ask her about her thoughts, but she would look up with a light comment. "I was just thinking about what a good, strong man my dad was."

*

During the first half of that year, the gaps in Colin's school achievement were closing, so that his extra tutoring was dropped. The old, rebellious Colin reappeared sometimes – Zoe was always quick to notice that. But often now her glance would linger on him, and her eyes would soften.

This was the Standard Six year for Colin, his last year in the primary school system. Next year, he would go on to a high school. He kept in touch with Hohepa, sometimes checking eel traps, sometimes on fishing trips. Many Saturday afternoons he would be sitting with his friend, honing his Maori language skills. One evening, when Hohepa knew Colin was at a church meeting with Aggie, he called on Zoe. His tap on the door startled her.

"Hello Zoe! I hope you'll forgive me for coming over unexpectedly. I just have something I want to mention to you. May I come in for a few minutes?"

Puzzlement showed in Zoe's eyes. It was rare that anyone came to her house. She nodded, stepping back to make way for Hohepa. She had just enough presence of mind to motion him to a chair at the kitchen table.

"You must be really proud of the young man Colin is growing into. He's made so many changes the last year or so. And he's been doing well with his school work. He has a sharp mind!"

"Yes." Zoe nodded again.

"Next year, Colin will be going on to high school. Have you thought about what school you want him to go to?"

What high school? If Zoe had thought about it at all, she just assumed he would go to the local public high school. "I suppose Wairarapa College. Isn't that where all the kids go?"

"Yes, it is. And maybe that's the best for Colin. But I've been wondering. You know, he's shown a lot of talent, the way he's turned himself around this year. Did you know there's a very good school especially for Maori boys? It's up in Hawke's Bay. It's called Te Aute College." He paused. "It's a live-in school."

Zoe stared at Hohepa suspiciously. "Sounds like one of those poncy high cost schools. Where the fancy big wigs send their kids." Zoe still had an abiding distaste for "big wigs."

"It is costly," Hophepa admitted. "But I believe Colin may be able to get a scholarship. I know a few people I could enquire with. No promises, but I think it's worth some effort."

Slowly, vaguely, some images of Colin as a graduate of a high-profile school began to form in Zoe's mind. It was such a different scenario from anything she had ever imagined. She was silent for some time.

"You said it's a live-in school? A boarding school?" Suddenly, amazingly, Zoe knew she would miss Colin if he went away to a boarding school. "Well, I dunno. I never thought ...." Her voice trailed off.

"None of us ever thought of something like this. But Colin has turned himself around in ways we never thought of. I'd like to at least check it out. What do you think?"

Slowly Zoe nodded. "No harm in asking I suppose."

"Okay Zoe, good. I'll let you know what I find out. Let's not say anything to Colin in the meantime, because it may come to nothing."

So, unbeknown to Colin, enquiries began for him to attend a school that would stretch him academically, and where his identification with his Maori heritage would be deepened.

Colin was still hesitant about faith. He was impressed and moved by what he'd seen, but, well, it was just so different from his experience up to now. He was attending Carrington

Church of God fairly regularly, especially the Sunday School. It was here that his friendship with Aggie became firm. They lost their shyness in chatting with each other, and sometimes talked about what being a Christian meant. Without her realizing it, these conversations helped Aggie refine her own understanding of her faith, and gradually clarified Colin's thinking too. Colin sometimes asked his mother to come to church with him. Zoe had many reasons for staying as far away from church as possible, but one Sunday in October she agreed to come. It was almost as strange for her as it had been for Colin on his first visit, but her major impression was the warmth of the people who greeted her. She had expected sidelong glances at the very least, if not open hostility. So she was softened towards coming to the special Christmas services, in which Colin participated.

That final year at primary school was one of the most important of Colin's life. He was amazed one day to realize how many people had been encouraging him as he worked at catching up on his school work. That day as he arrived home from school, and walked into the kitchen, he found Hohepa and his mum both sitting at the table. Hohepa smiled broadly as he looked up from a letter he held.

"Colin, come and sit with us! Your friend Mr. Te Koari has been working on something for you. Come and listen to what he's done!"

His mother's peremptory tone was daunting as usual, but Hohepa's smile was broad. What could this be? Colin sat down facing Hohepa.

"Kia ora Colin. This will be quite a surprise for you! It's a big idea, so you'll need some time to think it over. It's about your school for next year."

"Yes," said Colin, "Wairarapa College."

"Yes, that's the most obvious choice," replied Hohepa, "but there's another option. Have you ever heard of Te Aute College?"

For the next half an hour, Colin heard of a college where discipline and hard work were core values, where his Maori heritage would be embraced – in short where so many advantages were offered, that Colin's head reeled. And already, the letter

109

Hohepa held offered him a full scholarship!

But he would need to move away from Masterton, away from home! Was his mother just trying to push him away?

Colin looked up quickly at her face. What he saw astounded him. Zoe's eyes were soft, moist.

"If you go away to this school, I'll write to you every week. I swear I will."

Colin had seen movies of the interisland ferry passing out of placid Queen Charlotte Sound into the heaving, rolling seas of Cook Strait. For days his thoughts and feelings swirled, heaved, rolled. When he finally chose to accept Te Aute, it was partly trust in his friend Hohepa that decided him, but much, much more it was the glimpse into Zoe's heart.

"She wants the best for me! She cares about me!" He sat with his head in his hands, rocking back and forth as the love in her eyes replayed over and over.

When the time came for Colin to leave for college, Zoe really cried. Colin saw her tears, and Zoe Campbell cared not who else saw them. She watched him board the railcar that would take him to Woodville, and then on to Te Aute, dressed in his smart uniform. A fear gnawed at her deep down – among all those grand people, would Colin come to be ashamed of her, and their humble house? It was a real fear, but as Zoe considered the new character she had seen in him, hope began to flicker that he would be proud of her.

Chapter 11

An Overdue Conversation.

August, 1961

The cottage was a warm haven, as rain rattled loudly against the windows, and trees outside bent bough and trunk before the roaring wind. Years ago, Helen and Aggie had hauled in a small table, with four old kitchen chairs, to provide a few home comforts to their little hideaway. Other small comforts had followed, including the old cane couch where Helen sat.

"You remember our day off, when we found this room all full of dust and cobwebs?" As Helen spoke, Aggie turned from where she stood, staring at the water cascading down the window panes.

"Yes. I remember how a cloud came over, and we had this delicious feeling of refuge from a storm. It's the same today, only much more so. How old was I then? Just nine."

She joined Helen on the couch. Their thoughts ranged back over the years. Aggie knew she was still a very private person, her mind wandering often to her disfigured face, and to the ache of her missing hero father. She knew she was reserved, even towards her mother. But sometimes, grateful thoughts of how hard Helen had worked to be both mother and father to her swept aside the mist, and her face became soft and open.

"Thank you for bringing me up here that day. We had a special time didn't we." Her grey eyes spoke her gratitude. "And remember – the year Colin left for Te Aute – I was eleven then, and you told me it was time to prove Kelly Stephenson wrong, and buy my first bra. We went over to Shalari in Greytown. What pretty things they had there!"

Helen's eyes become moist. "Yes, I know how much you've missed your father. And I've missed having him there to admire your every milestone. So I've tried to make them all memorable. Those bras were rather expensive! But worth every penny!"

"And on top of that we celebrated the occasion with Stephanie Davis – you bought us each a huge ice-cream!" They both giggled at the thought of ice-cream commemorating a step into young womanhood.

"When my period started, you made that a milestone celebration too! You remember? Cassie Sanders and Pauline McKnight joined us at a coffee lounge. We had a girls' party swapping period stories, their own and others they'd heard. It was hilarious! I felt so special being welcomed to the club!" She paused a moment. "You were so wise. That milestone isn't an unmixed blessing, but Pauline and Cassie assured me that in spite of the PMS and all that, the ability to bear children makes the whole thing worthwhile. I often think of that."

Helen smiled again. "I'm glad that's a special memory for you. I think you're a very special young woman. I'm so proud of you."

In the fireplace, the remains of a burning log collapsed in a burst of falling embers. Aggie picked up the poker, and rattled it through the grate several times before arranging two more logs into the glowing redness. She returned to the couch, sitting turned towards Helen, their knees almost touching.

"Something else I really appreciate about the way you've tried to make up for my missing Daddy – you enlisted Pauline and Cassie to invite us often to their homes for dinner. We still go to one or the other at least every two or three weeks, just like we have for years. Even before adolescence started happening, you wanted me to watch some male role models – husbandly courtesy in action!" Aggie's voice was light, her eyes smiling. "It's worked too! I always come home feeling respected. Jon and Bill both make me feel like I'm valued, just like the other women round the table. And I think Cassie and Pauline enjoy seeing their husbands at their courteous best!"

Warmth flooded Helen's being. She felt closer to her daughter than she had for a long time. Agnes poised and confident, a respected, valued woman – the vision fed the longings of her heart. Eagerly, incautiously, she pushed on.

"Well dearest, this will be your last term at high school! I wonder what you will move on to next year?"

The soft openness of Aggie's face collapsed. Abruptly, she stood and faced the window again, the panes more than ever blurred by sheets of rain. After a moment, she turned, walked to the door, and went out onto the verandah. She unhooked her parka from a peg on the wall, struggled into it, and walked out into the storm.

*

About half an hour later, Aggie returned to the cottage. She left her boots, and her wet parka, on the verandah before stepping back into the warm room.

Helen sat at the table now, her head in her hands. As Aggie came in, she lifted a tear-stained face, then dropped her head again. Aggie moved slowly towards her, halting beside her chair. Soon she lifted an arm to rest across Helen's shoulders. Helen's hand came up to grasp Aggie's.

Eventually, Aggie spoke, barely more than a whisper. "I'm sorry Mum…... I'm sorry…..."

Helen's head lifted. "Precious, why can't we ever talk about your future? Why do you just withdraw like that? It was so nice, talking about our memories, and then …... and then…..."

Aggie squeezed Helen's shoulder, but said nothing. Eventually, she began. "Mum, I talked a little about feeling respected, valued as a woman. Then you went straight to talking about next year. It … it just feels like you have this picture of me as, as socially confident, here comes Aggie Betteridge, taking the world by storm. You don't say much like that, but I know you have hopes for a bright future for me."

She paused, pulling up a chair to sit close by her mother. "Mum, I'm just not like that. I'm just little Aggie, the one without a father, the one with the funny face, the one everyone laughs at."

113

She hunched in her chair. "I know you're not trying to push me, but, well, it seems like you have a vision of me that I'm not big enough to fill. So, I get guilty, and depressed."

Helen wanted to shout, "You're the one who shuts you in your private little world!" She turned instead to another thought. "Agnes, I've tried so hard, I've …."

Aggie sat upright. "Mum, don't blame yourself! You're right! You've done so much to make up. I love you!" Her hand grasped Helen's arm. "In my better moments I think of your grief for your husband, not just my grief for Daddy." She was hunched again. "No, it's me. I …. I don't know."

Aggie rose, peeled off her jeans, and hung them over a chair beside the fire. Wisps of vapor rose white to the mantlepiece.

Helen spoke again. "You're right Agnes, I do have bright hopes for your future. Just like any mother."

Something in her tone made Aggie glance sharply at her again. "Mum! Don't you get any thoughts about a man ever taking notice of me. Romance, and marriage …. I don't see it happening! I just don't!"

"And yet, a while ago you mentioned bearing children. As though that's something you look forward to."

Aggie's arms were folded, her head slumped forward on her chest. "I did, didn't I? And part of me does hope for my own children – I want that fiercely! But who would ever want me as a wife?"

Again, Helen resisted the temptation to argue. She walked to Aggie and drew her into her arms. They clung to each other. "We had a lovely time earlier today," Helen began. "Then we took a nosedive. But at least we've talked. I'm comforted by that. Agnes, my love for you is as fierce as your desire for babies!"

Aggie's arms tightened around her.

Chapter 12

An Unexpected Offer.

Aggie dropped her pen onto her desk with a satisfied sigh. Finished! Her last school assignment for the year. In just two weeks, the term would be over, and her high school career would be finished.

Since their afternoon at the cottage last August, she and Helen had talked a few times about next year. It wasn't easy, with Helen trying to be encouraging but not overpowering, and Aggie trying to listen while keeping her fears at bay. They had agreed that Aggie would have a break over Christmas and the New Year. Somewhere into January she would start looking for a job.

"So here I am, all prepared by my high school career. Prepared for what?" she mused. "Mum still hopes I'll start on some significant career. In a way I'd like to. In a way, I kind of sense that's what God is saying too. But for me, I'd just as soon start as apprentice machinist at Allied." She pulled a wry face. "Can imagine what Mum will say if I suggest that!"

*

Zoe and Colin Campbell joined Helen and Aggie to celebrate Christmas Day. Over the last eight years, Zoe had taken a long journey. The antagonism she felt towards Helen, and her scorn for the church and all Christians, had slowly been taken apart piece by piece. It was a slow and bumpy road, but finally, Zoe capitulated to the kindness and the miracles that were invading her life. She became fast friends with Helen, and with Aggie. Their friendship had grown especially in the last four years, when Zoe also became a supervisor at Allied Garments, and so was no longer Helen's subordinate.

Colin's time at Te Aute College had soundly vindicated Hohepa's faith in him. He became the school's star Rugby right winger, was captain of the tennis team, led the debating team and did well with his studies. For two years now, he had been working as a Forestry Cadet up at Kaiangaroa Forest. Zoe's best Christmas gift was to have Colin home for two weeks.

"Mrs. Betteridge, that Christmas Dinner was just the best! I'm stuffed." Colin pushed back his chair from the table.

"Sure, you wouldn't like a little more steamed pudding and cream?" Helen asked him.

"No thank you. I couldn't." Colin turned to Aggie. "Say Aggie, how's your learning of Maori going? You keeping up with what I taught you?"

"Not really," replied Aggie. "I don't have my tutor around these days. I remember what I said to you that day you first left for Te Aute. 'Poroporoaki. Kia ki a koutou te Atua.' And you said it back to me in English. 'Farewell. God be with you.' Am I still doing alright?"

"E tika ana," Colin replied.

"Let's see," said Aggie. "I think you told me 'that's right, that's correct.' Am I right?"

"Good job Aggie!" Colin grinned at her. "Do you still have that letter I wrote you in Maori?"

"Yes, I do," she replied. "I haven't seen it for ages, but I know where it's packed away."

"That was a long time ago," Zoe commented. "Do you see anything of the kids you knew back then? What about that girl who was suspended from school. What was her name?"

Aggie's face became sad. "Kelly. Kelly Stephenson. She got pregnant at the sixteenth birthday party her mum threw for her. I did see her once after that, with her tummy bulging. But I don't know what's happened to her since. I felt so sorry for her. Seems her dad had just cleared out. Kelly had so little going for her."

Zoe looked into Aggie's eyes. "She treated you so badly, yet you feel sad for her." It was just six months since Zoe had finally made her choice to be a Jesus follower, so that kind of forgiveness was still a wonder to her. Aggie's hair floated outwards a little as she turned her head to Zoe, prompting a different thought.

"Aggie, I'm glad you've grown your hair longer since those days. Down about to your collar. It's so soft and pretty."

Aggie dropped her head, blushing. "It helps to hide my birthmark," she muttered. Zoe didn't hear her.

*

The second week of January Colin was back in Kaiangaroa and Zoe was back at Allied, but Helen was taking vacation time to be with Aggie. On Tuesday afternoon they were at the art gallery, where the January theme featured interior furnishings design.

Aggie paused beside a drawing of a lounge room. "I like the color contrast here," she commented. "But with that pool right outside the French doors, the sunlight could get overpowering on fine days."

A couple, probably in their late forties, stood beside Helen and Aggie. The man glanced at Aggie. "It could," he responded, just as though introductions had already been made, and conversation already flowed. "But it depends which way the house is oriented. Is this the shady side of the house?"

"It might be," countered Aggie, "though as it's drawn, there's bright light pouring through those doors. The carpet square and the couch could fade easily in that position."

The foursome stood facing each other, making introductions. Immediately, Aggie's animation dropped away. She allowed Helen to introduce them. Their new acquaintances were Carl and Lorraine Sherwood, interior decorating consultants.

For the next hour, the four browsed together. While they discussed the drawings, Aggie was deeply engaged, often making spirited replies to comments from Carl or Lorraine. When at last Carl suggested they all adjourn to the café for Devonshire tea, she became reserved, retiring Aggie again.

Carl studied Aggie thoughtfully as she buttered her scone. His head turned towards Lorraine, his expression becoming quizzical as their eyes met. Almost imperceptibly, Lorraine nodded.

"Raspberry jam? Cream?" inquired Carl, passing the bowls to Aggie. She nodded gratefully. "Helen said you've just finished high school. And that you're taking some time to decide on a job to pursue?"

"Yes. I'm not sure what I might do." On this subject, Aggie was much less eloquent than she had been in their previous discussions.

"Aggie, how would you like to try out as an interior decorating consultant? Lorraine and I need someone with a good sense of what works in interior design, and what doesn't. You have good ideas, as you've been demonstrating over the last hour or so."

"Me?" Aggie could hardly believe her ears. "What would I do?"

"You'd study house plans, then come up with sketches of how finished rooms might look. You'd consult with owners to find out what their goals are. And sometimes you'd visit sites to get a first-hand look at the environment, and check on progress with the work. For a start, Lorraine or I would work with you, but I think before long we would probably give you a pretty free rein of your own."

Slowly, a picture formed in Aggie's mind of actually being paid to spend her days with colors, textures, designs, creating beautiful rooms. Initially, the part about consulting with owners flew over her head. She would be virtually hidden away, working just with all the things she loved!

"That. Sounds. Amazing. Do you think I could be good at that?" Aggie looked at her mother. Helen's eyes were shining. She looked at Lorraine and Carl. They both smiled warmly at her.

"Do you both have time to drive over to Carterton with us?" Lorraine asked. "You could come to see our offices, and where you would be working."

The Sherwood's drove their car, and Helen and Aggie followed behind, giving them an opportunity to share their thoughts about the afternoon's bombshell.

"It sounds perfect Mum. It's not something I would have gone after, but here it is almost being pushed in my lap! I hope I'm not jumping at it too quickly, but I do really feel peace about this."

"So do I dearest. This really could be the answer to our prayers. But let's see if we get the same sense in the offices."

Nearly two hours later, they left for home with a formal job offer for Aggie. She would begin with a probationary period of one month, at a salary barely below Helen's, starting the following Monday. Carl and Lorraine were used to acting decisively.

Helen and Aggie sat on their verandah long into the evening, chatting and praying. The longer they prayed, the more assured they became that this offer was indeed the answer to their prayers.

Chapter 13

Stranger at the Cottage.

Aggie was restless. She'd already been in her new job for two weeks, two exciting weeks that flew by. Lorraine and Carl were friendly and encouraging. Already her ideas and sketches were earning their praise. It was all going well.

Maybe a little too well. This job was so full of promise, of fulfilment. It contrasted sharply with the vague images she'd nursed up to now. "Me? Aggie? Am I really the kind of person this job calls for?"

"Nineteen. I'll be nineteen in just two weeks. That makes me nearly adult," she mused. "I should be self-assured, confident, a master of conversation ..... Sometimes I am! When I'm caught up with colors and designs, I talk up a storm! But apart from that, I'm still the sad-body."

She stared out her bedroom window.

"In fact, maybe I'm worse now than ever. Now when I sink back into my private world, I often get moody with it. A little sulky." She sighed. "Lord, I don't mean to be! Lord, you're still special to me. You still speak to me, show me things."

Memories of old times stirred. "Oh yes Lord! The cottage. I haven't been up there since that day with Mum back in August. I'll go hang out with you up there."

*

The man pushed his dark, wavy hair away from his eyes, as he knelt on the joists, measuring out another piece of flooring.

He was pleased with his progress, as the new rooms took shape. Already he'd extended the roof, so that he had at least some protection from showers. And the rest of his work on the property had gone well. He felt good.

Yet something was gnawing at him. "Lord, I'm looking forward to moving in. It'll be so nice and cozy here. A real little haven, tucked in right under the mountains."

He reached for the power saw, and lined it up with his pencil line. The sound crashed around him, as he depressed the trigger. "Amazing the noise these handsaws make," he thought for the thousandth time. He switched back to the previous thought, as he expertly guided the blade. "But Lord, I'm getting tired of living by myself. It'd be so nice to have someone share this cottage with me. A beautiful bride for instance. What do you think Lord? Hey, wouldn't it be great if I met someone today?"

The improbability of that thought brought a small smile to his face as he finished the cut, and laid the power saw aside.

He looked up. Not twenty feet away, immediately in front of him, a car was drawn up. The driver's side window was down, and from it a young woman stared at him, startled, her gaze loaded, if he was not mistaken, with indignation.

Their eyes locked, mutual surprise paralyzing each of them. Then her head snapped around, and the car accelerated forward, disappearing in billowing dust.

*

Helen sat at her kitchen table, thinking about Aggie's birthday. "Nineteen! I was only nineteen when I married Martin!"

"Mum!" Aggie burst into the kitchen. "Mum, I just drove up to the cottage, and there's a man up there, working on it! It looks like he's building new rooms, and changing it around, and, and ... Mum, someone's taking over our cottage!"

Aggie plumped into a chair, her face flushed.

"What's this Agnes?" asked Helen. "A man up at the cottage? Building on more rooms?"

Aggie exhaled through her nostrils, a small snort. "But Mum, that's been our special place for so long! How can someone else take it over?"

Helen gave a fleeting smile at her daughter's indignation. "Yes, sweetheart, we've spent lots of hours up there, had some happy times! But I guess it never really was our cottage. Who is this man? Anyone we know?"

"I don't think so," answered Aggie doubtfully, "though I'm not sure. He did seem familiar somehow. But it isn't just the cottage! He's done lots of stuff up there!" Aggie pushed herself up out of her chair and marched off to her bedroom.

Helen's gaze followed her out of the kitchen.

Chapter 14

A Birthday Hike.

It was just an hour after sunrise, but on this mid-summer February day, the warmth of the sun could already be felt. Wisps of vapor rose coiling above the roof of Mount Holdsworth Lodge, nestled below the bush-clad slopes of the Tararua Range. Aggie had decided to celebrate her nineteenth birthday by hiking from the Lodge up to Jumbo Peak, traversing south across the ridge to Mount Holdsworth, and back down to the Lodge. At a leisurely pace it would take most of the day.

Aggie didn't think of the mountains as her friends exactly. They were too huge and solemn to be friends. Yet the mossy forest floor, the busy streams, the towering trees, the jumbled outcrops of rock, the rough peaks all seemed to whisper some of their secrets as she stopped to listen. She couldn't think of a better place to celebrate her birthday.

Today, Helen would have joined her, but she was not feeling so well, and decided to pull out. Aggie was concerned. She knew her mother would not stay at home unless she felt more poorly than she was admitting to. But Zoe Campbell had stepped in to take Helen's place.

"I love the sound of the water!" Zoe's voice was lively as she closed the car door, and walked the few paces to the bank of the Atiwhakatu Stream. The stream at this point was large enough to form some invitingly deep pools as it swirled against the larger rocks on the far bank. But Zoe and Aggie had different business in mind. They retrieved their knapsacks from the car, and turned to set off into the bush. Crossing the suspension bridge over the stream, they both stopped short at the sound of a bellbird. It had joined the tuis finding nectar among the flax flowers a little downstream. Aggie and Zoe stood still, wordlessly drinking in the sounds they both loved.

They pushed on, crossing Donnelly Flat, then followed the stream. An hour or so later they passed the old Atiwhakatu Hut, and not long after came to Raingauge Spur Track.

Aggie took a deep breath. "This is where we really start climbing!"

"Yes, this is it," Zoe responded. "Let's fill our water bottles from the stream. We'll need some water to get us to the top!"

They knelt at the river bank, letting the cool water splash over their hands, gurgling as it filled their bottles. Then they turned left, away from the stream, as they began the climb to the main ridge.

*

They were wet with perspiration when they emerged into the clearing surrounding Jumbo Hut. As usual, there was a good supply of water in the tank catching rain water off the hut, so they refilled their water bottles.

"I'm soaked with sweat!" declared Aggie. "I'm going to find a secluded spot where I can dry off."

They walked to the southern edge of the clearing, where Aggie dropped her knapsack, then peeled off her shirt and bra, laying them on the grass to dry. She spread her parka beside them then lay down.

"Ah, that feels a little better. Warm sun, just a touch of breeze. This is so nice!"

Zoe lay back on the grass, with her knapsack under her head. "How's the new job going?"

"I love it! Just three weeks, but it's been exciting so far. Lorraine and Carl are good people." But her thoughts started on a different track. Her brow furrowed. "Zoe, do you think I'm hard? My heart. Is my heart hard?" She closed her eyes. "Like the rocks in the stream."

Zoe looked startled.

"I mean, I don't think so much about all the teasing any more, and about my dad. But I know it all affected me so much when I was younger. I thought about my dad so often. Too much really. And I think it's left me kind of hardened, turned in on myself. Sad. Maybe a little strange even. I know the old sadness still strikes at me. Sometimes I even feel kind of mean."

Zoe didn't know quite what to say. Her young friend was as simple as *The Listener* cryptic crossword. She lay like a carefree nymph, soaking in the sunshine, while her thoughts ran on the sadness that still dogged her from childhood.

"Aggie," she responded at last, "I surely don't think of you as hard-hearted. You're such a good friend to me." She paused before continuing. "There are a lot of years between us, yet I hardly ever notice that. But I think I know what you mean. You're often, what shall I say? Subdued? In a world of your own maybe? No, that sounds too harsh. You're often thoughtful about other people. Anyway, I like you!"

Aggie gave Zoe a grateful glance. "Well, like I said, I'm loving my job. But I'm a little scared too. I never imagined myself in a job like this. I'm still scared this kind of job is too big for a person like me."

"Aggie, it seems clear to me that God gave you this job. I think you'll do well at it. And perhaps one day, that sad, subdued part of you will be healed too."

"I hope so Zoe. I hope so!"

The breeze moved the tree tops gently. Aggie donned her bra and shirt again, then retrieved lunch sandwiches from her knapsack. They ate contentedly, saying little. At length Aggie stirred.

"I heard Kathy Pierce and Eric Paynter are engaged," she said. "Do you know them? They've been part of Carrington Church ever since I can remember. Or at least Kathy has. Eric came to Masterton about four or five years ago I think. He's one of the Hammer and Tongues men. And Kathy is a sweet girl. She was a year behind me in high school. I like her a lot."

"Yes," replied Zoe. "I don't know them well, but I know who you mean. Isn't she a bit young to be engaged?"

"Hmm. Eighteen. I guess she is rather, but they're not planning to be married for over a year. Eric has been negotiating to buy a property down in Te Whiti. Mum was talking to Mrs. Pierce, so she heard about their plans. The house on this place needs a lot of work, but they aim to give it a major overhaul."

"Well, God bless them," said Zoe fervently. "I think they'll make a great couple. Say, have you been up to your cottage recently, over near Dalefield Road?"

Aggie turned to face her. "Yes! You'll never guess what! I got a big surprise! Zoe, some man is taking over our cottage! Just a couple of weeks ago, I felt like doing something different, so I drove over there on Sunday afternoon. The first surprise was the track. It's been widened and upgraded. The part where it goes up the bank beside the waterfall even has a concrete surface now!"

"Goodness! What's going on over there?" exclaimed Zoe.

"Up the top, on the flat area where the cottage is, a lot has been happening! First, the stream has been piped, so that the water runs over a big water-wheel! About ten feet high I guess."

"It hasn't spoiled the waterfall has it?" Zoe asked.

"No. The pipe runs from further up, carries the water over the wheel, and the outflow goes over the waterfall."

"Now, what would a water-wheel be for?"

"I think I might know. Just listen to the rest! Right on the edge of the bush-line, close to the cottage, an area has been cleared, and there is a building – kind of a small barn."

Zoe was incredulous. "A barn? Up in the bush?"

"Well, I guess it isn't really a barn – it just gives that kind of impression. Actually, it doesn't look so out of place. The sides are rough-sawn timber, so it blends fairly well into the trees. I don't know what it might be for. But as well as that, the cottage is being rebuilt! There are more rooms added. I didn't stop to see much, but it's obviously being upgraded into a regular little living space."

Zoe sat up straighter.

"Someone's living up there," Aggie continued. "I keep thinking I've seen him before, but I'm not sure. Could be someone from the church."

"Well, there's a fine little mystery," said Zoe thoughtfully.

Aggie was still annoyed at the man who had usurped her cottage, the place of childhood memories. "Well, the cottage, and that whole space, is his space now," she said. "I felt a bit embarrassed I came blundering in, looking nosey, so I turned around and drove out again as quick as I could."

They paused, thinking about the developments over at Dalefield Road.

"Oh yes," resumed Aggie, "the water-wheel! I noticed that both the barn building, and the cottage had electric lights glowing! I think he must have a generator hooked up to the water-wheel!"

Zoe gave a low whistle. "Whatever he's doing, he's there for the long haul," she commented. "There's a collection of mysteries hanging around this man! I suppose all will be revealed one day!"

"I suppose so Zoe. But for now, it's time to get across to Holdsworth, and back down to the Lodge. How are your legs feeling?"

"Beginning to feel as though they've climbed a small mountain," Zoe smiled. "Now they just have to get me across the ridge, and back down the mountain!"

*

Aggie swung her car into Zoe's driveway. Zoe's house and yard were looking much tidier than they had a few years ago. The front fence had been replaced, along with her letterbox, which was now firmly attached atop its gatepost.

"Thank you so much for sharing my birthday hike Zoe! I can't remember a better birthday!

"It's been the best day I've had for a while!" responded Zoe. "Thanks for having me along!"

"I won't stay now. I want to get home and see how Mum

127

is. It isn't like her to be feeling unwell. She's been as healthy as an ox all my life! See you tomorrow."

A few minutes later, Aggie walked into the kitchen at home, and stopped short. The table was attractively set for three, with a small birthday cake as the centerpiece.

"Mum! I thought you were resting!"

Helen appeared smiling in the hall doorway. "Hello Sweetheart! Nice to see you home safe and sound. Yes, I've been doing some resting, and I'm feeling better. I arranged with Zoe – she's going to take a bath, and come back to join us for dinner. Happy Birthday."

Aggie surveyed her Mum. She did seem to be doing better than she was this morning. "Mum, are you alright? You were supposed to be taking it easy today, and here you've been working hard instead!"

"Truly, I'm doing much better. And it's been such fun preparing a special dinner for you. Tuna casserole, with our home-grown veggies, followed by jam turnover, with custard and whipped cream! Go get cleaned up now – it's nearly ready, and Zoe will be here soon!"

Aggie hugged her Mum. "Mum! You're the best! So, Zoe's known about this all day! But she hasn't said anything. The pair of you! Thank you, Mum!"

As she ran the bath water, she wondered about what had ailed her mother earlier in the day. It did seem to have passed, but a residue of concern lodged in the back of her mind.

Dinner was a fun birthday celebration. As they ate their dessert, conversation turned again to the mystery man at the cottage.

Chapter 15

Introductions

The face in the driver's side window drifted back into his mind every now and again. He wasn't especially drawn to the face, with its mix of surprise and indignation. But it was curious, quite curious, how she had appeared right there in front of him, just as that crazy thought occurred, of maybe meeting his intended that very day.

The incident did strengthen his thoughts about praying over finding a life partner. "Who do I know? I'm not even sure how to start praying about this Lord! How will you lead me?" His thoughts ranged over people he knew, but didn't find anywhere to alight. "Mind you, I haven't been trying to notice anyone. Guess I'd better turn on my noticer."

So the man at the cottage began thinking and praying more seriously about someone who might share it with him. At church three weeks later, he found himself sitting next to a young Maori man he hadn't met before. He believed this person must be a new-comer, so turned to greet him at the end of the service.

"Hello, I'm Ky Soames. Are you new here? I don't believe I've met you before?"

"Hello! Nice to meet you. I'm Colin Campbell. No, I'm not exactly a new-comer. I came to know Jesus through this church. But that was a while ago. I work for the Forestry Service now, so I'm usually up in Kaiangaroa. I'm home visiting my mum for three weeks – you might know her, Zoe Campbell? She's off in Martinborough today, visiting a lady who's something of a shut-in. Mum does laundry and such for her. She'll be back tonight."

"Oh, I don't think I know your mum. I've been part of the church about a year, but I haven't got to know too many here.

Glad to meet a man who works with trees. I'm something of a timber worker myself."

Colin's interest quickened. "Did you say your name is Kai? That's usually a Maori name, but you don't look as though you share my Maori heritage?"

Ky smiled. "No, my name is spelled K Y. I guess it is a little confusing."

"Hey, it'll be a while before Mum's back. Why don't we go find a place for lunch together?"

Before long they were sitting in a café, deep in conversation. Colin watched the man across the table from him. Strong, handsome face, framed by dark, curly hair. Earnest, hazel eyes, a quick smile. Not a large frame, but powerful shoulders and arms. This man could think decisively and work quickly, Colin decided.

During the afternoon, Ky learned much of Colin's story, and the people who were important to him. He heard of Martin Betteridge, a decorated war hero, killed in action, whose widow was a member of Carrington Church. Colin evidently held her in high regard, calling her Kaumatua Helen, a Maori name for a wise elder. Helen, and her daughter Aggie, had been influential in Colin's journey towards faith. Ky heard of how Aggie's prayers had once saved Colin's life. A recently-formed compartment in his mind stirred with interest.

"But with a name like Aggie? Why does she have to be called Aggie?" The thoughts circled round his mind. "Still, Colin admires her a lot. At any rate, I think I'll start attending one of the Sunday School classes. Maybe the Lord has a new friend waiting for me!"

*

"Hello! Do you have room for a new person in this class? My name is Ky. Ky Soames"

"Nice to meet you Ky. I'm Helen Betteridge. Yes, we're always glad to welcome new members."

130

Ky's mind did a flip. "Helen Betteridge leads this class?" he thought. His surprise must have shown, as Helen shot him a quizzical smile. "Oh," he stammered. "You're Helen. I, ah, a friend spoke well of you, so it's doubly nice to meet you." Helen nodded, and smiled again. She picked up a long white chalk stick, and wrote 'Kai Soames' on the blackboard.

"No, it's K Y," he corrected her.

Now Ky sat glancing around the circle of chairs at the other class members. Almost opposite him, he noticed a young woman looking intently back at him. Her eyes dropped as she encountered his glance.

"Is it her? No, the person who visited me up at the cottage, was glowering at me, face flushed. This one is, well, she's quite pretty! But, but I think she must be the one. Her hair is just the same." Another impression was pushing at his mind, not quite gaining entrance.

Ky's glance followed round the rest of the circle, looking for Helen's daughter, Aggie. Maybe she isn't here today. His eyes arrived back at his cottage visitor. The impression gained entry. Again, Ky's face registered surprise.

"It's her! She looks like Helen! This must be Aggie! Aggie Betteridge is my mysterious visitor. Well, well!"

Aggies eyes met Ky's again, momentarily confused, embarrassed. This time she gave the ghost of a smile before quickly looking away.

Ky looked at the floor, pondering. Now he had two images of Aggie Betteridge, conflicting images. He still didn't like the pouty, indignant cottage visitor. And the Sunday School class Aggie?

"She looks distinctly uncomfortable. Guess that's good in a way, if she's regretting her behavior that day. But, what is it? Just a little too embarrassed, like she wants to bolt into a hole. A scared rabbit. Where's the inner strength that Colin was talking about?"

Ky hazarded another quick glance. "Yes, she is pretty." Her summer dress was a kind of bold floral pattern of orange and gold, with bright, random splashes of green. Shoes kind of stylish, but not over-stated. Medium height and build. "Her eyes," thought Ky, "grey, magnetic. In spite of that timid, embarrassed look, there's still something strong, undefeated about her eyes. Intriguing."

As the class started, Helen welcomed newcomer Ky, and there were introductions all round. Ky nodded pleasantly as Aggie confirmed her name. By the time class concluded, initial surprise had subsided for both, and Aggie had recovered some composure. She approached Ky.

"Hello Ky. It seems we've already met. And were both surprised to realize it at the start of class. I must have startled you up at the cottage as much as you startled me. I'm sorry I was so, ah, abrupt. Glad to meet you properly now."

Ky's thoughts took a more positive turn. "Hmm, this is better. Not the startled rabbit now. Clear, pleasant voice. And the eyes, yes. Still something timid there, but something strong too."

"Hello Aggie. Yes, it's nice to meet you properly. And nice to be welcomed to the class. Your mum is a great teacher."

As class members dispersed, Aggie pressed close to her mum. "Mum, Mum!" she whispered loudly. "That new man, Ky! He's the man up at the cottage! The one who's been doing all the work up there!"

*

It was Wednesday evening, two days before Colin's return to Kaiangaroa. He and Ky made their way out of Carrington Church of God, where a visiting missionary had discussed his work. As they left the building, Colin noticed Aggie a pace or two ahead of them.

"Aggie!" She turned. "Ky and I are going for a cup of coffee. Like to come join us?"

Aggie hardly ever went out to restaurants or coffee lounges. Especially with two young men, one of whom she had only just met. She was surprised to hear herself say, "Thank you. That would be nice."

A few minutes later, their cars were parked on Main

Street, and they walked towards the coffee lounge. A young woman emerged from the adjacent shop, a grocery store. Her right hand clutched several bulging paper bags, while her left arm encircled a three-year-old child, with tear-streaked face. She staggered slightly, nearly bumping into Colin.

"Oh, may I help you with those bags?" Colin asked. Then, as the woman straightened up, "Why, it's Kelly! I haven't seen you for so long!"

Ky watched with interest. Colin and Aggie were clearly renewing an old acquaintance. Kelly seemed a little startled by Colin's courtesy, as he tried to help her with her groceries. Aggie too was gravely courteous to Kelly, though there was something else in her eyes he couldn't quite fathom. Kelly was introduced to him, and he sensed she was wondering about him, and how he came to be in Colin and Aggie's company.

And Kelly? There seemed to be grudging appreciation for their friendly words, and their offers of help. But also smoldering independence, the pride that said, "I don't need your help." Kelly straightened her back, and moved with a more purposeful step towards her car.

As they sat over coffee, Ky heard more of Kelly Stephenson, and her part in Colin's and Aggie's lives. His heart stirred with a deeper understanding of Colin, and especially of Aggie. "I'm beginning to figure out this strange mix of strength and reserve in her," he thought. "I'm beginning to be drawn to this lady!"

*

By the end of April, Ky's work at the cottage was almost complete. Walls were moved, and new rooms added, bathroom and kitchen were remodeled, and floors polished or carpeted. Ky's parents, Trevor and Melody Soames came to visit early in May. They ran a dairy farm in the Bay of Plenty, near to Kutarere, so it was difficult for them to take holidays. But seeing Ky's new home was worth the trouble.

133

Trevor looked every inch the weather-beaten dairy farmer, in his green felt hat, and red tartan swanndri. At nearly fifty years, Melody was charmingly feminine – not glamorous, but definitely feminine.

"So glad you could take the time to come down." Ky's hug enveloped them both.

"Good to see you son! Our manager, Max, has his son helping him, so between them they can manage the cows for ten days or so."

"Come have a cup of tea, and then I'll show you around."

Half an hour later, both Melody and Trevor were making approving comments as they inspected Ky's work on the property. Most of his do-it-yourself skill had been learned from his father, so he valued Trevor's suggestions for small improvements. Both parents were especially full of praise for his work on the cottage.

"This is so cozy and snug. The kitchen is well thought out – I could work in this kitchen. And I love the way you've finished the bedrooms." Melody wasn't one to hint too much, but she couldn't help adding, "Though you really need a woman's touch. Any thoughts of bringing someone to share your house with you?"

Ky smiled briefly. "As a matter of fact, I have been thinking more about that. I'm praying about it."

Trevor and Melody raised eyebrows at each other. "Are you?" Melody smiled back. "We'll pray with you."

The next five days sped by as Trevor and Melody became acquainted with Masterton, the Wairarapa's other rural towns, and the rolling hill country sweeping all the way out to the Pacific coast. They well understood how the brooding beauty of the Tararua Range, with its rivers and streams, had cast its spell on Ky's heart.

Ky had often told his parents of Carrington Church of God, so they were glad to accompany him on Sunday. Afterwards, as they sat at lunch, Trevor remarked, "It was great to meet Pastor Scott. We've heard so much about him from you. And that lady Helen, the one who leads your Sunday School class, she's quite impressive! I liked the way she led the teaching, and the discussion."

"Yes! And the girl Aggie, that's Helen's daughter isn't it?" Melody asked. "She struck me as rather special. Do you know her well?"

"Mum! Is that you hinting again?" Ky responded quickly.

"No! I ... truly, I just thought she seemed very focused. Original ideas, down to earth. I ... I wasn't hinting!"

"Well, yes they're both special people. I like them. But no, I don't know Aggie all that well." He paused for a moment, before adding, "I'd like to though. I'm thinking of asking her out."

Eyebrows raised again.

Ky resumed, "Oh, really? Well, I guess I have been thinking of asking Aggie out, though I hadn't admitted it to myself so far. But now, I've said it. Yes, I'd like to start getting to know her better."

*

Aggie quite liked Ky. She didn't see him very often – really only in the Sunday School class. He didn't say much during the class, but his few contributions were thoughtful. The conversation over coffee with him and Colin had given a more personal glimpse into Ky. He'd seemed deeply interested in the part Kelly played in their lives. She appreciated that about him. And she'd gotten over him being the man who commandeered her cottage.

But beyond those impressions, Ky didn't figure much in Aggie's thoughts. The idea that she would ever be swept off her feet by a man, and live happily ever after with him, was just not part of her thinking. It happened to people she knew, but, well, she was just Aggie. Perhaps some deeply buried part of her stirred with interest, but it was too deeply buried to affect her daily thoughts.

Ky was interested, but just as unpracticed as Aggie in the fair arts of romance. In many ways he was a man of flair, but when it came to asking a girl out, he was inexperienced, and rather reserved. As he grew into adolescence, he'd regarded the dating scene as a distraction. But now, it seemed the Lord was prompting him

For nearly three weeks, Ky thought about what to say to Aggie. Dinner at the Empire Hotel seemed to be the obvious thing. Having taken the step of deciding to ask her out, he found his feelings toward her were swelling quickly. He tried to rein them in, telling himself not to get carried away too quickly. He wanted to make her a small gift. But would that be jumping ahead too far, too soon? He debated that question as he worked on the gift for her.

Helen answered the phone a little after seven on Friday evening.

"Hello Mrs. Betteridge. This is Ky Soames, from the Carrington Church. I … err … wonder if Aggie is home at present? May I speak with her please?"

Helen's eyebrows rose half a notch. "Of course, Ky. She's right here."

"Agnes, Ky Soames from the church wants to talk to you."

Aggie and Helen exchanged a quizzical glance as Aggie came to pick up the receiver.

"Hello Ky. This is Aggie."

"Hello. Look I know we haven't talked very much at church, but well … I've come to admire what I've seen of you. I'd very much like to get to know you better. I was hoping we could get together, and … err … chat for a bit. Maybe have dinner together."

Aggie was silent for several long seconds. The idea that a man would be interested in her, want to get to know her, was so unthought of, it just wasn't registering. Some girls she knew went on dates. "Not me though. I'm Aggie Betteridge. What on earth does he mean? Dinner sounds nice though."

"Aggie? I … I didn't mean to offend you …." Ky felt a little flustered. Why would a girl like Aggie want to get to know him? This had been a bad idea. What was he thinking of?

"No Ky, you didn't offend me at all. That … that would be a lovely idea. Thank you very much!"

Relief flooded through Ky. His confidence started to return. "Would Monday be alright? I can come to your house at say quarter to seven. I've heard the Empire Hotel is very nice. Would you like to go there?"

"Yes, Monday is fine. At a quarter to seven? That, ah, well, thank you!" Neither of them had been to dinner at the Empire before. It sounded a little formal, and perhaps a little expensive. But Ky had asked her. What on earth could he be thinking?

Aggie replaced the telephone receiver and turned to face her mother. "Ky is taking me to dinner at the Empire Hotel." Her tone was neutral.

A smile slowly spread over Helen's face. It grew. It became the brightest smile Helen had smiled for many a long day. Of course, she had cherished deep down a longing that a very suitable young man would one day pay attention to her Agnes. But no such idea seemed to be on Agnes' radar. So the longing was buried away. Now it started erupting, bubbling up through her spirit.

"Whoa, whoa," she silently cautioned herself. "Slow down, slow down!"

"Agnes, that's wonderful! I don't know Ky well, but he seems very thoughtful, respectful." Like Aggie, her spirit had sensed depth in Ky. "And very handsome too!" she couldn't help adding mischievously.

At her last comment, Aggie glanced up. What did handsome have to do with it? This was just someone wanting to share a nice dinner with her.

*

Between Friday evening and Monday evening Aggie's thoughts wandered many times to her upcoming dinner with Ky.

137

It was still a puzzle to her, though she did feel some pleasurable anticipation. She wondered about what she would wear, but not nearly as much as Helen did. The mother heart in Helen wanted everything about this dinner to be just the best for her daughter. She tried to keep her thoughts and hopes on a leash, but she knew no-one she thought better suited to begin a romance with Aggie. In the end, she was satisfied with Aggie's choice of a slim-fitting teal blue suit over a plain white blouse, complimented by a paua shell necklace.

And now here they sat at their table at the Empire. The menu was a little more formal than they had encountered before, so the ice was broken for them as they joked back and forth over what the menu items might be like.

After they had ordered, Ky produced a small package. "I brought a small gift for you," he said, sliding it across the table. "I made it in my workshop. I hope you like it."

A gift? He was giving her a gift? Something he had made? What sort of thing would he have made? In his workshop? He had a workshop? A little color came into her cheeks. It was a small box, gift wrapped, with a bow tied at the top. A small card read "Made for Aggie, by Ky."

"Thank you so much Ky. You didn't need to make me anything!" She was undoing the bow, removing the wrapping paper, opening the white card box she found beneath. Inside was a carved wooden object, nestled in white tissue paper. She drew it out. A carved Kiwi! It was slightly stylized, a model of a Kiwi walking, beak lowered to the ground. It was carved from light tan-colored wood, with a darker brown grain rippling through. The matte surface was silky smooth to her touch.

"Ky! It's beautiful! You made this? I didn't know you made things like this!"

"Yes. That's what I do. I'm a wood carver."

Ky watched her turn the bird over, and note his name, Ky, burned in script under the base. "Yes," he said, "I put my signature on all my work. I guess you could say it's my brand. I'm just beginning to get some notice."

Aggie stood the Kiwi on the table. "Ky, thank you so much. You must have spent hours on this. It's so beautiful. I love how it feels to touch!" She traced her finger again over the bird's back.

Ky felt that warm glow again as he watched her obvious pleasure. "I'm so glad you like it," he smiled. "It's carved from Manuka. I like to work with Manuka – it's a very hard wood, and it takes a good polish."

They both leaned back from the table as the waiter arrived with their appetizer.

"Let's give thanks," said Ky. He rested his hands on the table. They both bowed their heads. "Thank you for a special occasion Lord, a special dinner, and that we can enjoy each other's company. Amen."

"You said you made it in your workshop," said Aggie as they began to eat. "Where is your workshop?"

"I built it just behind my cottage. You must have seen it when you visited me!" He smiled mischievously.

Aggie colored again. "Oh, so the barn is really your workshop!"

"Barn?" asked Ky. "Up there?"

"I knew it couldn't really be a barn, but it looks just like a barn, right there on the edge of the bush."

Ky laughed delightedly. "You know, I guess it does too! I think that's what I'll call it – in fact that can be the name for my whole space up there. So far, I've just called it 'the cottage' and 'the workshop'. From now on 'The Barn' is where I live!! And work!"

Aggie in her turn was beginning to feel some of that warm glow. He had given her a carving, she had given him a name for his living and working space.

Later in their meal, Aggie asked about Ky's name. "Ky can't be your real name? Is it short for something?"

"Do you know about King Hezekiah in the Old Testament?" he asked.

"Oh yes! He's one of my heroes!" Her eyes flashed. "What a man, holding out against totally impossible odds! What a courageous man!"

"Yes, he's one of my heroes too. And I have the honor of being named after him!" He smiled. "But Hezekiah is a bit of a mouthful. So, I shortened it to Ky."

Aggie looked at him admiringly. She was liking this man more and more. And Mum was right – he was a good-looking man! As she turned her head slightly, her hair swung back from the left side of her face. Aggie saw Ky notice the blemish beside her ear. He saw her notice him looking at it. There was a moment of awkwardness.

"I'm sorry," he said, slightly embarrassed, "I didn't mean to be rude."

"That's alright," replied Aggie, sweeping her hair back with her hand. "It's a birthmark. I've lived with it all my life."

Her gesture was confident, and her tone light. But cold fear wrenched at the pit of her stomach. Suddenly years of torment flooded back into her. She was little red-faced Aggie again. Now she would see the light fade out of his eyes. She would see the disappointment. Would feel him withdrawing from her. Already he was regretting spending all that time on the carving. Maybe she would just pick it up and toss it ....

"Aggie, you've had this all your life? I bet it cost you some teasing while you were growing up. It must have been tough for you. And yet .... and yet, it ... it doesn't spoil you." His gaze shifted back to her face. "Nothing could spoil you. You're still so beautiful!"

Beautiful? Had she heard right? Was he mocking her? Her gaze searched his eyes. She saw concern for her, softness, admiration. Unconsciously he had reached out to touch her hand. She knew it was a gesture of protectiveness.

Aggie's feelings were a jumble. Soaring through them was a hope, a hope that this man would ... would what? Love her? It was too big a word to use just yet, but it was forming, just beyond the edge of consciousness. There was confusion, embarrassment. This was the first time she had passed more than a few words with Ky, yet here he was calling her beautiful. Something was happening way too fast.

Ky felt the same embarrassment. He had not meant to come out with that word on their first real meeting. It had been a spontaneous response.

"I'm sorry, I'm embarrassing you! I didn't mean .... Oh

dear!" Ky was feeling that he had blundered badly.

"It's alright Ky. Don't be embarrassed. Thank you for being so courteous about it."

"Courteous!" he wanted to blurt in reply. "I feel so much more than courtesy towards you! I mean it!" But any further attempts to dig himself out would bury him even further. He looked down at his hands.

They were rescued by the arrival of their dessert. Gradually the relaxed feeling between them returned, though their conversation didn't flow quite so freely the rest of the evening.

*

Ky's car came to a halt in Aggie's driveway. He walked around the front of the car, and opened her door for her. They walked to the front door. Ky was still feeling anxious that he had offended her.

"Ky, thank you so much for a lovely evening. I really enjoyed it. It was a lovely dinner, and I'm ever so grateful for the carved Kiwi. Thank you!"

Her words sounded sincere, reassuring, but Aggie was opening the door as she spoke. She slipped inside, hardly giving him time to acknowledge her thanks. Ky was left standing uncertainly.

Aggie closed the door and stood still, her face crumpling. Slowly she started towards her mother's bedroom, from where she could see the light shining into the passageway. She left her gift from Ky on the kitchen table as she passed.

Helen heard Aggie coming. She rose with an expectant smile. But as Aggie appeared before her, a picture of misery, her smile vanished.

"Agnes! What is it? What happened?"

"Mum!" wailed Aggie, "he's so good, so gentle, the way he speaks is so strong! I think he really likes me! He likes me! He gave me this carving that he made especially for me!"

Helen had a hand on each of Aggie's shoulders. "He's

141

really good, and he likes you. He carved something for you. So what's so upsetting?"

"Mum! What if it doesn't work out? What if he doesn't ask to meet me again? What if he decides I'm not so beautiful after all? I don't think I could stand it."

Helen's arms went around her daughter, pulling her into a close hug. The smile returned to her face. After a few moments she drew back to arm's length again.

"Agnes my dear, if Ky Soames decides you're not so beautiful after all, I will personally gouge his eyes out!"

Aggie looked seriously into her eyes. Gradually her mother's serene assurance began pulling away her fears, like mist dispelled in the wind. They broke into their familiar shared giggle.

Chapter 16

Seeds of Hope for Aggie.

Helen and Aggie sat at breakfast, reviewing Aggie's dinner with Ky.

"It really was a nice time. We seemed to just start talking naturally right from the start. Up until he noticed my birthmark. He wasn't rude or anything – in fact he said it couldn't spoil me. That I'm still beautiful. It was a nice thing to say, but somehow, I felt a little panicky. It seemed like too much all at once. And then Ky got all embarrassed." Aggie sighed.

"First meeting jitters," Helen told her. "I expect you'll get back on track with each other easily enough."

"But Mum, I just left him standing at the door! I practically closed it in his face! What if he's all offended?" She paused. "Maybe I should call and apologize? But I don't know if he even has a phone up there! I suppose he must, if he's taking business orders."

Helen thought for a few moments. "Agnes, I think it would be best if you just sent him a nice card, thanking him again for a lovely evening. Trying to apologize for the awkwardness might just get more awkward than ever."

"But Mum, I don't even have an address! Maybe he has a letterbox up on Dalefield Road, but it's more likely he's using a Post Office Box."

They looked at each other for a long moment. There just didn't seem to be any way of reassuring Ky without appearing pushy.

"Maybe you're just going to have to wait this one out dearest," Helen said at length. "I'm sure he'll contact you again soon."

*

Ky wasn't offended, as Aggie had suggested, but he was troubled, confused. Had he really blundered so badly? Right through Tuesday and Wednesday he was going over the dinner conversation in his mind. By Wednesday evening he decided that he would try again. He needed to know where he stood. For early June, the days were still bright, so Ky thought the ice cream garden on Saturday afternoon would be a good option.

It was Helen who answered the telephone again. "Hello Mrs. Betteridge. It's Ky Soames. May I speak with Aggie please?"

"Of course, Ky. Just a moment."

"Agnes," she called, "It's Ky! I think he hasn't deserted you!"

Aggie hurried to the phone. She stopped, swallowed, and took a deep breath. Helen smiled, and gave her a kiss on the forehead as she handed her the receiver.

"Hello Ky. This is Aggie."

"Aggie, it's nice to hear you again. I … I wasn't sure how you felt Monday evening, after you got home. I didn't know …. But, anyway, I wondered if you would like to meet me again this Saturday? Do you like ice cream? Would you like to come to the ice cream garden?"

"Ky, yes, I'm sorry I seemed … abrupt when you brought me home. You weren't rude or anything. I did so enjoy having dinner with you."

Relief was surging through Ky. His anxiety was swamped by his smile.

"Did you? I enjoyed being with you too! So is Saturday alright?"

"Oh yes," responded Aggie. "I have good memories of that ice cream garden, going way back. What time shall I meet you?"

"Um. Let's see. Hey, why wait until the afternoon? What about eleven o'clock?"

144

"Yes, that would be just fine Ky. Look forward to meeting you there at eleven!"

Aggie replaced the receiver, spun around, and ran to fling her arms around her mother. "The ice cream garden on Saturday morning!"

Helen held her daughter close. "I'm very happy for you Agnes," was all that she said. But her heart warmed with gratitude watching the lightness of Aggie's step as she walked back to her room. She was even humming a snatch of a song, something very rare for Aggie.

This time it was Aggie who thought more about what she would wear on Saturday than Helen did. The realization that a rather special man admired her, and wanted to be with her, was gaining ground.

*

Aggie and Ky were seated either side of a small outdoor table, with their ice cream sundaes on the table. Both wanted to defuse the moment of tension that had ended their evening on Monday, but neither quite knew what to say. Eventually, Aggie tackled the issue on both their minds.

"Ky, I'm sorry I seemed rude when you brought me home on Monday. I didn't mean to. When you noticed my birthmark – you were very gracious, not at all rude. I've had so much rejection because of it throughout my life, and I was scared you might react like that too. When you were so kind – you said it couldn't spoil me, you even said I'm still beautiful – I was just rather overcome. I'm only just getting to know you and you spoke so … so compassionately. I guess it all felt a little … overwhelming. I got a little panicked. Thank you for being so kind."

Ky paused thoughtfully before responding. "Thank you so much for helping me to understand that Aggie. I did get too personal too quickly didn't I? I'm sorry. I didn't mean to."

They remained thoughtful for a few more moments.

145

Then Ky exclaimed, "Hey this ice cream is melting! We'd better eat up!"

The relaxed interchange of conversation was returning, and they told each other of their lives, their interests, their experiences. Ky was impressed to hear of Aggie's writing, and that she had published a few pieces in magazines. She was interested to hear how he became a woodcarver. She learned that his carvings were considered to have serious artistic merit – art connoisseurs were his market. Aggie told stories of the high-profile clients she had met in her home décor consulting work. For many of them, she supervised the execution of the designs she produced, ordering high quality materials, and coordinating a variety of contractors to the completion of the project.

Their conversation moved to Ky's discovery of the cottage, and how he obtained permissions to develop the site into a woodcarving retreat. He described the development of the site – the water wheel, the "Barn" as he was now calling his workshop, and the improvements he made to the cottage. He was very interested to learn that Aggie and Helen had also discovered the site years ago, and that it had become a favorite haunt, where they had many times sat and prayed together on the rocks right in front of the cottage.

"So that's why you came visiting that Sunday afternoon! Only to discover I had taken over your cottage!" He wanted to add, "Maybe it will become 'your' cottage again!?" Quickly he reined in his thoughts.

So, the talk, the laughter, the comments and questions ebbed and flowed between them, until Ky looked at his watch, and exclaimed, "It's after two thirty! Are you getting hungry? An ice cream sundae wasn't much of a lunch!"

"Hmm. Maybe something small," Aggie responded.

"Let's grab a hamburger each, and take them over to the Waipoua Stream. We can sit on the bank and watch the water."

"Sounds fun! Let's do it!"

The river bank led on to conversation about their love of the outdoors. Ky was an experienced bushman who loved to explore the Tararua Range. He knew all the tracks well, but would often leave the established routes, and find his own way to hidden valleys and pools. In part, these explorations were to search out fallen trees that still had timber sound enough for carving. He tried to avoid cutting growing timber - he would buy in cut timber if he was short of the types and sizes he needed. Aggie talked of hikes she had made into the ranges too. Once she had made a complete traverse of the Tararuas, from the Hutt Valley right up to their northern extremity at Shannon.

The afternoon wore on, but still Aggie and Ky were oblivious to the passing time. Eventually, at about five thirty, they began to talk of parting for the day.

"Would you like to go somewhere to eat again before you head for home?" Ky asked.

Aggie considered. She didn't want the day to end, but a restaurant just didn't appeal. "Say, would you like to come back to our house? I'm sure there are some leftovers in the fridge!" She had an immediate qualm about inviting her new friend to a meal of leftovers, but Ky promptly quelled that fear.

"Thank you! Yes! I'm so happy that I'm already friend enough to be invited for leftovers!" He gave her a delighted smile.

Helen too was delighted that Aggie brought Ky back to share an evening meal. If this friendship was going anywhere, she wanted him to feel very welcome in her home. She continued chatting with them, while she and Aggie quickly prepared a meal, and as they sat to eat together. But she didn't stay long after the meal ended. Wisely, she excused herself.

Aggie cleared the dishes off the table, then returned to sit beside Ky. They were quiet now. Finally, Ky spoke.

"Aggie, this has been the most wonderful day. We've talked about so much! And now I should be going. But one last question. On Monday, we talked about my name, shortened from Hezekiah. What about your name? I heard your mum call you Agnes while you were preparing our meal. That's your real name isn't it? Agnes?"

He seemed to be rolling the sound of it around inside his mind. Aggie nodded. Ky was silent again, his eyes closed. He raised his eyes to meet hers. "May I call you Agnes?"

Aggie returned his gaze, without replying. She was silent

for some time, though this time he knew she wasn't embarrassed, or offended. She was weighing her thoughts. Eventually, she responded.

"Ky, we've had a wonderful day together. We talked and talked and got to know each other so much more. It must be clear to you that I like you very much. My feelings for you are growing very quickly - I'll not try to pretend about that." She paused. "But I need to be sure that what I'm experiencing with you is not just my own feelings running away with me. I need to be sure that this new friendship really is a gift from Jesus." Aggie paused again, looking down at her fingers. Then raising her eyes again to his, she continued. "My name, Agnes, has been used throughout my life only by my mother. It's something very personal to me. When I admit someone else to my real name, that is a very personal matter. I need more space before I can say yes to your question."

It was Ky's turn to pause before responding to her. "Thank you, Aggie. You have all the space you need. For my part, I realize what a deep privilege I just asked of you."

As Ky took his leave, he was thinking, "A gift from Jesus. Yes, this friendship is already serious. I need to be at least as prayerful as Aggie."

It was still early, but Aggie sat on her bed, deep in thought. "Less than a week ago, I'd never dreamed of a man really liking me. But now .... Is this what you want for me Lord?" She was not really expecting an immediate, clear answer, but as she drifted off to sleep, she had the impression that Jesus had enjoyed her day as much as she had.

*

"So, Mum! What do you think of Ky?" Aggie asked as they sat at breakfast next morning.

"I suppose he's okay. Could be worse." Helen's eyes twinkled.

"Mum! He's much more than 'okay'! I saw the way you were chatting with him at the table last night!"

"Yes, Agnes my love, he's much more than 'okay'. You can tell he's quite the artist, but not the temperamental type. He's very well spoken, and he's obviously charmed by you!"

"Do you think so Mum? I like him a lot! Quite apart from his woodcarving, he must be good with his hands. Just look at the work he did up at the cottage, building the water wheel, and the workshop."

"He said he's only been a Christian for four years, but Jesus is clearly woven deeply into his life," responded Helen. "And into his wood-carving, if I'm not mistaken."

As they cleared the remains of their breakfast, Aggie remarked, "Ky seems a wonderful man to me. And I can see you think he's wonderful too, however much you might tease me! But maybe we're biased. Who else is there who knows him? I need someone to tell me I'm not falling for someone who's really not as great as he looks."

"Wise thought my dear," responded Helen. "Where did he live before he moved here? A farm up north somewhere wasn't it?"

"Yes, he grew up on a dairy farm near Kutarere. That's up near Whakatane. We don't know anyone from up there! Who has known him best in the last year, since he's been here?"

"What about Jon Sanders?" suggested Helen. "Ky joined Jon's Bible study group pretty soon after he arrived on the scene, so Jon should know him. Let's ask Jon and Cassie to come back for lunch after church."

*

"Great lunch – as always!" declared Jon Sanders. He and Cassie cleared dishes from the table while Helen fixed coffee for them all. Aggie went out of the room, heading for her bedroom. She returned as they sat down with their coffee, carrying a small carved object.

"How do you like my Kiwi?" she asked, setting it on the table.

Jon and Cassie both leaned forward. "That is one fine carving!" Jon declared.

"Any guesses where it came from?" Aggie asked.

Jon knew that Ky was a wood carver, and that his business was beginning to gain momentum. But neither Jon nor Cassie had seen any of his work, so they were not making any connections. Even when Jon picked up the carving, and saw the name "Ky" burned under its base, it took a few moments to register.

Suddenly, insight dawned. "Oh, Ky Soames! Is this his work?"

Aggie gave a small, shy smile. "He made it for me."

Jon and Cassie both glanced at Aggie, then at Helen, noticing her smiling, twinkling eyes, and back to Aggie. "He made it for you?" Jon began. Cassie continued, "So, he's .... he's .... You are ..."

Aggie came to their rescue. "We've been out together a couple of times."

"Aggie, that is wonderful! From what I've seen, he's a great guy!" Cassie's face was one delighted smile.

"Yes," Jon contributed, "Ky is a great asset in the Bible study. I've admired his depth, and his spiritual sensitivity – especially for someone who's been a Christian for only a few years."

"Wait a minute!" Aggie protested. "I like him very much too. Very much! But you two are supposed to be the objective critics! I need your cool appraisal, telling me all the faults I'm missing as my feelings run away with me!" .

Cassie and Jon's laughter cascaded around them. "Aggie, you are a treasure!" Cassie moved to her chair, putting an arm around her shoulders. "Sorry my dear, I really can't think of any terrible things to tell you about Ky!"

"Me neither," observed Jon. "Let's see. About six weeks ago, he was up at Mrs. Martin's house with me, repairing her back fence. Now Mrs. Martin is enough to try anyone's patience! We were both getting exasperated with her. But, you know, I think Ky stayed more patient and courteous than I did! Aggie, from everything I've seen, Ky is a fine man."

Aggie looked at them gratefully. "Thank you," she said. "But I'm serious about this. He seems a wonderful man to me, and everyone else seems to think so too. I just want to know that I'm not missing anything I need to know. If you do think of anything else, please tell me."

*

Ky and Aggie began getting together more frequently. On a fine Saturday in late June, Aggie drove up the Dalefield Road to spend some time watching Ky at his work. She noticed that bushes had been cleared, and beside the entrance to the track, a new sign proclaimed "The Barn," in large letters. And below, "Ky Soames, Woodcarver."

That day she watched Ky as he designed and shaped and polished the timber. He loved showing her the process from taking a raw block of wood, and transforming it into a delicately proportioned, silky-smooth work of art. On other days they left the workshop, and Ky showed her some of the trails he'd discovered into valleys, and onto plateaus where there were stumps and fallen trunks he meant to cut for timber.

Sometimes they sat beside a stream, sharing their thoughts and hopes. Sometimes they prayed together, sometimes they sat in silence. For Aggie especially, something new was happening. The depths of loneliness and sadness would not be fully healed for many a year. But for now, alpine orchids were scattering on the ground of her heart. She was grateful.

On the last Sunday in July, Ky and Aggie had spent the afternoon at The Barn. Now dusk was settling in. They wore jackets against the sharp breeze tugging around them, as they sat on the rocky lip in front of the cottage. Aggie was about to leave, but her heart wrestled within her.

They watched the shadows deepen. Finally, she asked, "Ky, would you still like to use my real name, Agnes?"

Ky had looked forward to hearing that question, but he was caught off guard. For a moment his voice failed him. Slowly

151

he formed the words, "I would be honored."

"I would like you to call me Agnes."

Ky reached across to touch her hand, their eyes meeting. "Agnes. Thank you for trusting me with your name."

They sat a few more minutes. As the daylight faded, Ky raised his arms in front of him, cupping his hands. He peered into them, as though some object was forming there.

"It's like a pearl. An amazing pearl!" His voice was filled with wonder. "It's growing, growing, filling my hands. It's bathed in a bluish glow, suffusing right through it. There's a flowing script across it, in dark blue, just one word. It's your name, 'Agnes'."

Aggie leaned towards him, trying to see into his hands. But the glow was fading.

"You saw my name? Written on …. on a pearl?"

They sat in silence, thoughts awhirl, not knowing quite how to respond. This time, Aggie's hand reached across to rest on Ky's arm. Soon, she gave his arm a slight squeeze, then rose. "Good night Ky." She walked to her car.

*

"Helen, may I talk to you for a few minutes?" Aggie was away overnight on a business trip, and Ky took the opportunity to visit Helen. They sat at her kitchen table.

"I want to talk about my friendship with Aggie. I've felt for some time now that God intends for us to be together. Maybe she told you that she gave me permission to use her name, Agnes. And right after that, I saw this picture of a huge pearl, with her name flowing across it."

"Really? No, she didn't tell me that."

"From the beginning, I've been very serious about our friendship. But now it's time for me to ask for your blessing, and perhaps your guidance. I have in mind to ask her to marry me some time very soon."

Helen sat watching him. "There's always been a part of

152

Agnes that I haven't been admitted to," the thoughts tumbled. "And now, here she is admitting a newcomer, sharing her real name, the name that has been only for our use up until now. But that's how it must be."

Slowly a smile formed. "I know there's nothing frivolous about the way you've treated Agnes. I'm confident that you're the right man for her. I'm very content with that." She leaned forward. "Ky, you have my blessing to pursue Agnes. Thank you for coming to ask me."

Ky nodded. "Thank you. Thank you."

Helen's face became serious again. "She's a complex person Ky. Please always give her space to come to her own conclusions. She's …. always been deeply affected by not ever seeing her father, or having him as part of her life. And the birthmark on her face, that was a huge burden to her early in her life. I always did my best for her, but …..."

"You've been a marvelous mother to her Mrs. Betteridge. I respect you. Thank you for being such a good mother to Agnes."

Helen paused, then smiled, "Just a warning Ky. When you ask her, I'm sure she'll accept!"

*

Signs of Spring were appearing. The first lambs of the season skipped in the fields, and white and pink blossom brightened bleak winter branches. The final week of August was busy for both Ky and Aggie. She had another business trip, this time to Wanaka, and he received two new commissions for carvings. They spoke by phone several times, but had not been able to meet. It was Thursday evening - Ky called Aggie again.

"Hey, I've been missing you!" They caught up with news since they last talked. Then Ky moved to plans for their weekend. "Agnes, I've been thinking about what we might do Saturday. I have something a little different in mind."

"A little different? What are you thinking of Mr. Ky?"

"We've been lots of places together, but I've never taken you out to Riversdale Beach. It'll be still rather wintry out there – we'll need to be bundled up with jackets. Are you up for a bracing walk along a lonely stretch of beach? I think it'll be just us, with the sea and the sky and the sand dunes."

"Hmm. It does sound different. The sort of challenge we like though."

"Good! But here's another challenge. I have in mind a special place for dinner. It's not too formal – not a suit and tie place, but kind of semi-formal. So, we'll need to be protected against the wind, but underneath, be just a bit dressy. What do you think?"

"Hmm, I think we can manage that. Looking forward to it!"

*

Ky drove to the southern end of the Riversdale Beach settlement, and parked the car. It was about quarter past four in the afternoon, so the sun was only just beginning to swing towards the west. They donned scarves, beanies, and jackets, before stumping their way through the soft, dry sand dune past the end of the road, finally reaching the damp, firm sand, where walking was easier. At first, they rambled north, with the wind at their backs, reaching as far as the Life Saving Club.

"Ready to face into the breeze now?" Ky smiled at her. She smiled back, pulling him round to feel the sharp, salt wind in their faces. Slowly they made their way back, savoring the intermittent swirling of a wave surging up towards them, the wheeling and crying of the gulls and terns. They passed the point where they had left the car, continuing along the wide sandy beach another half an hour. As expected, they had the whole seafront to themselves – a long, wide expanse bounded by the ever-moving surf on their left, and sand dunes, sparsely covered with marram and sedge grass, to their right.

Finally, Ky turned and stood gazing out to the ocean,

listening to the breakers, the wind, the gulls. It felt as though they were alone in a world bounded by surf, sand, and a sky that was just beginning to dim towards dusk. Aggie stood facing Ky. He reached down to take her hands, standing close to her.

"Agnes, just a few weeks ago you gave me the greatest privilege of my life so far. You trusted me with your name. Now I have another request. I love you Agnes. Will you be my wife?"

A stray beam of sunlight glanced over his shoulder, lighting up her grey eyes, as she gazed up at him. "I love you too Ky. Of course, I will be your wife!"

Their arms enfolded each other. Then Aggie stepped back again. "Wait a minute! Hadn't you better ask Mum about this?"

"She gave me her blessing weeks ago," Ky smiled at her.

"Did she! So you two have been scheming behind my back," she declared with mock severity.

"Not exactly my love. I've been sure about this for a while now, but I wanted to give you time. When you invited me to use your name, I knew I could move to the real question that was on my heart."

"I'd have said yes on the spot, if you'd asked me then!"

"I nearly did. But I wanted to go somewhere special, do something memorable."

"Ky, this is the perfect place for us! The mountains would have been nice – but this is so different, and desolate, and beautiful! I love you so much! Thank you!"

They knelt together on the sand, committing themselves and their future to God. Soon they moved higher up the beach where the sand was softer and drier. They sat together as the shadows began to lengthen behind them...

"Agnes, there's something I've thought about that we haven't talked of before," Ky began. "That was a special, wonderful hug we shared a few minutes ago. Up to now, we've hardly touched each other. Just brushing our hands together every now and then. I haven't wanted it to be any different, and I just assumed that you felt the same?"

"You mean if we'd been touching and kissing and hugging? No, that would have just complicated things. I'm so glad we've been this way."

"Good! I'm glad you've felt the same way. I thought you did. And y'know, I'd like us to go on that way. I dunno, maybe most people would think this is weird now that we're engaged, but it seems to me that most of that really belongs to after our marriage. I might give you a peck on the forehead, or on the top of your head now and again. Or we might have a hug now and then. But real kissing, and holding each other really tight, and everything like that – I want to save that for my wife!"

Aggie thought for a few moments. "I don't think I've ever put those thoughts together in my head, but now you come to say them, I think that's exactly what I would say too."

"I wanted to mention this, so we know we're on the same page. And we can talk more about it if we need to. I think we need to revisit all this closer to our wedding – we need to at least share our thoughts about what's ahead. But for now – well, as you said, all that will just complicate things."

Again, Aggie was silent for some time. Eventually she looked up at Ky. "Thank you for talking about this. I feel safe with you."

The sun had sunk below the hills behind them. The moon was four days before full, but a golden pathway had begun to shimmer across the sea, stretching almost to their feet. The moonlight began to give surf and beach and dunes a transforming sheen. Ky and Aggie slowly retraced their steps towards the car.

"You said we're going somewhere for dinner now?" Aggie asked. "I'm not sure I want this to end. Anything else would be an anticlimax."

"I do have something else for you," Ky replied. "I hope it won't be an anticlimax. At the Clearwater Station not far from here, they've renovated the old homestead into a bed and breakfast place. It's usually just bed and breakfast, but sometimes they do dinner if they get bookings from half a dozen or so parties, to make it worth their while. I managed to get us a booking."

"Race you to the car!" called Aggie over her shoulder as she set off running.

*

Ky and Aggie sat at a table for two in the corner of the Clearwater Station dining room. There were four other couples dining with them, but each was strategically placed, giving each a sense of intimacy. The candles on each table were the only illumination.

After they had ordered, Ky reached into his jacket pocket, and produced a ring box. "On our first real meeting, I gave you a gift, something I made for you. Tonight, I have another gift, something I chose for you." He handed it to her.

A prickle of gladness ran through Aggie, from head to toe, as she took the box from him. "Ky, you are so special," she murmured. She opened the box. The cushion-cut diamond sat on a raised setting above a gold ring. The polished gold sent back the flickering candle light, while small multi-colored sparks jumped from the clear depths of the stone.

"Beautiful. So beautiful." Aggie's voice was so soft, Ky could barely hear her.

"May I put it on your finger?" he asked. Aggie held out her hand. "I love you Mrs. Soames-to-be," he said, as it slipped onto her finger.

For the rest of the evening, Aggie could hardly keep her eyes off her left hand. This was definitely not an anticlimax, she decided.

Helen was still up when they arrived home. Aggie ran to her, holding out her left hand. Helen couldn't stop hugging them both.

*

They set the wedding date for early March. The months slipped by. Aggie and Ky wanted a simple wedding, and decided to make it a church-wide celebration, asking the whole Carrington congregation to join them.

In mid-September, Colin was home for a weekend again. On Saturday morning he drove to The Barn. As they heard the car, both Aggie and Ky emerged from the workshop, holding brooms.

"Hey Colin! Good to see you! You back for a week? Or more?" Ky hugged his friend.

"No, just the weekend. But I had to call by to see you. And I thought I would see your beautiful fiancée here too. So happy to hear your news!" He reached out to draw Aggie into their hug.

They sat on a bench against the sunny wall of The Barn, talking, laughing.

"Look, I don't have much time. I'm off back to Kaiangaroa Sunday night. But I wanted to see you both, and I want to see my old friend Hohepa. I don't think you've met him? He's getting on a bit, and seems a bit lonely these days, so I try to keep in touch. Would you have time to come with me now to meet him? I know he'd love that."

"We pretty much finished cleaning out The Barn," responded Ky. "What do you think Agnes?"

"Yes, let's," said Aggie. "I know what a friend he's been to you Colin. Would love to meet him."

Hohepa's eyes were showing his age, but they lit up as he saw his visitors. Ky's interest was caught immediately as he saw that Hohepa was carving a long narrow piece of timber.

"That timber, Hohepa, is that a piece of Tawa? What are you carving?"

"Tokotoko e haere. It's a walking stick. I'm beginning to need one! And yes, it's a piece of Tawa. You know something about timber, Ky?"

"Well, yes. I'm a woodcarver myself. You're making a beautiful job of that!"

Part of Colin's mission was to invite Hohepa to join him and Zoe for dinner at their house. He turned to Ky and Aggie. "And if you two, and your mum Aggie, could join us too, that would be perfect."

Before finding faith and friends, Zoe would never have

thought of hosting such a dinner. Even now, it was a stretch for her, but that evening, as they all sat after dinner in the lounge room firelight, she glowed with pride and happiness. Hohepa's eyes were moist as he sat in the warmth of their circle. At the end of the evening, as Colin took Hohepa back home, Helen stayed on for a few minutes, talking with Zoe.

"I was so glad to meet Hohepa. Wasn't he just so happy to be among a group of friends?" Helen commented. "He doesn't say too much, but what he does say is worth listening to!"

"Yes," answered Zoe, "I owe him a huge debt. He was the first one to take an interest in Colin. I want to keep in touch with him. Hope we can keep doing this – I hate to think of him sitting lonely at home."

*

On Labor Day weekend in October, Ky and Aggie sat together on the couch in Helen's lounge room. They had just finished dinner, and were chatting for a few minutes before Ky took his leave.

"Ky, there's something I've been wondering about," Aggie began. "You know how I've seen pictures the Lord has given me, and heard things he's spoken many times. But you know, there's just been nothing like that about our friendship, our engagement, our marriage. There's just been nothing."

She glanced quickly at him. "It's alright! I have no doubts that this is right for us. God has led us to each other. It's just that … Oh, I don't know. I wasn't expecting God would give me a complete picture of our life – surrounded by children and grandchildren!" She laughed. "It just seems strange, different. No little hints or glimpses of our future together."

Ky sat watching her face for a few moments. "I guess the Lord knows we're on the path he has for us. Maybe he just doesn't have any more to say to us for now."

Aggie leaned toward him. "I love you Ky Soames," she said.

Ky leaned toward her, kissing her forehead. "I love you too Agnes Betteridge."

*

One evening, Helen sat in her prayer rocker. "Lord, I'm so tired. And my back aches. I've had these spells for months, but it's getting worse. What is it Lord? I suppose I should go to the doctor. But I don't want to! There's a wedding coming up, and I don't have time to be sick!"

The next day at Allied Garments, Zoe Campbell came across Helen slumped across a table.

"Helen, what's wrong? What's happening?"

Slowly Helen straightened, composing the pain lines out of her face. "Zoe, can you come into my office for a minute?"

Helen closed the door, and sat back in her chair. "You're right Zoe. I've been getting pain in my back for quite a while now. And I get spells where I just go fuzzy. I need to get a checkup. I didn't want to admit it, with the wedding coming up. But … I'll phone the doctor now." She rested her head on her hands. "But Zoe! Zoe, please don't say anything to anyone! I don't want Agnes worrying. Not now!"

"Oh, Helen! This is so hard for you. Aggie needs to know, but I understand. I'd do the same I guess. But you get yourself off to the doctor quick smart!"

Helen's appointment was on December 15th. As Dr. Alders summed up, he told her gravely, "Helen, this is looking serious. I'll get you in for some tests before Christmas if I can. It's going to be next month before we get results from those."

So Helen summoned all her strength, along with discreet support from Zoe, to negotiate Christmas, and her part in preparing for Aggie's big day.

*

In January they all attended Kathy Pierce's marriage to Eric Paynter. It was different from what they were planning, but right for Kathy and Eric. The renovations at Eric's farmhouse at Shepherd's Rest were completed – the house waited to receive them.

*

Ky and Aggie sat on the warm rocks beside the Waipoua Stream It had become a favorite spot.

"Agnes," began Ky, "you remember when we talked out at Riversdale, how we're both glad that we haven't gotten into a lot of kissing and such. All that is for our marriage, not for now. Well, now our marriage is pretty close, and I ... well I don't feel well-prepared for this intimacy part. I want it to be nice for you – for both of us I guess. But what to do? You don't just blunder up to any old person, and say, 'Tell me what I need to know!'"

"You need the 'Sex for Dummies' manual," giggled Aggie.

"Yes, well, we've both read some of the books," Ky grinned back. "I just want us to be as well-prepared as we can be."

Aggie was serious again. "Ky, I really am glad you want to be thoughtful about this. Thank you for caring for me. We'll pray about it."

As though in answer to their prayers, Ky came across a magazine article about a marriage counselor living at Upper Hutt, who specialized in sexual issues. He found the telephone number and made an appointment. He was concerned that his request for guidance would seem naïve, so he was relieved and gratified to find that Dr. Wakeman was attentive and supportive.

"If every young groom was as thoughtful and respectful towards his fiancée as you are, most of my clients would disappear," he commented. "You seem relaxed and unembarrassed about your sexual self, and from what you say, it

161

seems that Agnes is too. I trust the ideas we have discussed – the things you need to talk together about, and the preparations you can make, will all be helpful. I don't think you'll have too many difficulties, but if you need further help, you know where to find me."

So, Ky and Aggie surprised themselves by the open, uninhibited conversations they were able to have about their coming intimacy. It was something they were always grateful for.

Chapter 17

A Wedding to Remember.

"Mum, who's going to give me away? You've been both Dad and Mum to me. There isn't any man who's been father to me."

"I know dear. I've been thinking about that. Jon Sanders has been closest to being a father. Do you want to ask him?"

"Hmm, I know it's supposed to be a man." Aggie frowned a little. "But we already decided, we won't have any attendants. So, it's already a creative kind of wedding. I think it has to be you Mum. I want you to give me to Ky."

Their eyes locked for a long moment. Helen's eyes became misty. "Thank you, sweetheart. I would be honored."

"But it would be nice for you to have a man as a kind of escort. A friend, a man you trust. Just so you're not all by yourself. I wondered … what do you think about asking Hohepa? I know we haven't known him very long, but he admires you! He thinks you're more 'Kaumatua' than he is himself! I know he'd be so tickled."

"Agnes, that's a lovely idea. Thank you for thinking of me."

*

Sprigs of white jasmine were fixed to the end of each pew. Aggie had chosen a simple dress of soft white cotton, with half-length sleeves, fitted at the waist, and full skirt curving softly outward to almost brush the floor. A single string of embroidered forget-me-nots began at her left shoulder, ran down the side of her bodice, then fanned out over the left side of her skirt. A sprig of white jasmine nestled into the left side of her dark hair.

Hohepa and Helen were a picture of dignity as they made their way slowly up the aisle, complementing the simple beauty of Ky's bride walking beside them. Ky stood in a light grey suit, white shirt, and grey bow-tie, watching their progress. His eye caught Aggie's - their gaze remained locked until she reached his side. Helen and Hohepa stepped back to join Ky's parents, Trevor and Melody.

During the service, a young woman slipped unnoticed through a side door. Tears wet her cheeks. If someone nearby had recognized her, they would have remembered her as Kelly Stephenson.

Ky and Aggie made their vows to each other. The whole church erupted as they shared their first kiss.

Colin stood beside Zoe in the congregation. Aggie's old friend Stephanie and her fiancé were there, along with a few other high school friends, her former school principal, Mr. Bradley, the McKnight's and the Sanders, members of her Sunday School class, Stephen Spenlow, and others from Allied Garments. At the reception following, the speeches were few, and the dancing, singing and conversation lasted long.

Helen's gift to Aggie and Ky was her prayer chair, the granny rocker that had sat in her bedroom for so long. Some guests wondered at that – would not the mother of the bride have given something more substantial than a rocking chair, and an old, used one at that? But Aggie and Ky knew that Helen had given her very most prized possession. Nothing could have been received with more gratitude – they placed it in their bedroom with something approaching awe.

So, began a marriage full of promise.

Chapter 18

A Peak and a Valley.

Ky and Aggie had decided on an unusual honeymoon. They planned to spend the first six days hiking in the mountains. But not their familiar Tararua Range – they would go further afield, and try a foray into the Te Urewera National Park, a very rugged area of bush and lakes up towards East Cape. They planned to take the Ngapakira Track, but before they reached its end, they would push north from the trail, making their way down into a stream basin Ky knew, where there were stands of bush, and also wide, grassy spaces – it seemed like a good place to camp, relax and explore. Following the hiking phase, they would drive up to a small guesthouse overlooking the sea near Pouawa, a few miles north of Gisborne, to spend another six days in more conventional comfort.

They devised this plan partly because they were both independent thinkers, likely to come up with something more memorable than predictable. And partly their idea was that a hiking trip would progressively admit them to small intimacies, preparing them for coming together in the comfortable privacy of their guest house.

The day was well advanced after a two-stage flight to Gisborne, obtaining a rental car, and driving the two hours down to Lake Waikaremoana. Aggie watched Ky scurry around in the dusk, finding a suitable place to pitch their small tent.

"Tell me what I can do to help," she called.

"Swing the car around a bit," he called back, "so the lights are showing us what we're doing."

With their site illuminated, Ky quickly had the tent

pitched and pegged down. Very soon they curled up in their sleeping bags, drifting off to sleep after a long and satisfying day.

Sunday dawned fine, though with a few scattered clouds that could bring some rain. Ky and Aggie woke soon after first light, but stayed in their tent for some time, reliving scenes from the previous day, enjoying their new closeness. In camping mode, they had shed only outer clothes before scrambling into their sleeping bags, so they were soon dressed, preparing to breakfast and move out. It wasn't a long hike to their planned camping base, so they were in no hurry. They packed the tent, and strapped it to the outside of Ky's pack.

For the first two hours, bush cover alternated with open spaces. They were covering the last of the open areas when drops of rain began spattering down. However, it wasn't enough to give them a serious wetting before they plunged back under the bush cover. The track wound back and forth as it traversed small ravines, each with its fresh chattering stream, but overall, it climbed hardly at all as it led along the western side of the Matakahuia Ridge.

Aggie and Ky stopped for lunch just before leaving the bush cover again. From there, they were looking out for a suitable place to turn north off the track, and drop down into the stream basin. The valley side was a gentle gradient, so they had no difficulty – soon they were down nearly at riverbed level, looking for a suitable site to camp. About half a mile further on they found a small clump of bush, and pitched their tent under its eaves. A small tributary stream bubbled just fifteen yards away.

For the rest of the afternoon, they lazed, read, and watched the wildlife around them. As evening drew on, three young deer came down to drink at the stream, unaware of two pairs of human eyes watching them. The clouds persisted, but didn't threaten further rain – instead they clustered in the western sky, turning the evening sunlight to orange and mauve.

Tuesday was spent rambling further downstream as far as the Ruakituri River. Just before joining the river, the stream they were following ran through a gorge, the banks coming down steeply on both sides. Aggie and Ky waded in the stream for this part of their journey, before emerging on the bank of the larger river. They could see the road on the far side of the river, but saw no vehicle pass while they were there. They were enjoying the isolation, the feeling of being in a world only they occupied. As they made their way back to their campsite, they talked of perhaps taking a more demanding hike up into the bush northwest of them. They would have to plan carefully, as many of the hillsides were steep, and they didn't have ropes. But with care, they thought they could find the passes.

When they emerged from their tent on Wednesday morning, the day was already hot, and promised to become hotter. They meant to make their way upstream, intending to reconnoiter a possible route to the northwest. But Ky remembered a spot a little downstream where two tributaries emerged almost at the same place. They swelled the stream, just where it surged against a rocky bank, creating a pool that practically begged any passer-by to come swim. The sun beat down as Ky and Aggie arrived at the spot, warming the sand under their boots.

Ky smiled at Aggie. "Anyone for a dip?" he asked, and began peeling off his clothes. Aggie looked around the streambed, the bush-clad slopes, upstream, downstream – all deserted. She glanced at the sky, as though checking for parachutists. She gave a shy giggle, left her clothes in a heap beside Ky's, and ran to join him in the pool. The initial cool-shock left them giggling and shivering, but soon they were plunging and jumping, glad to wash off the sweat of the last few days. Their wet hair clung around their faces.

Ten minutes later they lay face down, side by side on the warm sand near their clothes. The sun warmed and dried them. Before long, Ky raised himself on an elbow. He gazed at the form beside him, awed by the precious gift she was to him. For long moments, his eyes traced from top to toe and back again. At length, very tentatively, he reached out, touching her back. Slowly his hand moved down to her leg and up again to the small of her back. Aggie gave a contented wriggle, settling herself more deeply into the warm sand.

Now Ky knelt beside her, starting at her shoulders, touching, stroking, kissing, working his way slowly down to her feet. Tenderness surged through his heart. As he reached her feet,

Aggie turned on her back, and lay with her eyes closed. Ky's breath caught in his throat. He surveyed her again, his heart almost breaking with wonder and gratitude for her. His stroking, kissing, touching resumed, working slowly from feet to shoulders, brushing sand from her as he went. Aggie was filled with delight – delight in the strong, secure man who was loving on her, delight in the woman she was created to be. Her whole body hummed with a new awakening. As he reached her shoulders, she sat up, pushing Ky away, down on his back. She knelt beside him, taking her turn at touching, caressing, kissing from his face down to his feet. Now she sat astride him, slowly, carefully, slowly welcoming him into her.

*

Sometime later, Aggie opened her eyes. "Well Hezekiah Soames, I could easily cope with trying that again! But maybe in a more pampered environment. Where did you say is that guesthouse we booked?"

Ky's arms tightened around her. He raised his head, kissing her forehead. "At Pouawa," he responded.

"I'm suggesting a change of plans," she announced. "Instead of more hiking, we could pack up now, walk out to the car by about two o'clock, get to Gisborne by about four thirty, and call the guesthouse to see if they can take us a few days early."

Ky smiled at her. "Mrs. Soames, as always, your thoughts are a delight to my ears! Let's do it!"

They scrambled back into their clothes, and set off at a fast pace towards their tent. In the car, as they drove towards Gisborne, Aggie reached over, putting her hand on Ky's leg.

"Ky, I'm your girl. I'll always be your girl. I trust you," she said softly.

At Gisborne, they found a public telephone, and called the guesthouse. Yes, it would be no problem for them to begin their visit three days early. They were expected in about half an

168

hour.

The guesthouse was up a short side road, leading inland for about a hundred yards off the highway. It was on a slight rise, giving wide sweeping views of the bay. Kowhai trees grew around the sides and back of the building, giving it a cool, inviting appearance. They settled quickly into their room.

"Ky! Look at this!" Aggie was checking out the bathroom. "It's a shower. Some of the new houses are getting these."

"Let's try it! And look at these little bottles! Hair shampoo and conditioner."

The bathroom filled with steam and laughter as they tried the new innovations, emerging clean, refreshed and ready for dinner. Already, sharing the bathroom seemed so natural, as though they had always done it this way.

The next morning Aggie called her mum.

"Hello Mum! We're fine. I'm calling from the guest house. Yes, it was lovely. We had a good time, but decided we were ready for some comfort, so we moved here early."

"I'm glad to hear from you!" Helen was dreading the cloud looming on Aggie's horizon, feeling guilty that she had withheld her news so far. The surprise of a call earlier than expected was almost like being caught with her hands in the cookie jar. With an effort, she regrouped her thoughts. "Have a wonderful time the pair of you. Looking forward to seeing you!"

The rest of Ky and Aggie's honeymoon was spent reading, talking, sketching, cuddling, eating, making love. One day they drove further up towards East Cape. It was a long day, as both liked to explore the side roads they passed. Another day they drove down to Gisborne to wander around the city and do a little shopping. By the time they left for home, they were rested, and looking forward to settling together into The Barn.

*

The next five weeks brought adjustments for both Ky

and Aggie, as they became accustomed to life together. Routines they had established independently now had to be melded together. Like all newly-weds, they experienced the sharp pain of unexpected differences, testing their patience and forbearance.

Learning to be lovers also had its growing pains, but they were grateful for the approach they had taken, and the guidance they had received from Dr. Wakeman. In fact they both felt so blessed by their lovemaking that small hopeful thoughts played in the back of Aggie's mind that she might already be pregnant. But no, her period turned up as usual a week after their return. She knew her disappointment was unreasonable, and quickly dismissed it.

Aggie still liked to watch Ky at work when she could spare some time. His woodworking machines occupied about two thirds of his workshop. Then came a small gallery space, where clients could come to view his work. The remaining space was devoted to an office desk and chair, another small table where he would sit to sketch design ideas, and some comfortable chairs, where clients or friends could sit to chat and relax.

Aggie and Ky both enjoyed flexible schedules. Ky would usually disappear early into his workshop, where he would spend the day, often into the evening, sometimes quite late into the evening. But he was just a few steps from the cottage, so he could come and go easily. Aggie often worked from home at the cottage, sometimes from her office in Carterton, and occasionally she would be away for two or three days, visiting clients. But most of their activities could be scheduled or rescheduled around events they wanted to share.

Helen was of course a frequent visitor. They loved to see her, and she tried to make sure she didn't intrude on them too frequently. She had lost weight over the last few months, and seemed paler, less healthy. Several times Aggie asked about how she was feeling. On a Wednesday towards the end of April, Helen telephoned. She and Aggie chatted for a few minutes, then Aggie pressed her even more firmly about making an appointment with her doctor.

"Mum, it's very clear that you're not well. You can't put me off any longer – you really must get a check-up."

"Yes dear, I have an appointment on Tuesday." Aggie was surprised, concerned and relieved. Relieved that her mum was finally doing something about her health. But concerned, because Helen's admission that she needed to get a check-up made the problem, whatever it was, seem more real and immediate.

"I thought you'd be pleased I'm doing as I'm told," Helen continued brightly. "And now, I wonder if you could both come and join me after dinner on Friday. I have a really nice blackberry and apple pie here. Can you come over about seven to help me with it, maybe with some ice cream, and a cup of coffee?"

"Mum, that would be lovely! We haven't been to see you for a couple of weeks at least."

As she replaced the receiver, the thought struck Aggie that it was strange she was asking them to come over after dinner. Usually she would have had them come share a meal. Oh well. She dismissed the thought.

*

Aggie tapped on Helen's back door as she opened it, and called, "We're here!"

"Come in the pair of you. Dessert is on the table in the lounge room. I'm just pouring the coffee."

A few minutes later they sat with cups of coffee and plates of dessert on a low table between them. But before any of them could begin, Helen spoke up.

"Dear ones, I can't wait any longer. I have to ask your forgiveness." She glanced at each of them in turn. "I've been keeping something from you. You know I haven't been well – you were quite right. I went to the doctor late last year. They did some tests, and in January, well, they told me I have breast cancer." Again she looked at them beseechingly. "I know, I know! But how could I say anything when you were in the middle of preparing for your special day? I just couldn't spoil it all! I

171

couldn't!"

"Mum!" Aggie's throat constricted as she flew to her mother. She knelt beside Helen's chair.

"And since you've been back....... I've been planning to tell you. But," she burst into tears. "Do you know how much joy I've had, watching you so happy together?" Her words came in sobs. Ky had joined Aggie, kneeling in front of her chair. Helen's hand reached out to touch him. "Ky, do you know how grateful I am to the Lord, and to you? I can't imagine a better husband to take care of my darling Agnes! It's ... it's been so hard to break into all that with my sad news."

"Mum! Mum!" Aggie spoke up again. "Is it ... is it bad? Can they do anything?"

"Apparently I've had it for a while. It was slow for a start, so I didn't take much notice. But it's spread now to my liver. Agnes, precious, I don't have very much longer."

"How long?" Aggie could barely choke the words out.

"They think maybe three, four months."

Aggie buried her face in her mother's lap. Helen sat stroking her hair. Ky tried to get his arms around both of them.

As it turned out, Helen had already told Stephen Spenlow, her boss at Allied Garments. They had agreed that her last day would be the following Friday.

"Will you forgive me dear ones, for telling others before you?" she asked them again. "Do you understand? Is it alright?"

Aggie was emerging from her initial shock enough to realize what a burden her mother had been carrying. "Mum! You just kept it to yourself, all for our sake! That has been so hard for you! I love you Mum!"

The coffee was cold, the ice cream melted. But no-one took any notice. As Ky and Aggie drove home, she felt some of the old sense of isolation enveloping her.

"Ky my love. I don't mean to cut you out. I just feel wrapped in my own grief just now."

"I understand. I love you Agnes."

That night, as they lay close together, Ky's strong arms around her, her tears came slowly, a one by one procession.

In the coming weeks, Aggie cut back her work load to

spend as much time as possible with her mum. They agreed the best arrangement was for Ky and Aggie to move back to Helen's house, so that they could be on hand for her. It was preferable to moving her up to The Barn, as her house was closer for medical visits and appointments.

One day as Aggie moved in and out of her room, fussing over making her as comfortable as possible, Helen asked her to bring a chair, and sit beside the bed. She lay stroking Aggie's hand, watching her with love and gratitude. But something had been troubling Helen, ever since Ky and Aggie returned from their honeymoon. She couldn't quite place it, but now as she watched her daughter, the feeling grew.

Already, her mind was beginning to slow. Her eyes closed, a slight frown of concentration furrowing her brow. Gradually, a picture formed in her mind. She could see Ky and Agnes walking into the days ahead, full of love for each other, though as the road ahead lengthened, its verges narrowed, thorns and vines seeming to reach out to harass and tear at them. Then as the road stretched out further, she could see only Agnes. Somehow, Ky faded out of the picture. Helen's frown deepened. Gradually it smoothed again as sleep overtook her.

*

Helen's prognosis turned out to be only too accurate. It was just a few days beyond three months from when she broke her news that she left them. She had been in severe pain for over a month, but as Aggie and Zoe stood beside her bed, they saw a smile of such gladness come over her tired features. They knew she had left.

Aggie and Zoe stood sobbing, clinging to each other.

"She's free," murmured Zoe.

Aggie nodded. "Did you see her smile? Yes, she's free."

Aggie was surrounded with support, from Ky, from Zoe, the McKnight's, the Sanders, and Carrington Church as a whole. Those who watched said that it seemed a battle went on within her. The comfort of Ky's love was strong, but it was recent. Helen had been her protector all through those sad, isolated, childhood years. Slowly she trusted herself again to Ky, though it seemed a new layer of sadness settled on the old, and did not easily diminish as time went by.

At the Barn, two picture frames stood on the mantelpiece over the fireplace. One contained a photograph of Martin, dashing in his First Lieutenant's uniform. The other contained a sketch of Helen, drawn by a nine-year-old hand - Helen was sitting on the veranda of the cottage, with the clematis vine beside and above her. Beside the picture frames stood a small wooden case containing a Military Cross. And completing the little gallery was a carved model of a Kiwi.

Chapter 19

Though the fig tree....

Aggie didn't resume her full work load for some months after the funeral. During that time, her chief resource was her prayer chair. She would sit for at least an hour most days, rocking gently, recalling special times she had shared with Helen, inviting God to flood her with his spirit, healing her sense of loss. Ky's love was another major resource. Each night she lay in his arms, full of gratitude.

Stephen Spenlow had always been impressed by Helen's quiet strength, especially during the years she had been one of his shift supervisors at Allied Garments. He recalled how her quiet firmness had conquered Zoe Campbell. At the funeral service, he thought he had seen some of the same quiet strength in the Carrington Church people – he was impressed by the support they gave to Aggie. And, overwhelmed as she was, he could recognize something of the same strength in Aggie. Stephen began attending Carrington Church.

As August ended, spring bulbs all around The Barn were heralding the new season. Aggie's response was muted while the loss of Helen weighed heavily on her, but gradually she began to notice the bright golds, oranges and whites nodding in clumps on the grass.

One Sunday at Carrington towards the end of September, Ky noticed Colin Campbell sitting with his mum, two rows in front of them.

"Look, there's Colin sitting with Zoe. Would you like to ask them home for some lunch?" Ky asked Aggie. "Or maybe you'd like a little more space before inviting people up?"

"No, it would be nice to have them over. Zoe has been in

and out these last weeks anyway. She's a dear friend. And it will be nice to catch up with Colin. I have some soup, and we can get some fresh bread on the way home."

Zoe and Colin were glad to accept. Colin had visited The Barn briefly a year ago, but he had not seen Ky's work in detail. He was full of admiration.

"Ky, it's amazing what you've done here. What a great haven this is for you both. And what a setting for you to be working, each at your own art work! I love this view out over the valley, from the front of the house."

To Aggie he said, "Aggie, I was shocked and so saddened when I received the notes Mum sent about Helen's sickness, and then her passing. She was such a special person. Mum and I owe so much to her."

"Thank you, Colin," replied Aggie. "The card you sent was very thoughtful, very encouraging."

As they sat together over lunch, Colin had news to share. "The Lord has been prompting me about a change of career," he told them. "I've enjoyed my time with Forestry, and I've learned a lot. But I've decided to begin training with the police. I'm due to start at the police school at Trentham in two weeks."

Immediately a picture came to Aggie's mind of Colin in police uniform, striding purposefully through the bush. She didn't know where it was, but had the impression it was somewhere close to The Barn. She also knew it was something to do with an accident. Someone was in trouble up in the bush. "Now what could that be about?" she wondered. A faint memory stirred, a premonition she'd had as a little girl, back before the cottage was renovated.

"Colin, I feel a strong assurance that this is the right move for you. I wonder if you'll get posted to this area after your training? I have a feeling that you will."

"I'd like to be back in Masterton. And yes, I think it's likely, though they can send you anywhere."

"And I surely hope he'll be back here," Zoe exclaimed. "I've seen him for only short periods for long enough! It would be nice to have him home for a while."

They sat chatting through the afternoon. Much of their

talk was of Helen, their hearts still not quite believing that she was really gone. Helen had relied heavily on Zoe leading up to the wedding, and even more so on the day, as she managed to join in Aggie and Ky's joy, without letting her own anxieties intrude. She and Zoe became to each other the sister neither had known.

Their conversation moved to the subject of Carrington Church. Scott Lampton had been the pastor there for fifteen years, so a celebration was being planned. They talked of the weddings, funerals, and other events he had presided over.

"And there are so many new people!" said Aggie. "So many I see on Sunday, but I've no idea who they are!"

"Yes," replied Zoe, "the church is too small for everyone now. I'm so curious about the plans to extend the building, or maybe get a completely new church! I wish they'd hurry up and decide!"

Eventually Zoe and Colin made a move to leave. Aggie and Ky walked out to their car with them.

"Colin, next time you come up, I'll show you an old Matai log I found up the track not far from here," Ky promised. "It still has some good timber in it that I'm hoping to use."

"Sounds good Ky," replied Colin as he slid into the car. "I'll look forward to that."

Ky was grateful for the Campbells' visit. Their company seemed to shear away some of the heaviness hunched around Aggie's shoulders.

The next weekend they decided to revisit Riversdale. They hadn't been back there since the day of their engagement. Their walking pace was a little quicker on this Sunday afternoon, and soon brought them to about the spot where Ky had stopped and gazed out to sea. He stopped again, looking seaward, the onshore breeze pushing his dark curls back from his face. Aggie had her sketch pad with her.

"Hold it right there!" she called. She walked a few paces further along the beach, and a little towards the ocean, giving her the vantage point she wanted. Deftly her pencil strokes brought to life the strong, beloved face, and the rest of his form, against the background of sand dunes, and the low cliffs beyond.

As Ky examined her work, she commented, "I think this

sketch is going to be special to us. A special reminder of a very special day!"

Ky smiled and held her in a long hug.

*

As Christmas approached, Aggie and Ky's thoughts returned to their hopes for a child. The months had been going by with no hint of a pregnancy, but they were not concerned. They supposed it was to do with the emotional and physical demands Helen's death had brought. Now the pain in Aggie's eyes was more frequently softened by her small smile, and hopes for their first baby came back into focus.

As he thought of the responsibilities of a family, Ky began to consider a life insurance policy that would provide for Aggie and any children, in case of a mishap. It was early days for such thoughts, but Ky decided sooner was better than later, especially as premiums would rise as he got older. The policy he bought insured his life for six hundred thousand dollars. Aggie was surprised when he told her.

"Really? That seems like a very large amount. Isn't it very expensive to get insurance for that amount?" she asked.

Ky was a little bemused himself. "Did I really need to make it as much as that?" he wondered. But somehow, he felt no urgency to change it. It faded into the background of their thoughts, and the premiums were paid on their six-monthly cycle.

Christmas without Helen was a sad time for Aggie, but to offset those feelings, it was her first Christmas with Ky. Gladly they set about creating their own traditions. The cottage was decorated with Christmas cards, a tree, colored lights and a nativity scene. Ky's parents came down from Kutarere to spend a week at The Barn.

"We've visited twice before," said Melody as she hugged Aggie close, "but this time you're the lady of the house! And our new daughter!

Christmas passed, January came, and with it, warm

summer days. Aggie resumed a full work load, though her trips to client sites didn't occur more than about once a month at that time. Ky was busy with commissions for carved artwork, and with building his own collection. The display space in his workshop gradually filled. Some of his own work, as well as pieces commissioned for conference centers and colleges, called for larger carvings, five to six feet tall, so Ky ranged through the bush, seeking logs suitable for dragging back to his workshop.

During the long evenings, Ky and Aggie would often sit out in front of their house, watching the shadows lengthen over the valley before them, as the sun swung slowly around, turning the ridge behind them into a silhouette. Their conversation turned more frequently to their hopes for Aggie to conceive. By now, some concern was beginning to grow. Was something wrong? When her period turned up again in January, right on time, Aggie turned troubled eyes to Ky.

"When do you think the Lord will send us a child?" she asked. "we've been giving him lots of opportunity!"

Ky's smile was fleeting. "We have indeed my love," he responded. "Maybe we should think about a visit to the doctor," he suggested.

Aggie nodded soberly. Neither of them wanted to face the possibility that some medical factor was against them, so they felt some inertia about calling their doctor. But it seemed like a sensible move.

During the next two weeks, Aggie spent longer than usual rocking gently in her prayer chair, pouring her heart out, asking to know what was happening. No answers came, other than a renewal of her sense of the Lord's compassion and love for her. Late one afternoon at the end of January, she called and made an appointment for them both. The first available time was the third week of February.

*

During those first few visits, their doctor seemed optimistic. A few tests would isolate the problem, and all would be well. But the few tests turned into a long series of inconclusive tests. The only thing that was established early on was that Ky's sperm count was normal. So the focus turned to Aggie. As month followed month it seemed that the questions became murkier instead of clearer – what exactly was this latest test supposed to determine, and how long would it take?

Winter came on, and the bleak days began to mirror the bleakness of their hearts. Friends at Carrington Church knew of the trial they were going through – Aggie and Ky appreciated the support and prayers of the church folk. Aggie sat often in her prayer chair, waiting, seeking, waiting. Always she would receive fresh assurance that God felt her pain and cared for her, but never any vision or promise of a child. Each month as her cycle announced no conception, her disappointment cut deeper, and the one-by-one procession of tears would wet her face.

How often she recalled Pauline and Cassie's assurances that bearing children was the thing that turned the whole menstrual journey into a blessing. She had often thought of those assurances during her adolescence, especially when the monthly doldrums were upon her. Two of the articles she had published back then were on the subject of motherhood, long before she had real hopes of ever being a mother herself. At her marriage, that hope had come into full flower, but now the flower wilted.

For Ky, the sadness was partly to do with his desire for a family, but even more he ached for Aggie's pain. He poured himself into being the very best support he could be for her. Yet, even their relationship came under strain. In their love-making, neither placed demands on the other, but it had seemed for a long time that all the focus was on baby-making.

Aggie and Ky drove home from church on the last Sunday in September. Aggie turned a troubled face to Ky.

"Ky, we need to take a day to just be together. Can we take the day off tomorrow, and drive out to Riversdale again? What do you think?"

Ky was working to get a small dolphin carving finished for an overseas client. But Aggie's suggestion went straight to his heart – the stress had been telling on them both for so long. Maybe he could do some of the finishing on the dolphin that afternoon. That would save some time.

"I could manage that. Thank you for the suggestion!" Tears started to his eyes as he added, "Agnes, I love you so much!"

A little before ten on Monday morning Ky drew the car to a halt at the end of the Riversdale Beach Road. He and Aggie sat in silence in the car. Aggie's head was bowed, her eyes closed. She reached out her hand and rested it on Ky's knee. Twenty minutes later Aggie lifted her head.

"Ky, it's time we stopped this. Trying to have a baby has been consuming us for months. It's eating us up. We need to give this back to God. He can send us a child or not as he chooses."

Tears ran down Ky's face. He leaned towards Aggie, hugging her to him.

"How much it's cost you …" His words tumbled between sobs. "Agnes, how much it cost you to decide that. But you're right. Let's give it back to God."

As they sat and prayed together, it seemed that a small glow of peace, a tiny candle glow, began to brighten in a corner of their hearts. It was gradual, but they both felt its warmth.

Afterwards they walked on the beach, arms around each other, feeling closer than they had felt for a long time. It was the anniversary of the day Aggie had sketched Ky facing the ocean, while the wind ruffled his hair.

*

Slowly Ky and Aggie climbed back out of the pit that had threatened to engulf them. About six weeks after their day at Riversdale, Aggie had an unexpected visitor. She had known Kathy Pierce at high school, and now knew and admired her as Eric Paynter's wife. But somehow their paths had not crossed very much, so she was a little surprised when Kathy knocked on her door. Soon they were sitting at the kitchen table with cups of coffee. Kathy quickly came to the point of her visit.

"Aggie, I have some news that will soon become known at church, and you'll get to hear of it. I wanted to come tell you myself, before you hear it from someone else. Eric and I are expecting." Her eyes met Aggie's. "Aggie, I know you and Ky have been trying .... It must be hard for you to hear that I'm pregnant, when you so want to be yourself."

They sat with eyes locked together. Yes, it was hard to hear. Mixed emotions washed around in Aggie's heart. She stood up, moving to stand beside Kathy's chair. Kathy rose, and the two women held each other tightly.

"Yes Kathy, it does stab my heart. But truly, I want you to know I really am glad for you and Eric. Thank you so much for coming to tell me. That was so sensitive of you. Thank you!"

As they resumed their seats, Kathy marveled at Aggie's strength. She felt the genuineness of Aggie's response to her news, even while it stirred her own pain.

"Six weeks ago, Ky and I gave our fertility issue back to the Lord. It's his business. It's been easier since then," Aggie told her.

Later, as Kathy drove home, she thought, "Six weeks ago. That was when I conceived." There remained an air of .... What was it? Something mysterious, something not quite knowable about Aggie. Yet Kathy knew more surely than ever, that for all the trials that had dogged her life, Aggie Soames was a woman of God.

Christmas came, and was celebrated more joyously than Ky and Aggie would have thought possible a few months ago. They felt afresh the loss of Helen, and the absence of a crib in the bedroom, but gladness swelled in their hearts never-the-less. One event that added to their celebration was Colin Campbell's return to Masterton. His training had been completed with distinction, and he had been working as a rookie policeman in Wellington. Now he was transferred back to his home town. Zoe thought it her best Christmas present ever. Soon Colin became a well-known sight again in the streets – this time as a symbol of order and security.

So, another new year began. Aggie managed her home

design work so that it occupied her for three to four days a week. She learned to manage her sadness at having no child, though it still affected her, as each month reminded her. At these times, as she sat in her rocker, the slow succession of tears would sometimes wet her face again. But more and more, her loss came to deepen the bond she had with Ky. At night she lay, aware of his strength beside her, and was comforted.

She drew strength too from taking up writing again. One or two pieces were about fertility, her thoughts formed by studying characters from the Bible who had struggled with childlessness. She wrote also on children and childhood, in its exuberance and innocence, thinking of Jesus placing a child on his knee, and declaring that "the Kingdom of heaven belongs to such as these." But other pieces were on the world in which she lived, especially the brooding presence of the mountains under whose shadow she spent each day. They were huge and severe, yet they embraced those who dared to embrace them.

Chapter 20

Crushed.

Summer was waning. As May came in, leaves turned red and gold. With the autumn came rain. The bush dripped, and the stream turning the waterwheel at The Barn ran full.

"You going into the bush today?" Aggie asked Ky as they sat at breakfast one morning. She eyed the parka he wore.

"Yes. There's a big totara stump I've been wanting to get, but it's been so wet! The rain's stopped today, so I want to get it out."

"But Ky, it'll still be wet and muddy up there! Do you have to do it today?" They both stood. She moved round the table to stand in front of him. "What say we take the day off, do something together?"

His hands were on her shoulders. He looked at her in surprise. "Honey, what's up? It would be nice to spend the day with you. But …." Ky paused.

"Yes, I know. We can't just take days off, willy nilly. I just …. I don't know. You be careful, especially using your axe, while it's wet and slippery! I'll miss you!"

He hugged her close, planting a kiss on the top of her head. "I'll be careful! I'll miss you too! But I should be back in two or three hours. Love you!"

Ky set off up the track. Her heart swelled with love as she watched his confident stride. But she couldn't shake the uneasiness. "What's the matter with me Lord?" she prayed. "He knows what he's doing."

The place Ky was aiming for was about a mile from home. He'd already dug around the stump, using his axe to cut the surface roots that held it anchored. Now he encircled the remaining short trunk with straps, which he shackled to a hand

184

winch. The other side of the winch he chained to another strong tree trunk growing about twenty feet away. Ky began working the handle of the winch. The slack tightened, the stump began to lean. He moved behind it, checking to see the deeper roots becoming exposed, cutting them with his axe. He returned to the winch. Gradually the stump came up out of the ground. He checked the straps. They were holding firm.

Now there was a gap of about three feet behind and under the stump. Ky could see another root still holding. He took his axe and scrambled down into the gap, trying to position himself to get a swing at the root. The straps around the trunk slipped on the wet surface. He felt the tremor, and tried to scramble clear. The straps slipped again, this time sliding quickly over the wet bark. The stump fell back, crushing Ky, piercing and constricting his chest.

Aggie was not yet dressed. She sat in her dressing gown, rocking in her prayer chair when her spirit heard the cry. She leapt up, running for the door, a sob already in her throat. Ky had not told her exactly where he was going, but her bare feet flew unerringly. Along the track she ran, veering off into the bush at just the right place, dodging tree and vine, surmounting small rises, crossing small streams, until she came upon the stump where Ky lay trapped. She knelt on the wet earth and leaves beside his head and shoulders. He had not been able to breathe for several minutes, but somehow, he had held to life long enough for her to reach him. "Agnes!" He mouthed the word, no breath coming to aid him. His eyes held hers for a long moment before they closed.

"Ky!" Her silent scream shook the strong trees around her. She leapt up, running for the winch, agony bubbling from her throat. Blindly she fumbled with the strap, the steel wire, the winch.

"Stop! Think what you're doing!" Flip up the lug to release the winch. Pull the wire out. Loosen the strap, now rewind it round the trunk. Refasten the wire. Work the winch handle. She forced her trembling hands and arms to the task, trying to keep at bay the certainty that it was too late.

The stump was tilted back, opening a gap underneath.

She ran back to where Ky lay. Could she pull him free? But she could see that a root had pierced his chest, impaling him. She would need to raise the stump higher. She ran back to the winch, desperately working the long handle. Now she was back in front of him, hands under his arms. Ky's body fell free from the root penetrating his chest. Aggie's feet braced against a rock at the edge of the cavity, her legs pushing her upwards with all of her strength.

Ky's body slipped free, onto the wet ground. She dropped beside him, frantically calling his name. "Ky! Ky! Don't leave me! Oh God, don't leave me!" She looked at his broken chest, and suddenly her wild cries ceased. She lay beside him on the wet ground, pulling him to her.

Chapter 21

Auntie Aggie.

Aggie's dressing gown was wet through as she lay on the muddy ground beside Ky. The cold began to seep into her. She realized that Ky's forehead against hers was cold too.

Slowly, painfully, she disengaged herself, and stood up. She turned to go back to The Barn, but then turned again to Ky.

"I can't go and leave you here! Cold, alone, lying on the wet ground." She shivered. "I suppose I must. I have to get help. Oh Ky! Ky!" She took off her sodden dressing gown, and lay it over him, as though that would give him some protection. Then she fled back through the bush.

Back in the cottage, Aggie called the police, then quickly washed and dressed. In the distance, she heard a siren wail.

Colin Campbell was the first to arrive, his car crunching to a stop behind the cottage. He stepped out quickly, and saw Aggie coming towards him.

"Aggie!" Involuntarily, unprofessionally, he hugged her. Recovering himself, he stepped back, and asked, "Where is he?"

She led him up the track. At one moment, she glanced back, seeing him following in his police uniform, striding purposefully through the bush. They turned into the untracked part of the route, and came to where Ky's body lay. Colin took in the scene. He unclasped the small radio from his belt, and quickly summarized the situation to the backup car that was even now arriving at The Barn. He would walk out with Aggie to meet the backup team, and then guide them in to where Ky lay.

The men went to work. Quickly they examined and photographed the area, then laid Ky's body on a stretcher. Carefully, they carried him out.

Colin stepped back into the cottage to check on Aggie.

She sat on the floor of their lounge room. Her right leg lay with knee bent a little to the side. Her left leg was pulled up to her chest. Three picture frames stood on the floor in front of her – the center one held a sketch of a man standing on the beach, his curly brown hair pushed back by the wind. Beside the frames stood a small wooden case, and a small carved Kiwi. From the corner of each of Aggie's eyes came a tear, making its way down her cheek. At an interval, another tear would follow.

*

Colin was still in shock himself, but as he stood watching Aggie, his grief multiplied. He stood rooted to the spot for several moments. Then he turned and strode to her phone. He called the despatcher, asking to be connected to Stephen Spenlow at Allied Garments. When Stephen answered, he broke the terrible news.

"Stephen, Aggie is in unimaginable shock right now. Can you please cover for my mum, and have her come up here immediately?"

"You got it Colin. She'll be on her way in a couple of minutes."

Zoe arrived at The Barn, and let herself straight into the cottage. Aggie was still sitting in the lounge room, where Colin waited for his mother.

"She hasn't moved," he said. "Glad you could come. I'll leave her with you now."

Zoe sat on the floor beside Aggie, who turned to look at her friend. But it seemed to Zoe that her eyes did not really see her. If she had not reached out to touch her, Zoe would have thought that Aggie was not really aware of her presence. Aggie's head turned back to the picture frame in front of her.

Zoe shifted her position, so that she could stroke Aggie's hair. She murmured over and over, "Aggie! Oh Aggie. Precious woman. Oh Aggie, God be with you!" She thought her tears had never flowed so freely, or for so long. Eventually she thought of getting a cup of tea for Aggie. She tried to coax her into an easy chair, or to lie on her bed. But Aggie wordlessly resisted. She clutched the sketch of Ky to her, and would not move. The room wasn't cold, but Zoe thought the warmth of a blanket might be some comfort. She fetched a soft knitted wrap, and put it around Aggie's shoulders. By now some focus had returned to Aggie's eyes. She gave Zoe a grateful glance.

Another hour went by, and a car was heard outside. A knock came at the door, and Zoe led Pastor Scott Lampton into the room. Aggie still sat as Colin had left her. The succession of tears making their way down her cheeks had all but ceased for now. Scott knelt beside her. He tried to greet her, but choked on the words. He tried again. "Aggie, I'm so, so sorry!"

Aggie's head turned towards him. Slowly her eyes focused. "Hello Pastor." They were the first words she had spoken since she returned to the cottage. "Ky was killed. A tree stump fell on him." Her voice was soft, as though she were speaking from a far distant place.

"I know Aggie. I came as soon as I heard. I'm devastated." His hand rested on her shoulder. "Ky! I just can't believe it! Aggie, what incredible pain you must be feeling right now! But you are loved! Every member of Carrington Church will be folding you in their love." Again, his words ended in a choke.

Zoe spoke. "Pastor, she's been sitting on the floor like that for about two hours. Do you think we can encourage her to move to a chair?"

Now Aggie permitted herself to be led to the couch. She carried the drawing of Ky with her. Zoe took the opportunity to fetch the cup of tea she had mentioned earlier. While the water was coming to the boil, Aggie's phone rang. Zoe answered.

"Hello, this is Zoe."

"Mum!" It was Colin. "I called Pastor Scott. He said he would come."

"Yes. He arrived a few minutes ago."

"Good. Mum, I thought it would be good if you could stay there with Aggie for the rest of the week. She's going to need all the love and support we can give her. I can call Stephen

Spenlow and see what he thinks. I'm sure he'll be understanding."

"Hmm. Yes, we can't leave her on her own just now. I'll need a few things from home – can you bring them for me?"

So, Colin, Zoe and Scott rallied to Aggie's support. Scott called Ky's family in Kutarere, and arranged accommodation for them with one of the church families. Aggie drank the tea Zoe brought her, and further cups during the afternoon, but she couldn't eat anything. Zoe coaxed her to go off to bed a little after nine o'clock. At eleven, when Zoe checked on her, she was lying quietly on her back, her eyes still open, looking up into the darkness.

"Would you like me to sit with you a while?" Zoe whispered.

"No, I'll be alright. Thank you for staying with me Zoe." But before Zoe could move towards the door, Aggie suddenly turned on her side, half-sitting, propping herself with her arm. "Zoe, Zoe, he was so good! I loved him so much! So much! Why…. why?" Sobs shook her whole body. Zoe whirled back to her, and held her tightly. One by one, her tears made their solitary trail. Gradually, gradually, the sobs subsided, Aggie's muscles relaxing. She lay back again, her head resting on her pillow. Her eyes closed, her breathing evened, as sleep overtook her.

*

Aggie was already up when Zoe came to her early the next morning. She sat again with her picture frames, her medal case, and her carved Kiwi before her. But now she sat in her prayer chair, rocking, rocking, her eyes closed, murmuring words that Zoe did not understand.

Many of the Carrington Church members wanted to bring meals for Aggie, so Pastor Scott's wife Eunice set up a roster that kept her well supplied. At first, the meals were put in the refrigerator, where they stayed. But in coming days, when Aggie was able to eat again, she was grateful.

The funeral was set for Tuesday. Ky's parents arrived on Friday, coming straight to The Barn. They stood hugged together with Aggie for a long time. Other friends also came by on Thursday and Friday to sit a few minutes with her. Kathy Paynter wanted to visit, but she knew Zoe was there looking after Aggie, and realized it would be hard for her to deal with a stream of visitors. Besides, by now Kathy was nearly eight months pregnant, and didn't want to reopen another wound. Instead, she asked Eric to take a card to her that tried to express how deeply they felt her pain.

Aggie did not have so many close friends, but the shock waves that Ky's death sent through the community, and the respect in which they were both held, brought an over-flow crowd to Carrington Church on Tuesday. Allied Garments was closed for the morning, so that all could attend the funeral.

Aggie managed to say a few words during the service. "Up until Ky came into my life, I never for a moment imagined anything so wonderful would ever happen to me. But he came, and he was …." She stopped for a moment. "He was a most amazing gift to me. And now I suppose I have to say he's gone again. My heart can't believe that." A single tear rolled down to wet her lips. "Even my head tells me this isn't really happening. I'll … I'll wake up, and none of this will have happened. He can't be gone, he just can't." She stopped again, her head bowed. When she concluded, her voice was barely above a whisper. "Thank you all for being here. Thank you all for helping me get through this."

A young woman sat weeping near the back of the church, unnoticed by other mourners. She had been at Aggie's wedding, and had wept there too. But a careful observer might have noticed something different about her tears on this day. Perhaps for the first time in her life, Kelly Stephenson wept for somebody's pain other than her own.

*

In those first few weeks, Aggie's grief was black, crushing, indescribable. Ky's love had been to her like Spring bursting into mid-Winter. Now he was gone, and the bleakness of her soul could not be matched by the bleakness of any winter. She'd been Agnes to him – now, more than ever before, she was Aggie. Reserved, remote, isolated.

She might have continued, slowly dropping into the blackness. But imperceptibly, still so filled with pain, God began introducing something different - she was noticing children in a new way. Ever since she emerged from childhood herself, she'd felt a special affinity for children, that became part of her longing for her own children. Now it seemed, God was using her ache to give her a compassion for children that was quicker and keener than she'd ever experienced. On many days, her heart was still overwhelmed, but gradually, whether at church, in a shop, or passing a school, she would notice the children, and something in her would reach out. Love for these little ones slowly became a balm for her wounds.

Nearly a month after the funeral, Aggie experienced these new surges of love through an unexpected visit. Zoe had returned home, though she called on Aggie each evening. Aggie still spent a part of each day in her prayer chair – on this day she was rocking, praying, still occasionally weeping her one-by-one succession of tears, when she heard a car pull up beside the cottage. She went to the door, and found Kelly Stephenson standing with her twenty-month-old daughter on her hip. Aggie didn't quite manage to hide her surprise, but she welcomed Kelly warmly enough.

"I guess you never thought to see me come calling on you Aggie," Kelly began as she sat down at the table. "Truth is, I've thought about you a lot. Never quite been able to get you out of my head."

Aggie was making tea for them. She glanced quizzically at Kelly.

"I …. I treated you pretty bad at school. I just thought you were strange, and …. Oh, I dunno. Anyway, I came to your wedding. You didn't see me, but I slipped in. I couldn't believe you were really getting married. I came to, well, to mock, to see what sort of bride you were. What sort of wimp would be marrying you."

Kelly's words were raw, jarring. But at least she was being direct, unpretending. Aggie let her run on without interruption.

"Aggie, you were beautiful! And Ky, your husband – a strong, handsome man! I was so mad! It was all so ... so good! How could you, little Aggie, have done so much ...." Kelly bowed her head, as though struggling to say something that was hard to say. "So much better than the mess I made!"

Aggie's heart, sore and bruised as it was, opened to Kelly. She knew without being told, that Kelly had never before admitted to anyone that she had made a mess of her life. She moved to Kelly's chair, and knelt beside her.

Kelly pulled away a little. "Don't be sorry for me! I cried at your wedding! But it was mostly because I was so mad! And sorry for myself."

"Kelly, I have a feeling you're being more honest about yourself right now than you've been for a long time. You've no idea how much I appreciate that."

Kelly couldn't quite believe she was hearing a soft answer. But she continued. "I've been mad at you for a long time! It seemed like you were so happy, and I was .... Well never mind. But then, then I heard about Ky. It ... it shook me, I can tell you! Suddenly, all those feelings of being so mad at you, they just went! Suddenly, I was sorry for you! Truly! No one deserves that! No one! I just want you to know, I'm very, very sorry that your husband died."

Aggie still knelt, meeting Kelly's gaze. Kelly was unsettled by the acceptance she saw in Aggie's eyes. She moved to stand, taking her leave.

"Wait Kelly! You haven't shown me your little girl!" The child had been dozing on Kelly's lap. She stirred as Kelly began to stand, and looked with sleepy, curious eyes at Aggie. "This is Debra," Kelly said. Aggie noticed brittleness in her voice, and in her glance at her daughter.

"Kelly, what a beautiful daughter you have!" Aggie felt

the wave of love for this little one wash over her. Debra began to push at Kelly in a whining, petulant way.

"Yes, well she can be a little brat." Kelly confirmed Aggie's impression. "Just like her brother Peter. He's at school. Peter's six."

Aggie wondered at how hard life must be for Kelly, struggling to raise her two children by herself, with little support, and few parenting skills. And she wondered also at the strength of the compassion that was swelling within her for these two children. She would like to keep in touch with this little family, if Kelly would let her.

"Kelly, thank you so much for coming to visit me. You're right, it's been overwhelming for me." Her voice broke momentarily. Recovering, she spoke softly. "Thank you for coming to tell me how ... how you felt when you heard about Ky." She reached to touch Debra's hair. "Kelly, please visit me again. I really would be glad to see you. And meet Peter."

*

Yes, Aggie wanted to meet Peter, even if his mother described him as a brat. She thought of other children, those she knew at the church. Many different children. Some from families with a high quality of love and nurture. Some not so. And the compassion within her continued to swell.

At Carrington Church, Sunday School for adults as well as children began an hour before the service. On the Sunday following Kelly's visit, Aggie arrived at church at her usual time, but instead of going to her own class, she went to find the class of five and six-year-old children.

"Do you mind if I just sit at the side, and watch the children, and pray for them?" she asked. The teacher wondered at her request, but warmly invited Aggie to find a chair. During the activity time, some of the children noticed her, regarding her with curiosity. One turned to the teacher, and asked, "Who's that lady? What's she doing here?"

"Oh!" he replied, "That's umm … that's Auntie Aggie. She loves to watch the children, and pray for them. She's praying for you while you work!"

And so, Aggie became known, at first to the children, and then to adults as well, as Auntie Aggie. Whenever children gathered, Auntie Aggie was likely to be present. She interacted very little, but her grey eyes followed each child, her lips often moving soundlessly.

*

Aggie became more of an enigma than ever. She was known, trusted and admired as a kind of guardian angel to the children. Yet her love for these little ones never fully rescued her from relapsing into the old sadness. As Ky's bride, the mists had all but dissipated. At that time, she was gladder and more spontaneous than anyone had ever known her. But wisps had reappeared when Helen died, had strengthened during her struggles to conceive, and now, oh especially now, with Ky's death, the air of sadness and reserve was back.

The children became used to Auntie Aggie's presence in their Sunday School classes. Those who dared to approach, found themselves welcomed - they would sit on her lap, receiving smiles and hugs. But most kept some distance. She was just Auntie Aggie.

*

Kathy Paynter delivered her first daughter, Alexi Louise, on Sunday 3rd of July. When Aggie heard the news, she was stabbed again by her own barrenness and widowhood. But the stab merged also with a rush of joy for Kathy and Eric, gladness for the miracle of a new life. When Aggie arrived to visit on Tuesday morning, Kathy was sitting propped up in bed, cradling

Alexi in her arms.

"Aggie! Thank you for calling in! I didn't expect a visit – I mean, you must be feeling … feeling very vulnerable yourself. I'm glad you came!"

"Kathy, I'm so happy for you and Eric. You doing okay?"

"I'm fine," Kathy replied. "It was awfully hard," she grimaced. "But that's normal, right?"

"I guess so," Aggie said, with a small smile. She moved closer to the bedside. "How beautiful she is! So tiny. So perfect!" They were both silent, gazing at the little form.

"Kathy, may I hold her?" Aggie glanced at Kathy. Immediately, Kathy was apprehensive. She admired so much about Aggie, knew her to be a woman of strength, a gracious woman. Yet, there was that aspect of the unknown about Aggie. She felt possessive, protective, unwilling to give Alexi into her arms. Then she saw the love in Aggie's eyes, and felt ashamed of her hesitation. It lasted only an instant – now she was smiling, holding Alexi up for Aggie to take.

Kathy watched as Aggie held her baby. She saw the joy in her face, heard her crooning words of love and blessing. Then, as she watched, a troubled look came over Aggie's face. She still looked intently down at Alexi, but her brow was furrowed. Her blessing merged into a language Kathy did not know. Kathy was aware of the love that still flowed from Aggie to her daughter, but knew that for a moment, a cloud had passed over Aggie's spirit.

The moment passed. Aggie's eyes showed only gladness again. She gave Alexi back into Kathy's arms, and soon after took her leave. Kathy was not unduly alarmed - she knew Aggie to be a good and godly woman. But she did wonder. What had Aggie seen that had troubled her? Something in Alexi's future? Her own brow furrowed a little as she held her daughter closer, and prayed for her again.

And so dear reader, we have walked quite a while with Aggie, and those she knows. Let's now step forward again about five years, to rejoin Kathy, Hannah, and Alexi in the kitchen at Shepherd's Rest.

Chapter 22

Alexi Paynter.

"Lexi! Be careful with your orange juice! You'll spill it!"
Alexi drained her glass.

Auntie Aggie a witch? What a question! Yet Kathy
couldn't deny that shadows of Auntie Aggie tip-toed around the
edge of her own fear. She still remembered the time Aggie held
Alexi as a new-born, and seemed to see something disturbing in
her daughter's future. Was that it? But nothing had come of that,
not so far at least. Kathy was a little angry at herself over the
three or four bouts of irrational panic she'd felt.

For Alexi, well, she could understand how young minds
would come up with a word like "witch". To the children, Auntie
Aggie must seem strange, sitting quietly to the side whenever
they gathered, watching, rarely saying anything. They must feel
almost invited to add something scary, witchy to the scenario.

Kathy turned to face Alexi. "Honey, Auntie Aggie is a
really nice lady. She loves all the children, and prays for them.
Lots of sad things have happened to her, so that's why she often
looks sad. But she's certainly not a witch!"

Concern filled Alexi's face. "What sad things have
happened to her?"

"Well, her daddy was a soldier fighting in the war, and
he was killed, so he never came home again! Auntie Aggie never
had a daddy at home when she was a little girl like you. And
when she grew up and was married, not long after, her husband
was killed in an accident. She was terribly, terribly sad about
that."

Alexi continued thoughtful about Auntie Aggie as her

mum finished clearing breakfast, and prepared her and Hannah to leave for the Young Mum's group at Carrington Church. Auntie Aggie often took care of the children while their mothers met to relax, chat, listen to a speaker, and enjoy a cup of tea together. That day, as Alexi watched her, she thought maybe Auntie Aggie wasn't quite such a cross person after all. Part way through the morning, Alexi approached her.

"My mum said you didn't have a daddy when you was little, and your husband got died in a accident. You can have my second teddy so you won't be so sad."

Aggie knelt before her. "Lexi, that is so kind of you! I would love to have your second teddy, if your mum says it's okay. Are you sure you won't need him?"

"It's alright. I got my other teddy that sleeps with me."

On the way home, Alexi told Kathy about the gift she meant to make to Auntie Aggie. Kathy was pleased and touched. However, thoughts of the second teddy were displaced later that afternoon, as Kathy went into labor. She called Eric, who came home immediately. Kathy's mum Jan arrived shortly afterwards to stay with Alexi and Hannah.

Alexi watched anxiously as a frown of concentration covered her mum's face. Kathy stood braced against a chair, her breathing deep, quick, measured.

"Mummy! What's wrong?" In her concern, Alexi relapsed into the diminutive. She ran to hold her mother's skirt. The contraction was passing off, and Kathy managed a quick smile at her daughter.

"It's alright Alexi." Her voice was still a little breathless. "I'll be okay in a minute. Having a baby is hard work!" A few more moments, and she straightened her back, hugging Alexi to her. "Dad will take me to the hospital in a few minutes, where there will be lots of people to help me. Don't you worry, they'll look after me real well! You and Hannah have fun with Grandma while I'm gone!"

Everything was a whirl of unusual activity, but no-one seemed alarmed. Alexi's anxiety soon faded. When she woke the next morning, Grandma Jan tried to keep her from making too much noise. "Your dad didn't get much sleep last night, so he's asleep now, trying to catch up. He was there when your new brother was born! Yes, you have a new baby brother! You and Hannah can come have some breakfast, and a little later we'll all go to see him and Mum!"

Hannah was too young to understand much of what was going on, though she knew she had a new brother, and after breakfast they would be going to see him. At almost five, Alexi had watched lambs being born, so during breakfast she gave Hannah the benefit of her big-sisterly knowledge. Grandma Jan smiled to herself as she listened.

Eric appeared in the kitchen already dressed as the children finished their breakfast. He sat with them over a quick cup of coffee and piece of toast. Shortly after, they were all in the car on their way to the hospital.

Kathy was dozing as they came in, but roused as she heard them. "Hello my special little ladies," she greeted them. "Have you come to meet baby Edward?"

"Edward? Is that his name?" asked Alexi. "Where is he? Oh, in there!" She noticed the small crib at the end of her mother's bed, and ran to look in it.

"Yes, Edward. Do you like that name?" Eric asked her. "Be careful. He's sleeping just now."

"He's all wrapped up! I can hardly see him! Can I hold him?" Alexi wanted to know.

"Sorry Honey, you'll be able to hold him when he comes home in a few days. We don't want to disturb him while he's sleeping," Kathy told her.

A brother who slept, almost completely covered with blankets, was not what Alexi had hoped for. However, she contained her impatience until Friday afternoon, when Mum and Edward came home. Now she could watch, and run little errands, as Mum nursed, and bathed and changed little Edward. If she sat very still in one of the big lounge chairs, Mum would let her hold him for a few minutes before he was put back in his crib.

With all the excitement of a new baby, Alexi had to be reminded of her morning task of feeding the chickens and collecting the eggs. But when Sunday came, she didn't forget to take her teddy to Sunday School to give to Auntie Aggie.

"Alexi, I'm glad to have your teddy to look after! What's his name?" Aggie took the bear in her arms.

"He's called Bagley," replied Alexi. "He's very good at cuddling up when you get into bed."

"Do you think you'll need him back soon?" Aggie asked. Alexi's kind act deepened the bond she already felt with this little girl.

"No, I won't need him," replied Alexi. "You can give him back when you stop feeling sad."

Aggie mused to herself, "Do I really project so much sadness? Out of the mouths of babes!" To Alexi she said, "Tell me about your new brother. What's he like?"

Alexi began a recital of life with a new baby, delighting Aggie with her matter of fact descriptions, not forgetting to mention how Edward's anatomy differed from hers and Hannah's. Soon she moved on to talking of her birthday, just two weeks away. And after her birthday, she would start school!

Alexi was still thinking of school when she arrived home from church. She went to find Kathy, who had just put Edward down in his crib.

"Mum, will I have lunch at school?"

"Yes, honey. I'll make some sandwiches each day for you to take to school. We'll buy a lunch box to put your lunch in. Would you like to help me choose a lunch box at the store this week?"

"Hmm, yes! That will be just like Dad. He has lunch at work." Alexi felt having to take your lunch with you was a very grown up thing. Being five, and going to school made her feel very important. Maybe that was why she changed from calling her father "Daddy" at that time – now he became "Dad".

So the big day came at last. The Paynter family had a small party on Sunday 3rd of July, in honor of Alexi's birthday, and the next day, Kathy took her off to begin her school career. Everything was very new for a few weeks, but she settled in well. It was not long before other new students started, and Alexi became one of the old hands. Kathy's heart warmed as Alexi told of how she helped the new students feel welcome. It was clear there was something sensitive and caring built into Alexi – it showed in the way she looked after animals, as well as her concern for people who seemed to have a need of some kind. Giving her teddy to Auntie Aggie was just one example among many.

*

Since Ky Soames died, Eric Paynter had visited The Barn each spring to check on the water wheel, and other equipment Ky had installed. Making sure that all was well-maintained was one way the church family supported Aggie. This year, he took Alexi with him. Often, he would look after one or more of the three children on a Saturday morning to give Kathy a break.

Eric mused about Aggie as he worked. "I wonder what I would be like if my life was anything like hers. Never saw her father, carried that birth mark on her face all her life, harassed throughout her schooling. Losing her mother so early, and then her husband! What a godsend he must have been to her, only to be whisked away again!"

He glanced at Alexi, watching him work, as she sat on a rock beside the stream. She was showing some signs of restlessness.

"Lexi, do you want to take a walk along the track towards the cottage? Just don't go near the stream, okay?"

Lexi nodded, and started slowly up the track, wandering from one side to the other as she examined its borders.

"I won't be too much longer," Eric called after her.

The yearly visit to The Barn made him one of the very few people who ever came there. At church on Sundays Aggie's strange blend of reserve and warmth hung about her. She could hardly have been described as outgoing, but to those who conversed and interacted with her, she seemed friendly and interested. But when it came to anyone visiting her at home, it was as though Aggie still regarded The Barn as private to her and Ky.

202

Eric was sure she had never gotten over Ky's death. "And," he thought, "it seems that all of her griefs are still raw." When Eric arranged to come up for his machinery maintenance visit, Aggie thanked him, and told him to go straight to the task. He was not sure whether she would be home at the cottage – if she was, he didn't see her.

The bright September sunshine followed Alexi along the track. Eric watched her making her way up towards The Barn, the building that had been Ky's workshop. "The Barn" was the name of the whole property, but it was still used to distinguish the workshop from the cottage.

Alexi stood at the door, wondering if she dared go in. She hoped she might see Bagley if she ventured inside. She reached up and pulled at the door handle.

Eric saw her disappear inside. He wondered momentarily whether he should stop her, but thought Aggie would have no objection. He could watch the door from where he was working, so he would see her when she emerged.

Aggie had given Ky's bandsaw, his bench saw, and his lathe to different families where she heard there was a need. The rest of the machinery had been pushed further towards the back of the building, leaving more space for the display of his carvings. The office-lounge area was also a little more spacious. Aggie sometimes used this area for reading, praying, or sketching. No-one else ever came there.

The door clicked closed behind Alexi. She stood with her back and her hands pressed against it. The windows in the room facing her were wide, so the interior was well-lit, all except for the back, where machinery clustered in semi-darkness. Alexi strained her eyes to see into the shadows.

"Maybe she's hiding back there somewhere! She might jump out at me!" Auntie Aggie had spoken kindly when she gave Bagley to her. But this was different! This was a large, silent room, partly inviting, partly scary. She stood quite still for a minute or two, her eyes roving over the carvings, the dark recesses at the back, and the chairs, the table, the desk closer to her. Bagley was nowhere to be seen.

Soon Alexi dared to walk further into the room,

examining each carving in turn. She walked back to where the chairs and couches stood in a rough semi-circle. Choosing a wide, comfortable-looking chair, she sat down. A large open fireplace was recessed into the wall opposite her. A draught stirred some of the fine ash. Alexi stood again, and moved to each of the windows in turn. On one side, she looked across a short grassy space of just a few feet to where the bush began. On the other side ran the track leading up to the cottage, and beyond was tussocky grass, running as far as the rocky area on the edge of the plateau.

Outside the window, two magpies screamed at each other. Alexi's heart leapt in her chest. She ran to the door, and wrenched it open. Back down the track she ran, almost upsetting Eric's balance as she charged into him. Eric was just finishing using a grease gun to lubricate the water wheel bearings.

"You alright Sweetie?" he asked, smiling down at her. "I'm about done. You ready to go back home?"

Alexi nodded. Her somber mood gradually lifted as they drove home.

*

Eric took Alexi with him on each of his visits to The Barn over the next three years. During those years, the silent, big room became almost a place of pilgrimage for her. The carvings and comfortable chairs, the table and couches, were kept dusted and cleaned. Evidently, Auntie Aggie came often here, though Alexi never saw her.

As she grew older, her understanding told her more and more firmly that there was nothing to fear from Auntie Aggie. But emotionally – well, there was always something deliciously scary about allowing the word "witch" to creep into her mind.

"Lexi!" she would say to herself, "you should be ashamed of yourself! It just isn't kind to think those thoughts about Auntie Aggie!" But there it was, a strand of feeling that didn't completely die out for many years.

*

As she grew, Alexi made friends easily with other children. Her birthday party each year at Shepherd's Rest was an event her friends looked forward to, as Kathy put imagination into finding activities that were fun and memorable. Sometimes the activities included a visit to places such as Third Creek on Jon and Cassie Sanders' property. On one of these visits, Alexi discovered the cave that Auntie Aggie had found years earlier.

Of course, Kathy put the same effort into birthdays for Hannah and Ted too. Yes, "Edward" was shortened to "Ted" at about the time he began to walk and talk.

One Sunday, in the winter of 1974, just after Alexi's eighth birthday, the family were driving home from church.

"Auntie Aggie came into our Sunday School class today," Alexi announced. After a pause, she added, "Her eyes are grey."

Kathy wondered why this was worthy of comment. "Does she often come into your class?"

"No, she used to when I was in Miss Lillian's class, but now she hardly ever does." Another pause. "I thought at first she was kind of scary. She just sits and watches. Seems like she's talking to herself. But then, when you really look at her, her eyes seem kind of, well, soft and smiley."

"Auntie Aggie was touched when you gave her Bagley to look after," Kathy told her. "She prays for you, and for the other children in the class."

Alexi often thought of Bagley and wondered about him. But her path hardly ever crossed with Auntie Aggie, so she never asked.

"That was a long time ago. I was just little then." The kind grey eyes watching her today merged with the memory of long ago. "I think she's nice really," she added.

Later, as Kathy and Eric prepared lunch, Eric commented, "We're so blessed by our children! Alexi's becoming a sensitive little girl."

"Isn't she just," smiled Kathy. "She's good with Hannah and Ted. Patient, usually not bossy with them. I'm glad we got Sandy for her." Sandy was the pony they bought when their stallion, Old Joe died.

"She's a natural rider. She's coming along nicely with her piano lessons." Eric caught Kathy in his arms, and kissed her, before calling the children to the table.

*

Another four years passed, and Alexi was in her second year at her intermediate school. Next year she would begin high school. She was passing her adolescent milestones, learning from Kathy's affirming guidance, and gaining confidence from the praise and appreciation of her father Eric.

One day, at Sunday School, Auntie Aggie visited her class again. "Alexi, you're becoming a young woman!"

Alexi blushed, but pleasure at the compliment washed through her.

"Yes, my dear, I was glad you won those awards for your Bible knowledge. But as I watch you, it's not just your head being stuffed full of knowledge. Jesus is growing in you. I can see that. I love to hear you laugh! Makes me want to laugh too!"

Her arm was across Alexi's shoulder, giving her a squeeze. Alexi thought there had probably been some hugs from Auntie Aggie when she was quite young, but nothing like a shoulder squeeze had happened since then. This was quite a privilege!

"I've watched you with the other youngsters too. Especially the ones no-one else notices. The ones who don't get invited to anyone's party. You notice. You care, and comfort. You try to help them." Aggie knew what those left out ones felt like.

Alexi blushed again, and Auntie Aggie's eyes twinkled for a moment, then became serious again. "Lexi, stay with Jesus! There are some bumps in the road ahead for you. You're going to need him!" She patted Alexi's arm, and turned to go.

Alexi frowned a little. What could she mean? Bumps in the road? Her mother had never told her of the shadow passing over Auntie Aggie when she held her as a new-born baby. Kathy still thought of it sometimes, and wondered. But for now, Alexi let "bumps in the road" pass out of her mind, and was care-free again.

*

Kelly Stephenson did not respond to Aggie's invitation to stay in touch, but continued to struggle through life as a single mother. She had another daughter now, Naomi, three years younger than Alexi, by a father different from either Peter's or Debra's. Kelly had shown a flash of genuine concern when she heard of Ky's death, but mostly she retained her spirit of headstrong independence. She had no contact with either her mother or her father, but lived a lonely life. Kathy continued to show friendship to Kelly, and gradually gained occasional admittance to her house. Perhaps it was her mother's example that inspired Alexi to befriend the isolated, needy people.

Alexi's love of horse-riding prompted Kathy and Eric to buy a full-sized mare for her, allowing Sandy to be passed on to Hannah. Both girls were responsible for caring for their horses.

Alexi named her new horse Cloud. Eric took care to guide her as she became accustomed to the more powerful horse, and taught her to tackle more ambitious jumps. Soon she and Cloud were galloping on the grass-covered road verges all over the southern outskirts of the town.

*

At the end of that year Alexi bade farewell to her primary school career. With the new year came the adventure of high school. Now her skills and interests began to take on a greater maturity. As she progressed through her high school years, she began to take personal interest in her studies, often going beyond the research required by class assignments.

Horse-riding continued to be a strong interest for her through her first three years at high school. In her final two years, her studies and other activities began to crowd out her riding, but up until then she was often at a local gymkhana. Cloud also became her means of visiting The Barn. She would leave the horse tethered near the door, then go inside to sit for a while, thinking, praying, lost in her own thoughts.

One day, just after her sixteenth birthday, Alexi finished saddling Cloud, meaning to take a gallop up to The Barn again. But she was ill at ease. Something was bothering her, and she didn't know what it was. She was about to swing herself into the saddle, when the feeling intensified. She stood beside Cloud, uncertain. She closed her eyes. "Lord, what is going on?" she prayed.

At once, a picture came to her mind. She saw Auntie Aggie standing at the door of The Barn. It seemed she was looking across the intervening distance, looking straight at her.

She spoke, "No Alexi, don't come up here today. Go to the Stephenson's."

Alexi was startled. She didn't know the Stephenson family well. She knew her mother went to visit Kelly sometimes, and she knew thirteen-year-old Naomi would begin high school next year, and become eligible for youth group. But the picture was as real as anything she had ever experienced. Somehow, she knew also that she was to take a First Aid kit with her. In a moment, she was on Cloud's back, all hesitation gone, cantering over to the stable where she stopped just long enough to fetch a small, red tin box containing first aid supplies. She stowed it in her saddle bag, and was away, galloping for the lonely Stephenson house, about a mile beyond the town border.

The house was run down and overgrown with trees and bushes. As Alexi pulled Cloud to a halt, she saw Naomi painfully hobbling towards the broken front steps, blood running down the back of her right leg. Her tear-stained face turned to see Alexi running towards her.

"Alexi! What are you doing here?" Surprise, and a little fear were in her voice. Her mother didn't encourage visitors.

"What happened to you?" Alexi replied. "Let me see your leg! It's bleeding badly!" She was on her knees, opening the First Aid box. She grabbed a cotton cloth, then ran to a tap standing at a drunken angle near the steps to the house. She carried the wet cloth back to Naomi, and began cleaning the blood from her leg. Two deep gashes were revealed, running from below her knee, down into her calf. Alexi found a tube of antiseptic ointment, and managed to slow the bleeding enough to apply some of the ointment down each gash. Then she took a long bandage, and began winding it around Naomi's leg.

As she worked, Naomi told her, "I was sitting on the fencepost out the front there. I sometimes sit out there just thinking to myself, when Mum isn't home. I thought she might be coming, so I tried to get down quickly, but I lost my balance, and my leg caught on the barbed wire. One of the barbs caught me, and ripped me!"

Alexi thought of this lonely girl, sitting lost in her thoughts, afraid that her mother might find her sitting there. She was glad she'd been able to help. Naomi was pathetically grateful for the kindness. Somehow, Alexi knew she wouldn't have found much sympathy if it had been her mother who found her bleeding.

Later, Alexi told Kathy about the picture she had of Auntie Aggie directing her to go to Naomi's house, and of how she had bound up her leg.

"Good for you Lexi," Kathy told her. "I'll go over there tomorrow, and see if I can get Kelly to take her in for a tetanus shot."

*

Alexi's visits to The Barn continued every two or three months throughout her years at high school. The Barn had a kind of attraction for her; she came to love these times, when peace would seep into her soul. She would examine again the array of carvings, wondering about the man who had been Auntie Aggie's husband. She didn't announce her visits, and didn't see Auntie Aggie while she was there. She was trespassing really, but she also had a sense that Auntie Aggie knew of her visits, and didn't mind them, especially after the incident with Naomi. She wondered if Auntie Aggie knew of the picture that had come to her. Was she aware that she was speaking to Alexi across that distance? It wouldn't be until years later that Alexi would ask her about it. In Alexi's mind, there was a kind of unspoken acceptance of her visits – Auntie Aggie knew she had been, both of them were okay with that, and neither of them said anything.

And she was right. Aggie often thought of Alexi, and prayed for her. In her spirit she knew that somehow, some day, their lives would connect in an even more special way. She didn't know what it would be, though she knew it was somehow connected with the shadow that had entered her heart that day she first held her in her arms. So Aggie was glad to see Cloud tethered outside, and would pray for her young visitor.

*

"Lexi! Those young guys at Youth Group taking notice of you?" Eric gave her a playful punch on the arm as he watched her rubbing Cloud down after her ride.

Youth Group was one of the highlights of Alexi's week. "Yeah Dad. Some of them do." She grinned at her father.

"What does that do to your heart strings? It's nice when a guy thinks you're special, huh?"

"I guess. But mostly I don't take too much notice. Paul's nice though. I like him."

"Yes," Eric replied, "Paul's a good kid. Sensible, fun. But you know how it is!" His eyes twinkled. "Any guy who's interested has to respect my beautiful daughter as much as I do before he gets past the gate."

"Aw Dad!" Alexi smiled. But she was glad of her

father's strong, protective admiration. "I know, some of the girls are kind of boy crazy. Always talking about who's in love with who. As though their lives depended on it."

Eric nodded soberly. "So many of them starve for real affection. Their lives do just about depend on any crumbs they can get." His arm went across her shoulders, giving her a brief hug. "Lexi, you're a precious woman. I'm proud of you!"

By her fourth year in the youth group, Alexi began to take on some leadership responsibilities, such as leading prayer groups and discussion groups, and helping to plan and arrange for activities. As she reached out to befriend the younger teens, Naomi Stephenson especially caught her attention. Since that day a year ago when she bound up Naomi's bleeding leg, Alexi had often wondered about her. She began to take Naomi under her wing.

*

Kathy's persistence in befriending Kelly Stephenson had borne some fruit. While her children were young, Kelly had occasionally attended the Young Mothers group at Carrington Church, so she had at least a passing acquaintance with other mothers her age. Every few months, Zoe Campbell hosted a gathering for women of around Kelly's age, helping to foster a sense of inclusion for her. Zoe's and Kathy's friendship had encouraged her to begin attending Carrington Church again, a place she thought she would never return to after leaving at the age of sixteen. She was beginning to soften a little towards the story of God's love for her.

Kelly's son Peter had been known as a tearaway child as he passed through the Masterton school system, and her daughter Debra was similar. Both Peter's and Debra's way of coping with their deficient home life had been bravado and swagger. Peter had left home at age twenty, crossing the Tasman Sea to discover what life might have to offer him in Sydney, Australia. Debra followed him when she turned eighteen. Neither of them had more than brief, irregular contact with their mother.

Naomi was different - her strategy for coping with life had been to retire into herself. Throughout most of her schooling, she was the quiet, retiring child whom nobody noticed. Her grades, like her clothes and general appearance, were average to poor.

That is, until adolescence discovered her. As her body began to change and develop, it seemed that Naomi discovered some things about herself that she liked very much. Somehow, she found it possible to keep her hair groomed. Somehow, she managed to find more becoming clothes. Her demeanor changed – she smiled, was much more outgoing, there was some bounce about her.

Kelly watched the change in her daughter, not sure whether to be pleased or alarmed. "You're becoming quite the young miss, aren't you," she said as Naomi prepared for youth group one Saturday. "You talk a lot about Alexi. I guess that's alright. Her mother's okay, so she's probably the right sort. But mind! There's lots of boys go to that youth group. I know! You just keep away from those guys, you hear?"

"Yes Mum!"

"And cover yourself up! You look like a young flirt!"

It was true. Alexi was her hero – a popular, older girl, who took an interest in her, and encouraged her. She respected Alexi. But Naomi was also excited by her blossoming womanhood, so that attention from the boys at Youth Group was like cool, fresh water to her parched soul. Naomi appeared each Saturday with her young round breasts pushed high, and generously displayed.

Alexi nearly despaired. She sought out her mother's advice.

"You're right Alexi," Kathy told her. "It's great to see her take pride in herself. But she's never had anyone to teach her about tempering that with modesty. Remember all the talks we've had about taking pride in your body, and respecting it – respecting it far too much to put it on display. Keeping yourself for the time when you're safe in your own married nest." She smiled at her daughter. "Now you're being called upon to pass on the wisdom to Naomi. God bless you Lexi. Proud of you."

So Alexi worked hard to encourage a change in Naomi's style of dress, without dampening her gladness in herself. Naomi tried to pay attention, but it was hard. Alexi's friendship was very special to her, but it wasn't quite the same as the admiration of the young males.

*

The crisis came towards the end of June, that first year of Naomi's participation in the youth group. Ben was a member of a loose group of youths who hit the town each Saturday evening, cruising in cars or on motorcycles. Ben had noticed Naomi at the ice cream store where she had a part-time job. His eyes lingered long on what he saw, and he started looking out for her, following her movements. On this Saturday, Ben had somehow contacted Naomi, and persuaded her to accept a ride home from youth group on his motorcycle. When she agreed, he gleefully advised some friends to meet him at a lonely spot outside the town, where he would bring something choice. Nobody noticed Naomi slip out shortly before the evening's activities ended.

Police Sergeant Colin Campbell was in an unmarked patrol car that evening. As he passed Carrington Church, he saw a young woman climb onto the back of a motorcycle, without a helmet. By the time he turned the car, the motorcycle had already moved off, so he used flashing lights and siren to give chase.

"Oh no!" groaned Ben to himself. "A cop! He's too fast for me. But if I don't get her out to Tony and the others, I'll catch it from them."

He tried to quickly flick the bike into a tight turn down a side street, leaning as far as he dared. He nearly made it, but some loose gravel on the intersection came under the front wheel, and the bike went sliding across the roadway on its side. Ben and Naomi also slid in different directions. Each of them was still lying prone on the roadway as Colin stopped close by, and stepped out of his car. With his torch, he quickly inspected each. He could see some blood on Naomi's jeans and on her arms, so he returned to his car and called an ambulance. His initial thoughts were that apart from the bleeding, neither seemed to be seriously injured, though both were stunned. He walked back to Ben, and heard him muttering, "Tony! Tony will kill me! I have to explain!"

Colin knew the group he was dealing with. He knew who Tony was, and guessed that Ben had been intending to take Naomi to him, and probably a few more, waiting at some location where they didn't expect to be disturbed. Colin also knew most of the places these boys frequented. As soon as a backup team and medics had taken control of the accident scene, Colin left to check out the most likely place the boys might be waiting. Sure enough, as he arrived at the end of a short, graveled track, he could see two cars and a motorcycle parked there. Tony and three other boys regarded him suspiciously as he approached. He flicked his torch at them.

"Hello Tony. Hank. Justin." The other boy he didn't recognize. "And who are you?" he demanded. Mike Trask. Mike could see that the other boys knew Sergeant Campbell, and knew he was not someone to mess with. He supplied details for Colin to note down. "Mike, if you'd like to live a long and happy life, you better say a quick farewell to these guys. They're not good for your health."

To all of them he said, "Well guys, Ben had a nasty spill off his bike on the way out here. He's not too badly hurt, and neither is his passenger. They're being treated at the hospital right now, but I think they'll be sent home when they've been patched up." He looked at each of them, shaking his head sadly.

"Listen up guys. You need to be very thankful that Ben came off his bike. That saved you all from committing a serious crime, that would have put you behind bars until well into your twenties." After a brief pause, he continued, "Like I've told you before, when you guys want to wise up, and realize that you're losers if you continue with this way of life, come tell me about it. I'd be glad to help you get a fresh start. A friend helped me get a fresh start once, and I'm glad of it. Now, beat it!"

Naomi suffered some deep bruises and some cuts and scratches that took weeks to heal. But she had no other injuries. She didn't know it until years later, but a wise, godly woman with grey eyes was sitting rocking in her prayer chair that night, praying urgently for Naomi. She did learn about the place Ben had been intending to take her, and the fate that she would have suffered there. Now she understood better what Alexi meant by attracting the wrong kind of attention. She began to button up. And the incident bonded her more deeply with Alexi. She still had many years of neglect to overcome, so it would be a long journey, but from that time Alexi became more firmly than ever her friend and mentor.

During the second half of the year, Naomi's heart still reached out for the affection that had been in such short supply in her life up to now. Friendship from Alexi and some of the other girls filled some of her need. But romance was such a strong temptation, so she was constantly in a "going steady" friendship with one of the youth group boys. At least she knew enough now to confine her affections to young men from the youth group. It was a growing experience for Alexi to give the best guidance she could to Naomi, while still giving her freedom to make her own choices. On some issues, she was almost obliged to become the boundary-setting parent.

"Does he respect you? Does he cherish you? Is he a real man? A man of leadership, and strength and courage? Is it really respectful to you when he …...? Does your friendship with him help you to know Jesus better?" So her questions to Naomi went, over and over. Gradually, Naomi gained a deeper respect for herself, and correspondingly demanded a deeper respect from any boy who wanted to take an interest in her.

As the new year came in, Naomi was more than ever the pert, bubbly teenager, but beneath the bright exterior, a stronger character was growing. She was becoming more thoughtful, and her faith in God was beginning to form. Her mother wondered more and more at the changes she saw in Naomi. Kelly began to question Kathy Paynter more about her faith, and what she thought was happening to her daughter. During that year, Kelly began attending one of the women's Bible study groups, as well as Sunday service.

*

The year passed, and another year opened - Alexi's last year at high school. She began to think in earnest about the next chapter of her life. She investigated several career options – some of them raised initial enthusiasm, but as she continued to pray, none seemed to be the right path for her. The months went by, and the year ended with all the mixed feelings of a final farewell to her school days, but no sure path forward.

January however, brought two major developments. The first was The Mission Connection. This was a new organization being developed by Jerry and Jayne Lawson, a mission-minded couple from Tauranga. God had laid on their hearts to begin an agency that would collate and disseminate information on missionary opportunities. It would be a resource for people considering some kind of missionary commitment. The objective was partly vision-raising, laying the needs and challenges before the church, getting the attention of those people God might be calling to missionary service. And partly it was to establish a central information point, holding stocks of information sheets and fliers that could be mailed to inquirers. Jerry and Jayne believed God had directed them to establish the first center in Masterton.

When Alexi heard of the new organization, and that the Lawsons were seeking the right person to take charge, she immediately felt that this was what she had been waiting for. Jerry and Jayne agreed. It took few inquiries for them to establish that Alexi was a young woman of deep faith, with a strong track record of care for others, and with the administrative and relational skills necessary for the task. They had already bought a house on Renall Street that was being renovated to provide both office space, and living quarters. The plan was that the appointee would live on the premises. Eric and Kathy were enthusiastic about Alexi's appointment, but felt she needed a little more maturity before she left home to live independently. It was finally agreed that she would commute from home until July, when she turned nineteen, and make the move at that time.

January's second major development was David. David Manning had a family connection with Bill McKnight, so he came to stay with the McKnight's when he arrived in Masterton to take up a job with the Borough Council. The Parks and Reserves Department was expanding, with the requirement for new staff, so David's training and experience in horticulture won him a position.

Alexi noticed David the first Sunday he attended Carrington Church. He found a seat across the aisle and one row forward from where she sat, so it was hard to miss the warm greetings being exchanged as he sat down. Alexi was not inclined to be swept off her feet by any eligible-looking young man who happened to appear, but she did find her eyes straying in his direction, noting his quiet, confident demeanor, his thick blond hair, and the way he was clearly participating in the service.

Two weeks went by, and Alexi hardly thought of the young man she had noticed. But on Saturday as she arrived at Youth Group, there he was, holding a guitar, warming up with the music team. "Hmm," thought Alexi, "So he's a guitarist too. I wonder who this guy is?"

The program began twenty minutes later, and the newcomer was introduced to everyone. His name was David, and he had moved from Auckland to take a job in Masterton. Before his move, he worked with at-risk youth in the Auckland suburb of Panmure, and was really interested in becoming part of Carrington's youth group. Later in the evening, Alexi was sitting chatting with David. She could see he had been watching the group, already forming some quite accurate impressions of the teens, noting the quiet, reserved ones, as well as the more boisterous ones. Her heart warmed to him as she recognized the same concern for these young people that she felt. She chatted about the ones she had especially worked with, the ones who were responsive to guidance, and those who were not so much. She talked of Naomi, and how far she had progressed during the last two years.

As she drove home that evening, Alexi realized how much she had enjoyed talking with David. Her thoughts and, yes, her feelings towards him were warm. She took herself firmly in hand. "Come now Lexi Paynter," she told herself, "the first time you have spoken with this man, and you're in danger of letting your feelings run way out ahead of you!" She sighed. "But, really, he's obviously a man of faith. He loves those kids already! Pretty cute too, with those flashing eyes, and blond hair! Good singer, great guitarist! Twenty-two – he's just four years older than me." She stopped again. "Lexi! Stop it! Pull yourself together!"

And so she did manage to pull her thoughts back into line. Until next Saturday. And the one after. By now, Alexi knew she had some real praying to do. "Lord, I like David a lot! He seems to me a really good man. But Lord, you know I don't want my heart to run ahead of you. I'm trusting you to show me what you have in mind."

Alexi began to be just a little more reserved when she got into conversation with David on Saturday evenings. She tried to avoid chance meetings with him at church. She wanted to give herself a chance for some objectivity. She didn't suspect it, but David was going through the same process. His heart had warmed to Alexi at least as strongly as she had warmed to him. He thought she was beautiful, capable, thoughtful – he respected her deeply, and loved talking to her as much as she enjoyed talking with him. But he didn't want to rush into a special friendship either. And unbeknown to either of them, a third person had somehow discerned the way their thoughts were going – Auntie Aggie was praying for both of them.

*

There was no clearly defined starting point for David and Alexi's relationship. They began stopping off for coffee together after the Saturday night youth group meetings, and began sitting together in church. David had not heard a very clear answer to his prayers, but the slow, step-by-step growth in their friendship felt right to him as he continued to pray. Alexi heard a more definite answer – she believed God was saying to accept the steps of friendship as David offered them. And so, before long it came to be understood, both by Alexi and David, and by the folks at Carrington Church, that there was a special friendship happening.

Their bonding grew mostly around their shared love for the youth at Carrington. They spent many a conversation planning the programs, and discussing the hopes, concerns, triumphs and disappointments they experienced with the lives of the teens in their care. Naomi was frequently in their minds. She was continuing to grow in self-confidence and trust in Jesus, but it was a roller-coaster ride. Alexi tried to encourage her to enjoy friendships with the boys, without falling into a new "in love" experience every month or two.

David and Alexi also encouraged each other as they grew into the responsibilities of their respective jobs. Alexi enjoyed her work with Mission Connection, her methodical mind and her imagination combining to build an efficient new organization. Jeff and Jayne Lawson were well pleased.

David too was fitting well into his responsibilities with the Borough Council. His supervisor, and a few of his co-workers, were not so easy to get along with, but David was working prayerfully on growing his relationships with them. Gradually he and Alexi began to enjoy regular "dates" together – going out for a meal, or touring around the small rural museums. Once, she took him to visit The Barn. They did not see Auntie Aggie.

Alexi helped David settle into his own flat late in March, adding a woman's touch by advising on curtains, mats for the floor, and cutlery and crockery. When July came, David helped Alexi move to the house in Renall Street. It was the day of the move, as they were relaxing at the end of the day, that David first took her in his arms and kissed her. Alexi was surprised. The kiss was wonderful – it seemed to tingle all the way down to her toes. Was this alright? She supposed so. It seemed to be generally understood that young, in-love people would enjoy kissing each other. Besides, God had told her to accept each step of friendship as David offered it. From now on, some cuddling and kissing became a regular part of their week.

So, for David and Alexi, life was full of happiness and promise. Auntie Aggie thought of them often, and prayed for them.

Chapter 23

Dilemmas and Diamonds

March, 1986.

Alexi was troubled.

And she was annoyed with herself for being troubled. So much of her life could hardly be better. She had been working with Mission Connection for more than a year, a very satisfying year, in which she had grown personally with the job, and the organization had grown in scope and vision with the hard work she put in. As a leader in Carrington Church's youth group, she was having a significant impact on young lives, and had the satisfaction of seeing many of the teens avoid pitfalls, growing instead in depth and Christian character.

Alexi was known more than ever as a fun-loving girl with a ready laugh, who could also be serious when the occasion demanded. She would often sleep at home on a Friday night, and spend most of Saturday with her family. At those times, she might sit at the piano for part of the afternoon, letting the music seep into her, relaxing her. Or she might go riding on her mare, Cloud, returning with her face flushed, her hair swept back by the wind. She loved her environment, living between the beautiful Tararua Range, and the coastal hills stretching east to the Ocean. She was an experienced hiker, familiar with the trails and huts in the southern stretch of the Tararuas. Habits of bush safety were second nature to her.

And there was David. Alexi was deeply in love with David Manning. She admired him immensely, and loved working with him as they shared their deep commitment to the youth of the church. He seemed to be doing well at his job as horticulturist with the Masterton Borough Council, where he was earning praise for his initiative. He was admired and accepted at Carrington Church, not just for his work with the youth, but also as a worship leader, and by his participation in one of the men's Bible study groups.

But Alexi had some nagging, half-formed thoughts about David that were starting to concern her. She didn't want to admit it. She didn't want to solidify the thoughts by clearly formulating them. But there was something – how would she describe it? Something a little woolly about the way David went about some things. She remembered that when their friendship blossomed into a romance, it was more like a slow drift than a deliberate, articulated transition. Not that that mattered much now. She was sure of his love, and his loyalty. She felt secure with him. Still, it would have been nice to have him declare a new level of commitment to her at that time – or something like that.

"Oh, what did I really expect of him? I don't know! Is it just me?" So her thoughts went.

Marriage had been mentioned between them a few times, not in an immediate way, not as though marriage was already on their horizon, but enough that they knew they each regarded their friendship seriously. Alexi didn't want to escalate the pace of their romance. At this point, she wasn't quite ready for much focus on marriage. But, well, there was never any discussion, there didn't seem to be any opportunity to even comment on how they each felt about the state and direction of their friendship.

"I think I need to talk with David about this," she thought. "I wish he would bring it up, take a lead on this himself. But never mind, I'll mention it."

But before she made an opportunity to raise these questions, a new concern superseded them. It was about kissing. When David first kissed her, about eight months ago now, Alexi felt wonderful. She felt safe and cherished in his arms, and the sensation of his lips on hers rippled right through her, deepening the bond she felt with him. But through the summer, and especially in the last two months, they seemed to be taking longer over their kissing and cuddling times. It was getting to be more than she felt comfortable with.

"But why?" she asked herself, "is there something wrong with me? Why do I feel like this?"

Several times, Alexi had disengaged herself, laughingly bidding David good night. And sometimes, he had protested – light-heartedly of course. It wasn't an argument between them. But it was something else that was adrift, with no sharing of their thoughts together.

And the thoughts about kissing and cuddling were harder to bring up with David. From what Alexi had gleaned during her growing up years, most adults, including the Christian adults inhabiting her world, just seemed to expect that a girl and a guy in a serious relationship would indulge in some kissing. So what was bothering her? And how did one go to one's boyfriend, and say, "I'm not happy with you kissing me?" What would he think? In a way, she was glad about his kisses. She always had been. She thought of herself as pretty mature regarding sexuality in general. Making love as a married woman was something she looked forward to. But was she really all bent out of shape? Why did she often get these uneasy feelings after David said his final goodnight, and left her at the Mission Connection house?

Alexi did find an opportunity to talk with David about where their relationship was going. The conversation went well. David seemed to be glad she had raised the matter. As he realized these questions had been bothering her for a while, he even apologized that he had not raised them himself. But the disquieting feeling that kissing was beginning to take on more urgency and passion than she was ready for – that was too confusing for her to deal with. It faded uneasily into the background.

*

"What do you think of Naomi's piece on Jesus' feelings the night he was arrested?" David's question broke into Alexi's thoughts as they sat together in the ice cream garden one Saturday afternoon.

Oh, yes. The Easter pageant the Youth Group had been preparing for Easter Sunday just two weeks away on March 30th. Naomi was in the Sixth Form this year. She was still as full of sparkle and adventure as she had been when she arrived at Youth Group four years ago, but now her character was more tempered with thoughtfulness and sensitivity. She had become a modest, strikingly beautiful young woman. Naomi still attracted attention from the boys, but now the attention was based on a more sober admiration. And she no longer felt the need to respond to every scrap of male attention coming her way.

"Wasn't that something?" Alexi responded to David. "She's amazingly sensitive. I think it comes from her memories of how life was for her while she was growing up."

"That must have a lot to do with it," David agreed. "Have you noticed the closeness that's growing between her and her mother? Whoever would have believed it? Kelly Stephenson is becoming a much sweeter, kinder woman. Lexi, your mother deserves so much credit for that. She's really hung in with Kelly, being a true friend to her."

"Yes, she has," Alexi responded. "It's easy to see how proud Kelly is of her daughter. She glows with pride whenever Naomi takes part in something at church."

The Easter service was a memorable event. Carrington had built a new sanctuary, dedicated in the same year Scott Lampton celebrated twenty years as pastor. That was seventeen years ago now, but most folks still referred to the building as the "new" sanctuary. It was an impressive structure, with a roof that swept to a peak rising high above the front platform and communion table. Acoustic panels across the ceiling were suspended from polished timber scrollwork, curving up to the central apex. The effect was modern, though the apex of the roof, rising into dimness, introduced the hint of a lofty cathedral.

That Easter, the musical instruments, the singing, the readings and the spoken pieces blended beautifully, as the central story of the faith settled upon the heart of every hearer. Kelly Stephenson was deeply moved, not only as she watched and listened to her daughter Naomi, but by the age-old story of the

Cross. That day, Kelly left her tired, self-centered life behind, and became a follower of Jesus.

Naomi was beyond thrilled by her mother's decision. "Lexi, I can't thank you enough for all the help and all the prayers you've prayed for me and my mum!" she said as she greeted Alexi the next Saturday at Youth Group. "Already she's changing the way she talks. I know she loves me, and we've been getting closer for a long time, but up until now, she usually had this kind of sarcastic way of talking. Now, she smiles, and she's so much kinder. I'm ever so grateful to you, and to your mum – she's been a good friend to my mum for so long."

Alexi smiled. "Yes! I'm so happy for you and for your mum. Auntie Aggie was the one who prayed with her last Sunday. They knew each other when they were school children."

"Hmm," replied Naomi, "I think I've heard that before."

Aggie came and sat in with the youth group about twice each month. As always, she would watch from a corner, sometimes talking with a leader, or one of the teenagers if they spoke with her. But mostly, she watched. Sometimes her eyes would follow Alexi, her lips moving in prayer; sometimes it would be one of the other leaders, and often it would be one of the teens. She was never obtrusive. She just came to be accepted as part of the scene.

"Auntie Aggie," Naomi continued, "well, I don't know her very well, but when you get talking to her, it's like …. like so much love flows out of her! You can see it in her smiley eyes. I'm grateful to her too."

Alexi smiled and nodded. Her heart swelled with encouragement as she watched Naomi's gladness that her mother was now a Christian. Giving time and prayer to Naomi, and to other young lives at the youth group, was deeply fulfilling.

*

The days became shorter, the leaves turned to red and gold. Alexi's uneasiness about kissing still muttered away in the background. She and David had always discussed their hopes and concerns for the youth of the church, but more often now, their talk would turn to their own friendship, and their thoughts for the future. Thoughts of marriage were getting more focused. And David had backed off a little in his eagerness for holding and kissing her. It was still more than she really wanted, but it seemed she was getting used it.

Autumn turned to winter, and Alexi's birthday was getting close.

"Lexi, your birthday is on a Thursday this year." David and Alexi were sitting in a coffee lounge one evening in mid-June. "It's also the anniversary of you moving into your own place at Mission Connection. I thought it was worth doing something a little special. Do you think you could get the day off?

"The whole day off? For my birthday?"

David smiled a little awkwardly. "Yes. There's this kind of excursion I've been thinking of taking you on. I think you'll like it. And we haven't been out and about for a while. It seemed like your birthday would be a good excuse."

"Sounds like fun," replied Alexi. "Though Mum and Dad might want part of the day on my birthday."

"Yes," agreed David, "I thought of that. But I was wondering if they might give you some kind of party on the Saturday night. That's what they did last year. Oh, no, it was Sunday night. Youth Group was on Saturday."

"Yes. I think that would be fine." Alexi looked up at him. Her face took on one of her impish smiles. "So, where are we going?"

"Not telling! It's a surprise!"

"What'll I wear? Formal, hiking, casual?"

"I'll tell you nearer the time." David smiled in a mysterious, pleased way.

So, they joked and teased for the next two weeks as July 3rd approached. On the Wednesday evening, David phoned Alexi.

"Casual dress for tomorrow," he told her. "But we'll be outdoors, so dress warm. Scarf and jacket, gloves and woolly hat! I'll see you at eight in the morning."

"Sounds exciting!" Alexi giggled. "I'll be ready!"

As Alexi piled into David's car next morning, she exclaimed, "You've tidied your car! And vacuumed the floor! All in honor of my birthday?"

"You won't turn twenty ever again in your life," David grinned. "We have to make the most of it! Okay, we're off to Wellington. We're going for a drive around the harbor."

Alexi looked at him curiously. A drive around Port Nicholson, Wellington's harbor. She hadn't done that for a while, but there had to be more to this day than that.

"Alright sir. Just as you say!" She settled down to enjoy the ride. It was a grey, wintry day, with a cold wind gusting, so the warm interior of the car felt cozy as they crossed the Rimutaka Range. Emerging from the Hutt Valley, they began skirting the northern side of the harbor. A few whitecaps were scattered across the sea. Soon they were passing through Wellington City, and on towards Oriental Bay. As they reached the Royal Port Nicholson Yacht Club, David pulled into a parking space. Alexi glanced quizzically at him.

"Well Lexi, you beautiful person, how would you like a yacht cruise on the harbor?"

Alexi's eyes opened wide. "Today? Isn't it a bit stormy?"

"A little," agreed David. "But we're adventurous souls! Both pretty good sailors, so some plunging through the waves will just make it more exciting! The sloop I chartered is a thirty-two-footer, so it has a small cabin if we want to escape the worst of the wind and spray."

"Are we going to sail her ourselves?" Alexi wanted to know. Both she and David had some experience with yachts, but she wasn't sure about them managing a thirty-two-footer on a squally day.

"No," David replied. "The skipper and one crew member come along for the ride. We have two hours."

"David! All for my birthday? This must be rather expensive!"

"Lexi, you're worth it!"

Neither of them would ever forget the next two hours. They braced against stays and stanchions as the wind whipped by them, the yacht plunged willingly into the swell, the taut sails sighed softly, and gulls screamed overhead. As they turned for a downwind leg, David put his arm around Alexi, his head close to hers.

"Lexi, you're right. This isn't just about your birthday. I love you Lex. Will you be my wife?"

Alexi's breath caught in her throat. For a few weeks now she'd been hoping to hear that question, but had no idea it would be today. Her eyes shone. "I love you too David. I would love to be your wife."

As they drove home that afternoon, Alexi couldn't take her eyes off the diamond that sparkled on her finger. "David, thank you so much! That was the perfect setting for us – facing the raw challenges together! I think we were made for challenges, don't you?"

Chapter 24

The Crash.

Alexi was reliving their harbor experience. She felt again the yacht heeling to the breeze, the spray bursting over the bow. She'd hooked her arm around a main stay while she tugged off her glove, holding out her left hand to David. She studied the diamond on her finger again. "He's a good man! Strong, a man of faith! He's in it for real, for keeps."

The celebration with Alexi's family on the Sunday following her birthday became both a birthday party and an engagement announcement. Eric and Kathy were pleased and proud to give their blessing to David as a prospective son-in-law, and Hannah and Ted were excited to welcome him as a brother-in-law.

The wedding was set for February 14th, giving about seven months for all the preparations. Alexi and David plunged into a whirl of activity - guest list, checking on a venue for the reception, designing invitations, and discussing their wedding service. Alexi had excited discussions with her friends on the dress design she would choose. Naomi was deeply honored when she was asked to be a bridesmaid.

The concerns Alexi had felt earlier about David had all but disappeared. It seemed they were able to discuss much more readily the issues Alexi felt to be important. The future they each envisioned together, the possibilities for service in their church and community, or perhaps some overseas Christian missions experience were frequent topics of conversation. Where they would like to live, and their thoughts about how many children they might hope for. David was even initiating these discussions almost as often as Alexi did.

But there was still that nagging question about the cuddling and kissing. Alexi still felt a little pressured that David looked for more than she did. She'd mostly become used to the way things were, assuming her unsettled feelings were just something unexplained about her. But towards the end of July, the niggling frustration was growing again. Wedding planning was a pleasant, manageable kind of pressure, but somehow it seemed to snag on this other, less manageable stress, building the two together into a tangled ball in the pit of her stomach.

Yet the kissing and cuddling question seemed even more difficult to broach with David. If it seemed awkward to ask your boyfriend to back off from kissing you, how much more awkward to say that to your fiancé? One day she asked him whether he had other girlfriends before they met.

"Yes," David grinned at her. "I dated a few girls in my teens. Why, you jealous?"

Just a slight frown creased Alexi's brow. "Oh. In your teens. Like, how old were you when you started dating?"

"Let's see, I was sixteen when I dated Saffron. That was my first kiss! But it only lasted a couple of months. Then Missy – we were going together for, oh, nearly a year."

David was about to mention a third former girlfriend, but something about Alexi's expression stopped him.

"You okay Lexi? That was when I was young – just puppy love! I didn't have any girlfriends after I got involved with the groups we ran up in Panmure – the groups for kids who'd been in trouble with the police. And anyway, you're the only really serious relationship I've had! You're different! You're special!" He paused for a moment, before adding, "Does it worry you that I had girlfriends when I was younger?"

"Oh, no!" she responded. "I guess I should've expected that you would have." But she was trying to convince herself as much as David.

Now Alexi's confusion deepened. Part of her mind told her she was being very petty to be bothered about girls David had kissed as a teenager. But part of her definitely felt cheated.

"He said it was just puppy love, as though that somehow makes it alright! If it was just puppy love, why was he kissing

230

them?" So her thoughts ran. "He said I'm his first serious relationship – but it almost feels like I'm the next in a long line. Is it really any different when he kisses me, different from how it was with them?"

"So then, what say he did have a serious relationship in the past?" Alexi continued to argue with herself. "What if he'd been engaged before? What if he'd been married before? Does that mean you wouldn't want him?"

"Hmm, no, I think that would have been alright. That would mean he'd genuinely entered into a serious relationship, and for some reason it came to an end. So, he had to deal with that in a thoughtful way, and come out the other end. I could cope with that. But this kissy, puppy love! Oh, I don't know! Why does it even bother me?"

About that time, Alexi made a discovery. It came to her that she had really known this all along, but now it became a focused thought. She noticed that the feelings she was experiencing were very physical. It was her body that was on edge, restless. She noticed this especially on those evenings after David left, when she undressed for her shower before going to bed.

"Oh! That's it!" The thought hit her. "I'm aroused, ready to go, but I'm not going anywhere." It came as a revelation. "When we've been kissing … I suppose that's what it does to me."

The discovery was partly reassuring, partly not.

"So, I guess I'm pretty normal then. My body is telling me I'm good to go! But, but, should I be aroused by a bit of kissing? Am I super-sexed or something? Everyone seems to expect that we'll be kissing, but no-one ever hinted that … that it would affect me like this."

The discovery about herself led Alexi to another discovery, one that left her even more shaken. A question had been nudging around the corners of her mind for weeks. Now it clarified. When she and David were standing close together, with their arms around each other, she'd noticed something hard against her leg, or her tummy. As this realization came into focus, she suddenly knew what the something hard was.

"He's aroused too!" She was incredulous, yet she knew it must be true. "And yet … yet it doesn't seem to bother him! He's never shown the least embarrassment. Surely, he must know? Of course, he must know!"

Now Alexi was really confused. She'd never heard anyone talk about this. She and David had never talked about their boundaries. They'd both just assumed they were on the same page. Some kissing was in order, but everything else was reserved for the time they were truly bonded as a married couple. Yet this arousal she experienced, and especially as she realized David was experiencing something the same, seemed to be an anticipation of married love-making.

"I know David's a good man! He's a godly man! I'm sure he would never … that he doesn't get all lusty over me. I would see it in his eyes, I'm sure I would! So, why does he let this happen?"

Her thoughts went to her parents. How had they managed all this before they were married? Maybe she would ask her mum. She'd always been pretty open with her mum, but this? This seemed so deeply personal.

"Is there someone else I could talk to about what's happening? Eunice, Pastor Scott's wife? Hmm, she's much older than me. I don't know how things were back in those days."

"Auntie Aggie. Auntie Aggie? Why on earth would her name come to mind? What would she know about it? Oh, yes, she was married wasn't she. Hmm, seems strange – I wonder how her romance was?"

A small hint stirred in Alexi that Auntie Aggie's romance would have been very intense, and at the same time very circumspect. Still, the notion of going to Auntie Aggie with this problem didn't seem at all realistic.

"I need to share this with David. After all, we'll be getting very intimate in a few months, so I guess I should take the plunge, and try to tell him how I'm feeling."

But it was still so confusing, and Alexi was afraid there was something strange about her. She couldn't think of a way of bringing it up with David. And now it was even more difficult, now she had realized that kissing left them both aroused. Was it the same for those girls he'd kissed during his teens? Did they get aroused? Was he aroused by them? Did they notice it, as she had? The vague feeling that she had been cheated by those early romances became a little stronger. It began to feel as though she might not be able to have this conversation with David without sounding like she was accusing him.

The next evening, she made a visit to The Barn. She wasn't going to visit Auntie Aggie, but it was so long since she had been up there. On this evening, she sat for a long time, thinking, praying, pondering. It refreshed her to sit, soaking in that quiet atmosphere. She could just feel that Auntie Aggie often prayed in that room. As always, she somehow felt sure Auntie Aggie knew of her unannounced visit, and was happy for her to sit for about two hours, before making her way back home.

Yes, Aggie did notice her visitor, and was pleased to see her. She sat in her bedroom, in her prayer chair, focused on Alexi while her visit lasted. She knew of course of the excitement of wedding plans going on for Alexi, and was glad for her. But this visit told her that something was troubling her young friend.

Alexi resolved several times in the coming weeks to voice her concerns to David, but it never seemed to be the right time. She began to find pretexts for missing or curtailing their goodnight cuddle. She found she was good at masking her feelings, so David was not alarmed. But the pretense bothered her too. She didn't want to pretend about anything to David.

Throughout August, and into September, Alexi made several more visits to The Barn. She knew Auntie Aggie would notice the sudden increase in her visiting, and would probably wonder. But she felt safe with the unspoken arrangement they had, and found The Barn a real solace. Aggie noticed and wondered, and prayed.

During the second week of September, Alexi knew she had to say something to David. On Saturday evening he brought her home after Youth Group. It had been a demanding evening, but now she tried to refocus her thoughts on what she needed to say. David didn't usually go inside with her when he brought her home. Again, it was not something they'd discussed, but rather a tacit agreement that being alone in her home together, especially after dark, was not a wise idea. So, with rare exceptions, it hadn't happened. Tonight, was one of the exceptions. Alexi wanted to give David some documents about an upcoming conference, so he went in with her to get them.

David placed the papers on the table while he took Alexi in his arms. She drew breath, but he was already tilting her face up for a long kiss. David was aware that by coming inside with her, he had crossed their unspoken boundary, so he stepped back, intending to take his leave after just one kiss. His hands rested on her shoulders. He smiled at her. Alexi drew breath again, to speak to him. David let his hands drop.

It was completely unpremeditated. He'd not thought of any such thing, but David's right hand stopped over Alexi's breast.

Now his mind was a confused whirl of thoughts. "Oh! Why did I do that? Is this alright? This is outside our boundaries. I'd better take my hand away. Is she okay with this? She hasn't moved. I think she's okay with it."

David moved a little to his left. His hand went under Alexi's sweater, touching her through her shirt.

"Hmm. I'd better not do this. But she hasn't moved. She hasn't said anything. Hey, we're nearly married. Maybe we can take a little step in this direction. Dear Lord, she's so soft, so precious. Okay, I'll take my hand away. Maybe just a tiny squeeze. Then I'll take my hand away."

David's hand flexed ever so slightly.

Something inside Alexi snapped. Something thick, stretched, taut. She almost heard it snap. Her hands went to her sweater, sweeping it off over her head. Her fingers were on her shirt, unbuttoning, unbuttoning. The shirt slipped from her shoulders. Her hands met behind her back, unfastening. Her bra followed her sweater and shirt to the carpet.

Her fingers were on David's shirt, unbuttoning. His shirt met the floor.

All the while, David was trying to protest. "Lexi, we can't, we mustn't …. Lexi don't do this … Lexi, stop."

But other thoughts contested. "I started this. If I stop her now, she'll think I don't want her. She'll think there's something wrong with her. Oh Lord, Lord, why did I do that?" His protests died inarticulate in his throat, as Alexi pulled him to the floor. Their chests rubbed together.

They didn't remember afterwards just how the rest of their clothes were discarded. They did remember his entry - hurried, inexpert. His response came almost immediately, a few jagged peaks of pleasure, that left him unsatisfied.

Alexi felt shafts of sensation sweep through her. But she was not nearly ready for David to finish. The sensations died. He tried to thrust. She tried to move under him. To no avail. Angrily she pushed him off her, and lay on her side, knees hugged to her chest. Her body ached with readiness and frustration. Her sobs choked her – sobs of devastation, of guilt, of betrayal, of overwhelming anger.

David was behind her. As he looked at her, he knew he was in territory more private and intimate than he had ever been. He was trespassing. Embarrassed, he looked away. On all fours, he crawled around her, in front of her. Her sobs wrung his heart with almost physical pain.

David too was devastated. The wreckage of their glad ideals seemed to engulf them. "Lexi," he croaked, "Lexi!"

At the sound of his voice, Alexi's eyes flew open. She pushed herself up to a sitting position, ankles crossed in front of her, knees still clasped to her chest. "David! Get out of here! Stop looking at me! Stop looking at me! Get out of here!"

The rage in her voice crashed into him. He'd never heard anything like it from her. If David was already devastated, this reaction from Alexi told him the devastation was only just beginning. Fragments of thought whirled in his brain – fragments of protest, of guilt, of desperate desire to comfort her, to commiserate together at their undreamed-of blunder.

"Lexi!" He tried again. "Lexi!"

"Get out! Go away! Get your clothes and get out!" If anything, her rage was even more intense.

David stared at her, unbelieving. Dumbly he turned to find his clothes, gathered them, moved towards the door to get himself dressed, stumbled down the steps and out to his car. Alexi heard the car door open, the engine start. The sounds faded into the distance.

*

David drove back to Alexi's house early the next morning. He hoped that at least she would talk to him by now. It was six-thirty, but already he'd missed her. Her car was not there. David didn't know such depths of grief and shame and worry were possible. How he longed to be with Alexi, and at least somehow try to cope with their disaster together.

Alexi had slept for two snatches of about half an hour each. She was awake at four, knowing only that she wanted to get away, to be by herself. She wasn't suicidal, but the notion of just disappearing somewhere, never to reappear again, played around the back of her mind. She didn't know quite where she was going, but she knew it would be somewhere wild and desolate. Instinctively more than by design, she stowed jacket and warm clothing, sleeping bag, groundsheet, and several water bottles into her backpack, before heading for her car. She was away before five o'clock.

He knew she wouldn't be at church, but David tried to watch for her just in case. He didn't want to see or talk to anyone else either, so he turned for home when he didn't see her.

Alexi took back roads, driving through Gladstone and Longbush, finding the narrow, dusty road through Tora, and so to White Rock Road. She was in Southern Wairarapa now, east of Martinborough. When she reached the coast, she turned north, finally reaching the end of the road at Te Awaiti. There was nowhere more remote than this, unless one left road access behind, and went on by foot. Which Alexi proceeded to do. Taking her backpack, she walked up the valley into the hills. By early afternoon, she reached the top of a ridge, from where she could see the sweep of the coast, stretching south to north. Alexi took out her jacket and put it on, then lay on the ridge, her pack under her head, staring at the sky. Mercifully, she drifted into a fitful sleep.

236

*

David was almost frantic with worry. It was Tuesday afternoon, and Alexi hadn't returned. He phoned her at every opportunity, without any response. Could she have had an accident somewhere? Should he call the police, just in case? Ah, Colin Campbell! He knew Sergeant Campbell. He would call him this evening. But before David made the call that evening, his phone rang. It was Alexi.

"Lexi!" David sobbed into the phone, "where are you?"

"David, I'm sorry! I just had to escape. I've been down on the coast. I'm back in Martinborough now, so I wanted to call and let you know I'm alright."

"Lexi! Thank you for calling. I've been out of my mind with worry for you! And so sorry for … for everything!"

"Me too David. Listen, I bet Mum has been calling, and wondering where I am. I'll call her from here and tell her the pressure has been building, so I just needed to bolt for a few days. If anyone asks, just tell them that, okay?"

"Yes, okay Lexi." In his relief at hearing her, together with the huge upheaval since Saturday night, David couldn't keep from sobbing still.

"David, I'm coming back now. I'll have to put in a day at Mission Connection tomorrow. But meet me tomorrow night at The Barn. About six o'clock. Is that alright with you?"

"Oh yes, yes! I'll see you then Lexi."

The next evening Aggie watched gravely as first David, and then Alexi arrived, and let themselves into The Barn. Aggie didn't know what was happening with Alexi and David, but her heart told her the first scene was opening in the drama she had glimpsed when she held Alexi in her arms, just two days after her birth.

*

237

Both Alexi's and David's minds still felt numbed, overwhelmed by their blunder. It still felt unbelievable, though by now some thoughts were emerging from the fog.

The theme in David's mind circled around how they could have betrayed themselves, their hopes and their ideals so badly, together with his overwhelming sorrow that he had so disrespected and hurt the woman he loved. A similar theme ran in Alexi's mind, but her concern was also for the future, and what they would do from here.

As Alexi arrived, David hastened to her, but she stepped aside, saying, "David, please don't touch me. Come, let's sit down."

This didn't seem a promising start to David, but as they sat opposite each other, Alexi's next words were not quite so discouraging.

"David, I've been beastly to you, I know. I'm sorry. I've been swamped with fury. Fury that we betrayed ourselves, fury with you for doing that to me, fury with myself for practically dragging you into it. I'm still furious, more than I've ever been about anything. But I'm beginning to get a few glimpses of perspective."

David dropped to his knees before her. "Alexi." He was unconscious of using her full name. "It was my fault. Why did I touch your breast? I'm so, so sorry. I had no idea what I was doing. What it would do to you."

The angry tone crept back into Alexi's voice. "I was already uneasy about the times you spent kissing me. All the times we spent half an hour or more kissing and holding each other, and when you left I would go inside feeling so … I don't know … so, on edge. It took me ages to settle down to sleep."

David moved back to his chair, aghast. "You were? I never knew that!"

"I tried to tell you. But it was so confusing. Everyone seems to think kissing for courting couples is okay, so I thought something was wrong with me that it got me so aroused. But … but so did you!" she accused. "Sometimes I felt you against me, and I could feel that you were ...." - she hesitated over the word - "were aroused. But it didn't seem to bother you! You just seemed to smile and leave. But I was left restless, feeling prepared for something, with nowhere to go!"

David was looking at her, amazed. "Lexi, Lexi, yes I did sometimes get ... But guys get hard sometimes and it's no big deal, and it goes away. Oh Lexi, I had no idea! And then when I touched you, and it .... Oh Lord, why was I such a fool!"

Alexi was looking at David, trying to take in the idea that a guy's body could respond that way without it meaning he was feeling the sort of arousal she'd felt. She struggled to accept the notion. She shook her head, trying to regroup her thoughts.

"Well, anyway," she resumed, "what are we going to do now?"

"You mean ... I don't know .... What are you thinking of?" David was confused. He knew something had fundamentally changed, but he hadn't started grappling with the implications.

"David, can you see me walking down the aisle, all smiling and radiant, just as though nothing had happened? I just bought the most beautiful dress I ever dreamed of! How can I wear it now? What a sick pretense that would be!" Her face was wet with tears again.

David's gut turned to stone all over again. Oh, yes, he hadn't thought of that. As he looked at her wet face, he thought that he'd never known it was possible to feel so wretched.

"But if you don't, if we change anything, how are we going to explain that?" David sat, his head bowed over his knees. "Alexi, do we own up, tell everyone what happened? It's my fault! I'll take the responsibility and defend you!"

"David, it was hardly a rape! You can't take all the blame!" She cupped her hands over her eyes for a moment, trying to sooth their redness. "But thank you for wanting to protect me. I've thought about coming clean, telling everyone. But then I think of all the kids we've counseled, and prayed with, and taught – how can we betray them?"

"Maybe we already have betrayed them." David's voice was very low. He sat in silence, then slowly, painfully, he rose and moved to kneel again in front of Alexi. "Lexi!" His voice broke. He tried again, speaking slowly, separating each word. "Lexi, God knows I don't want to lose you. But, but if you need to break off with me because of this, I'll, I'll understand."

Alexi looked at him kneeling in front of her. "I won't say I haven't thought of it David. But you're a good man. In spite of everything, I think we're meant to be together. That's if you still want to be with me!"

"Oh yes, Lexi! I do. I wouldn't leave you now!"

After a pause, Alexi spoke again. "I don't know what to do. The way people believe in us! They have confidence in us. We can't blow all that up. I just can't decide. Guess we have to think about it some more."

David sighed and nodded.

"But David," Alexi continued, "until we do decide, you'd better be good at not giving us away! I just had a day at work, being my bright bubbly self to all the people who phoned. In fact, I was dismayed at how well I could pretend. Mum called late in the day. She's still a bit curious about why I suddenly took off for a few days. I nearly blurted out the whole story to her. If I hadn't had the day's practice at talking sweetly to all the Mission Connection callers, I would have!"

They left shortly afterwards, undecided, heavy-hearted. As Aggie watched them go, they lay heavily on her heart also.

*

The next few days were exhausting for both David and Alexi. All the joy had gone out of their wedding plans – they both felt this, but especially Alexi. It was her day, the day on which she would be presented as a beautiful gift to her husband. But now, now if she went through with it, it would be a day of sham, taking every ounce of her energy to keep up the façade. But on the other hand, dropping the bombshell of their shattered ideals was just too big. She couldn't face it.

Saturday evening was the worst. Maintaining the role of the confident leaders among the church young people, leading prayers, singing, teaching, being bright and affectionate with each other – they felt guilt sweating from every pore. It wasn't that they thought of their blunder as unforgiveable, but there was a deep, unadmitted inconsistency between their own behavior and all that they taught and represented to these precious young ones.

Alexi badly needed someone to confide in, to help her decide on what to do. But it was impossible – who could she talk to? Auntie Aggie's name continued to pop into her mind occasionally, and strangely, Auntie Aggie did seem to be the one person she could have confessed to. But really, she hardly had a close, confidential relationship with Auntie Aggie. She continued visiting The Barn most evenings at that time. It was a place of solace, though she never went with the object of meeting its owner.

So, David and Alexi drifted into accepting that they would go ahead as though nothing had happened. They were both deeply unhappy at not being authentic, as most people believed, but getting it all out in the open was just too hard.

They kept up appearances well. Only two people knew that something was amiss. One was Alexi's mother, Kathy. Kathy had no idea what was wrong, but she knew something was. Every now and again she gently probed, but Alexi always deflected her questions. She didn't know what to do with her uneasiness. Most of the time, Alexi seemed excited about her upcoming wedding. But occasionally, Kathy caught a tired, hunted look in her daughter's eyes. She prayed often and fervently that God would heal whatever was troubling Alexi.

The other person who discerned the cloud over David and Alexi was Aggie. Aggie prayed too – rocking in her prayer chair, walking the bush trails or sitting at vantage points overlooking the plain, sometimes sitting in The Barn, among the beloved carvings Ky had left her.

*

Two weeks later, a new concern cropped up for Alexi.

241

Her period was late. Just twice that she could remember, she'd gone three days past her usual time. Today she was three days over again. The next day, she had a moment of hope that her fears were wrong, but no, it was just a little spotting. That evening she called by the chemist store for a pregnancy test.

Just after eight o'clock, David answered his phone. "David, meet me tomorrow evening at The Barn. Six o'clock." The phone clicked as she hung up.

It wasn't a request. It was an instruction. Once again, foreboding crashed into David. What was going on? He was angry at being spoken to like that, and considered calling back. No, maybe this wasn't the right time.

David spent a miserable day. Clearly, the storm-cloud of anger and withdrawal was enveloping Alexi again. Why had she lapsed back to this?

He was sitting at the table in The Barn when Alexi came in. David looked up apprehensively. Alexi drew a card from her handbag and threw it down on the table in front of him. David picked it up.

"What's this?"

"It's a pregnancy test." Alexi's words seemed to bounce, one by one, clattering onto the table. "It's positive."

David stared at the card, while its meaning seeped into his brain. He looked up at her. "Lexi!" he whispered. His head sank. Then, "Oh, Lexi!" This time almost a shout.

"I'll never wear that dress now!" she stormed. "I'll never fit into it in February! A fine couple we'll be! Everyone's ideal of the wonderful Christian leaders! What a great Christian home they'll have!"

She sank into a chair. "David, I'm sorry! You're no more to blame than you were already. But I'm just so crazy angry at you, at myself, at the ruins of our dreams!" After a moment, she went on. "As though the dress means anything. But it does! It does! It's a beautiful dream, given to me, and now it's snatched away again!"

They both sat, head in hands. Finally, David spoke again. "Lexi, it looks like this is out of our hands. We thought we could ride it out. But now, everyone's going to know."

"David!" Now it was her voice that was almost a shout. "Can you see me telling Naomi about this? After all the times I've encouraged her, and prayed with her! And now I have to tell her, 'Oh by the way, Naomi dear, I'm pregnant! Just do as I say, not as I do!'"

Alexi subsided back into her chair. They were silent again, faces covered. Finally, she spoke again.

"Yes," she said slowly. "Everyone's going to know. Unless …. Unless."

Their eyes met, both of them knowing what 'unless' meant. The word hung in the air between them.

No! Never! They couldn't! But being exposed, being crushed, being shamed! Both alternatives were unthinkable.

David sat, still with head bowed.

*

Alexi sat, watching David intently. She waited fully five minutes, then rose, went out to her car, and drove away.

*

David was surprised to hear her go. They hadn't brought this to any conclusion. He supposed she just couldn't cope with any more for now. A few minutes later, he rose, walked to his car, and drove away also.

As David's car turned onto Dalefield Road, Aggie was musing about this, another visit from him and Alexi. She walked over to The Barn. She picked up a card lying on the table. In a circle in the middle of the card, was a blue oval. Nothing quite like this existed when Aggie was struggling with fertility testing, but she realized in a moment what the card in her hands meant.

"Oh Jesus, dear Jesus," murmured Aggie. She put the card back on the table, returned to her cottage to get a jacket, then walked across the springy grass to the rocky outcrop opposite her front door. She prayed there until well after the stars became bright in the sky.

An urgent thought struck Alexi as she turned into her driveway. She stopped, grabbed her handbag, and peered into it. Oh, no! Quickly, she drove back to The Barn. She leapt out of her car, and ran into the room. Thank goodness! It was still there. She swept the card into her bag, and returned home.

For the next two days, David didn't hear from Alexi, and he didn't try to contact her. He thought she wanted space to try to come to terms with the situation. By the third day, a Friday, he decided they needed to get together and talk about moving forward. He tried to phone her during the day, but she didn't pick up. David arrived home from work, planning to freshen up, then try to visit Alexi. When he cleared his mail, he found a small envelope with "David" written across it in Alexi's hand. He took it inside, and tore open the envelope. It contained an index card, with three lines written across it.

"I took care of it."
"I won't be at Youth Group Saturday. Please cover for me."
"See you at church Sunday."

Bam! Bam! Two more body blows slammed into David. Yet he was already so punch-drunk, so emotionally frozen, their effect was lessened, halved even. The first punch to his gut was the horror of what Alexi had done. Yes, they'd let that idea float between them, but he'd not imagined she would act on it. And the second blow was the realization of how alone Alexi must feel. He'd failed her again. Her anger had been such a barrier, cutting him off from her – now he realized he should have somehow tried to reach through it, to connect with her.

David had no idea where Alexi was. And the note he'd just read overwhelmed him. He had to flee somewhere. He wasn't hungry, but made himself prepare something – a couple of eggs, with toast and coffee. He ate quickly, grabbed a water bottle, sleeping bag and groundsheet, and headed for his car. He remembered Alexi showing him a cave at Third Creek, up at Jon and Cassie Sander's property. The darkness of a cave seemed just what he needed.

The daylight was fading when David arrived at the cave. He was finding his way by torchlight as he reached the entrance. He flicked the beam into the cave, and heard a startled gasp. The light fell on Alexi's face.

"Lexi!"

"David! I, I needed to escape. The blackness of the cave seemed to match the blackness of my soul."

"I felt exactly the same Lexi." David stepped into the cave, and moved toward her. At last she allowed him to wrap her in his arms. They stood together, clinging to each other. "Are you alright Lexi? Are you … hurting, sore?"

"A little," Alexi replied. "I'll be okay."

For a long time, they stood, eyes closed, hugged together. Eventually, they spread their groundsheets on the sandy floor of the cave, scrambled into their sleeping bags, and lay huddled against each other.

"David, I just did the most wicked thing I've ever done. I never, never, never thought ...." Alexi's voice trailed off. "And yet, strangely, since you arrived, I almost feel like I could pray again. Nothing much – just a word or two. I've hardly prayed at all since that night at my house. David, do you suppose God could ever take a moment's notice of us, ever again?"

"I don't know Lexi. If I were teaching a Bible study, I'd say, 'Yes, of course he could. God always forgives, no matter what.' But for me right now, I just don't know."

Chapter 25

To Have and to Hold, From This Day Forward.

So, David and Alexi carried with them the dark secret of their lost virginity, and the darker secret of their lost baby. At first, it took a super-human effort to maintain a bright exterior, while they carried their grief and guilt within. Not quite all their joy at their approaching marriage was stolen, though most of it was. Trying to cover up the deficit, as they joined with friends and family to plan, arrange, anticipate their special day – it all demanded so much emotional energy.

And at Youth Group, encouraging the teens to be authentic and vital in their faith, while they felt so inauthentic themselves, was a hypocrisy that ate at their hearts. They considered resigning immediately, but agreed that an abrupt resignation would seem strange. Instead, they made it known they would finish their Youth Group leadership at the end of the year. That gave them the pretext of their impending marriage, and the need to take time for each other.

A major distraction from the heaviness of their hearts was the purchase of a house in the north-east corner of Masterton. The house was much in need of renovation, but for that reason it was just barely affordable for them. David spent every spare hour he could find repairing and modernizing the kitchen, bathroom, and main bedroom. He would like to have done more, but three rooms were a start, and Alexi was well pleased with them. She spent many hours working alongside him, sanding woodwork, and painting.

The stresses that had exploded around them left David and Alexi feeling raw, even in their attachment to each other. But working together at the house did much to build the bonding between them. They began to have glimpses of hope that all might not be not lost for their future. Maintaining the façade was so foreign to them both - they hated it, but accepted it as their only option.

Gradually, the black pall of guilt receded a little. It was still there, waiting to envelop either or both of them whenever they were reminded of it. But it didn't dominate their days quite as much as it had. One Sunday afternoon they took the Mikimiki Track into the Tararuas, walking alongside the stream, to a beautiful grassy clearing they knew. They knelt together beside the stream, pouring out their hearts to God.

"Lord God," prayed David, "we have cried out over our shame and guilt so many times. We know you forgive us, but, but…. We know we're playing a dishonest game with everyone – it's so hard. Should we tell Pastor Scott, change our wedding plans somehow? Lord, who would be helped by that? Anyway Lord, please bring us through all this somehow."

No major revelation came to them, and not much changed following their afternoon of prayer, but they did feel some small renewal of their sense of being loved and accepted by God, no matter what happened.

*

As the weeks went by, Aggie became more and more concerned. Alexi's pregnancy test had been positive. Could it have been a false positive? She didn't think so. It was clear to her that David and Alexi had somehow betrayed their ideals of coming to their marriage as virgins, and that Alexi had consequently become pregnant. Her heart ached for this young couple she loved so well.

But it seemed nothing was happening. A pregnancy wasn't something that could be kept hidden indefinitely from the

Carrington community. Aggie knew her church well enough to know its leadership would not respond with harsh judgement. A few in the church would gossip – she hoped it would be only a very few. But as wedding plans went ahead as before, as nothing became known of the issue, as nothing seemed to change, her heart grew heavy indeed. A spontaneous miscarriage perhaps? Aggie was not at all deceived by the bright exterior David and Alexi tried to maintain. She discerned they were coping with almost intolerable pain - pain that was not quite accounted for by a miscarriage. Gradually, Aggie became sure that Alexi had aborted her baby. And the realization cut her more deeply than any knife could have reached. She had prayed for Alexi all through her life, joying in her successes, aching over her losses. The tangled knot of love and grief she now carried each day was barely lighter than Alexi's own anguish.

Kathy had no knowledge of a positive pregnancy test, as Aggie did, so her worries for her daughter were less focused. But her concern that all was not well with Alexi and David continued to deepen. She talked about it sometimes with Eric.

"I just can't shake it off. Alexi's not herself, she's worried. There seems to be some shadow hanging over her. She's full of the wedding coming up. But I often get the feeling she's …. Oh, I don't know … Forcing it somehow. What do you think Eric?"

Eric couldn't quite match Kathy's womanly intuition, but he did share her concern. "You don't think there's some rift between her and David?" he asked.

"I don't know," worried Kathy. "I just don't know. She's taken Cloud riding several times recently. She always enjoyed that. But I had the impression last Saturday, that there was a 'cloud' hanging over her, and she was galloping as hard as she could to somehow shake it off, leave it behind."

They sat at the kitchen table, facing each other.

"When you've been working with David, helping him at their house, how has he seemed then?" Kathy asked.

"Hmm," responded Eric, "I've helped him up there, let's see, four times now. He's always very grateful for the help. And he seems thoughtful and, yes, I'd say cheerful. But maybe more, ah, preoccupied with his own thoughts. Not quite so fun as he used to be. I don't think I've heard him joke in quite a while."

"I haven't heard either of them talk about the Youth Group for a long time," Kathy worried. "But I suppose the house and the wedding are their main concerns just now."

"Yes, and when they're up at the house, working together, they seem happy enough with each other," said Eric thoughtfully. "I've seen them, oh, lots of times, just holding each other. I don't mean kissing and cuddling, but just hugged tight, and staring into each other's eyes. They're sharing something deep with each other."

Kathy remembered the stabs of panic she'd experienced when Alexi was about five years old. The aching anxiety her heart carried each day felt a lot like those old fears.

*

Kelly Stephenson continued to build on the faith in Christ she had discovered at Easter time. It was a step-by-step process as she gradually shed the old cynical habits, but with Kathy's ongoing friendship, she persisted. Kelly was a well-known attender at Carrington Church now. In the months following Easter, Colin Campbell became a regular visitor at Kelly's house.

Colin was now a senior sergeant with the Masterton Police. So far as anyone in the Carrington Church community knew, romance had never been a part of his life, so no-one was yet construing his friendship with Kelly as a mid-life romance. But he was definitely known as a person who cared for those on the margins of life. In Kelly's case, perhaps it was the memory of their early school days. He'd been given the hand up that he needed, but Kelly had been either unwilling or unable to accept help. Whatever the motivation, Colin was certainly a good friend and encourager to her, often attending to household maintenance tasks. Besides Kelly, Naomi also enjoyed his visits. She appreciated his quiet humor and wisdom. Sometimes he reviewed school assignments with her, suggesting small improvements.

About mid-October, Kelly's son Peter surprised the community by arriving home from Sydney. Peter had matured beyond the tearaway youth most people remembered. He'd discovered an unexpected flair as a salesman, a talent he put to good use at several car sales outlets in Sydney. After some initial poor choices, Peter learned the value of restricting his spending, and building his savings, so he returned home with a respectable bank balance.

Never-the-less, Peter was still a rather hard-nosed young man of the world. He was bemused at the way his mother and younger sister had "got religion." It wasn't such a surprise that Naomi had gone that way, but as for his mother, well, he could hardly believe she had gotten so soft. He wasn't quite sure how to relate to her – this new courtesy was so different from the old sarcasm and aggression he was used to. Strangely though, he really liked his mother's friend Colin. Peter didn't want to admit to himself that he enjoyed the company of one of these Christians, so he tried to maintain some reserve with Colin. But often he would find, in spite of himself, that he was joking or discussing something of interest with this wise, astute policeman. It was through Colin he found a job as car salesman with Fagan Motors.

*

Spring was especially beautiful that year. The daffodils and jonquils grew in such profusion, the blossom on the fruit trees promised abundant apples, peaches and apricots, and the grass seemed to be more lush and green than anyone could remember. As October merged into November, people began to remark to Alexi that summer would provide a perfect day for her wedding. The world was conspiring to provide the most beautiful setting for a beautiful couple. Alexi would laugh gaily, but inside, her heart would die another death. As January passed, and the day grew closer, she and David felt their duplicity more strongly, yet they also grew more hardened at shrugging off the guilty feelings.

250

Since that terrible night in September when their ideals shattered around them, there had been many hugs as they clung close to each other, but no more kissing, or anything remotely sexual in the way they related. As their wedding approached, each of them privately began to wonder how they would feel about connecting as a married couple. At length, David opened up his thoughts to Alexi. It was Saturday 7th of February, just one week before their big day. David had spent most of the day putting the finishing touches to the house, doing all he could to make their new home ready to receive them. After returning to his flat to shower and freshen up, he drove to Alexi's house. They were sitting now on a garden seat at the back of the house, enjoying the cool of the evening.

"Lexi," he began, "you've been amazing the way you've coped with everything over these weeks. I appreciate you!"

"I feel more wretched than amazing," responded Alexi. "But I guess we've got through so far. You've done pretty well too."

"There's something I've been thinking about." David paused for a moment, then continued, "Our first attempt at making love was a stunning failure in every way I can think of. And as from next Saturday, I guess we're supposed to carry on from where we left off. I don't know about you, but I just can't imagine …. I mean it won't be anything like it would have been … I, I just don't know how you'll be feeling, or how we're going to handle this."

"Oh David," Alexi responded, "I've been wondering and scared about all that too. Thank you for mentioning it!" She turned toward him earnestly. "David, I don't want to deny you, or, or … But when I try to think about all that, my mind just won't function. Could we, do you think, could we just go slow on all that? Could we leave it for a while? Would that be alright?"

"That's what I've been thinking Lex. Let's not rush it," David said to her.

"Really David? Could we? Really?" Alexi could hardly contain her relief.

"Do you still want to sleep together in our nice new bed?" David asked her.

"Yes David, yes I do! But would that be fair to you? Could you stand to be close in bed, but without …"

"I, I think so," replied David. "I'm not sure how it would be. But I know I don't want to rush anything."

"Oh David, thank you, thank you!" Alexi snuggled against him, tears of relief wetting her face. "Let's just get through this wedding. We can start thinking about all that later."

"Love you Lexi. Proud of you." David held her close.

As he held her, another small deposit of gladness dropped into Alexi's heart, beside her relief at their intimacy being deferred. She felt it, but in her exhausted state, she didn't quite identify it immediately. Slowly her thoughts cleared. Oh yes, David had shown leadership in mentioning the issue. He was changing. Not so long ago, he might have just let it go by without saying anything, leaving them to flounder along.

She snuggled even closer. "Thank you," she said again.

*

It was the hardest day of Alexi's life. Though a tiny part of her managed to enjoy it. The weather kept all the promises made for it – a bright blue summer sky, with hardly a cloud, and just enough breeze to stir her veil a little. She knew she was a beautiful bride, and was glad of that. She was glad of the love of family and friends, and the depth of their well-wishes. She was glad to be united with a man she loved and still respected deeply.

It was a special wedding for Pastor Scott, both because he thought of David and Alexi as a couple full of hope and promise, and because it was the last wedding he would preside over as Carrington's pastor. After many years of greatly appreciated service, he would retire at the end of February. As he led them through their vows, the tension inside David and Alexi grew. How could they deceive this man who had been such a strong friend to them, a friend they deeply respected?

The youth group were there in force, showering David and Alexi with their love and gratitude. How deep the dishonesty felt to them as they matched laugh for laugh, smile for smile, with these precious young ones.

For Alexi, the hardest part of all was playing the excited, happy bride with her bridesmaid Naomi. How proud Naomi was to take that role! How she looked up to Alexi, her friend, mentor, the one she trusted, who had prayed for her, and with her, so often. How black and wretched Alexi felt as she pretended.

Keeping up the pretense for her parents was hard too. Alexi knew that her mother suspected that all was not well. Kathy had gently probed many times, so concerned to uncover the pain she discerned in Alexi. As Kathy watched Alexi on her wedding day, she was almost reassured. Almost, but not quite. Her mother's heart knew that this was not quite the day she had hoped for her beautiful daughter. Alexi saw her mother watching her once or twice, with an unreadable expression. And her heart wrenched once again in guilt and grief.

Kathy couldn't hide the worry she felt as she and Eric chatted with Terry and Esther, David's parents down from Auckland. Esther moved to take Kathy's hand in both of hers.

"I know Kathy, we feel it too. You see them more, so you catch the undercurrent more, whatever it is."

Kathy nodded, managing to blink back a tear. Terry's arm rested across Esther's shoulders; Eric's arm encircled Kathy. The worry hung between them.

"We still don't know what this shadow is about," Eric said at last. "But today, we each support our children as best we can."

*

To Alexi, the reception seemed to stretch on interminably. At long last, the speeches, the chatter, the well-wishes and congratulations began to wind towards an end. The guests began to take their leave. At most gatherings, Auntie Aggie would be among the first to take her leave, but today something kept her until nearly the last. At length, she approached David and

Alexi as they stood beside the exit.

"You're such a beautiful bride my dear," she said to
Alexi, reaching to take both of her hands. Aggie's smile was
gentle, her voice soft. Yet Alexi had never been more aware of the
wells of pain hiding behind those grey eyes. "You've been special
to me ever since I held you as a baby," she told Alexi. "I've
prayed for you most days of your life. And since this wonderful
man came on the scene…" She turned her eyes toward David.
"Since then, I've prayed most days for both of you. I love you
both."

A deep response stirred in both David and Alexi. Neither
of them really understood it, but both knew Auntie Aggie spoke
truth from her heart. What would she think if she knew what they
knew?

"Thank you. Thank you for coming." They spoke almost
in unison. And both were aware that their response was no mere
formality. Their appreciation for her presence, and her words,
came from somewhere deep within them.

"Alexi, I still have Bagley, the teddy you gave me when
you were five years old. That really touched me." Auntie Aggie's
eyes twinkled as she spoke.

Then one last sentence before taking her leave. "You're
welcome at The Barn any time." She dropped Alexi's hands and
was gone.

David and Alexi looked at each other. It was the first
time there had ever been any acknowledgement of their visits.

*

David had rented a house on the bank of the Akatarawa
River, nestled into its bush-covered valley north of Upper Hutt. It
was only about two hour's drive from Masterton, but it felt out-
of-the-way, quiet and restful. Alexi and David welcomed the
respite more than they could have imagined. For the first two
days they did little but lie dozing on their bed, letting the stress
and anxiety of the last weeks slowly seep out of them. The next

day they drove further into the hills, emerging at last on the western side of the range, at the little town of Waikanae. They spent the day browsing and snacking at the shops, before returning to rest again. Another day they spent on the beach at Waikanae. Then there were some bush trails to explore along the river. By the end of the week, they were feeling they had done enough relaxing, and were getting restless. The progress they had made on their house was encouraging - they were looking forward to their return, to settling in, and making a start on the next renovation project.

On Sunday they found a church service in Upper Hutt that helped refresh their spirits. Afterwards, they sat over lunch at a small café.

"Well Lex, have you done enough relaxing? Do you feel like getting back home? We can still have a relaxing week at home before we get back to work again."

"I do feel a bit restless now," agreed Alexi. "Yes, let's go home tomorrow. I want us to be together in our house."

They didn't hurry, but arrived home by mid-afternoon on Monday. They stood in their new kitchen, holding each other closely.

"From this day forward," David whispered in Alexi's ear. "For better, for worse. Dear Lord, please may it be for better."

Chapter 26

Alexi's Despair.

Gradually, friends noticed changes in David and Alexi. In the months leading up to their marriage, they had worked hard at being the same cheerful, outgoing Christian couple they had always been. But as they settled into married life, maintaining the old buoyancy became just too costly.

The change wasn't dramatic. Faith in God was still foundational for each of them, sustaining and motivating them. But gradually they withdrew from leadership roles. Resigning from leadership in the youth group came first. Then in March, Alexi resigned from Mission Connection.

"I can't do it any more David," she said one evening as they sat at dinner. "It was a super job. I loved developing Mission Connection. There was always some action going on. I hate to leave. But it isn't me anymore. I'm not the person I pretend to be while I'm there. I have to escape!"

She took a job as sales assistant at Leighton Furnishings. Alexi's job change came as a surprise to those who knew her – selling furnishings didn't seem like her, not nearly as much as her role at Mission Connection. So, people began to wonder.

For Kathy, the job change was the strongest confirmation yet that Alexi was troubled. She just knew it wouldn't have happened if their daughter was still her energetic, cheerful self. Alexi phoned one day, trying to drop the news casually into her conversation. Her mother was not at all deceived, and spent the rest of the day with tears frequently welling in her eyes. Eric noticed her sadness as soon as he came in after work.

As they sat at dinner, Eric asked, "You feeling sad Honey? What's up?"

Kathy began to tear up again. "Alexi called today. She

told me she left Mission Connection, and she's working now at Leightons, selling curtain material and carpets. Eric, what's going on with her?"

"What did she say about it? Why's she done that?"

"She said she just needed a change. To broaden her experience, try something different. But if that was all, she would have been chatting about this before. She wouldn't have just suddenly gone ahead like that."

Eric frowned. He was worried about whatever was going on with Alexi, and he was worried about the way Kathy was becoming so burdened.

"Lexi's been different for a long time now," agreed Hannah. "She's often moody, until she catches you looking at her, and then she puts on her smiley face again."

Ted looked at the anxious faces around the table. He too knew that something unexplained had happened with Alexi, but he wasn't sure what to say. He tried to lighten the atmosphere with a small joke. "Well, I guess Lexi's an old married lady now."

Eric spoke again. "Let's all pray right now for her and David. And kids, in your own prayer times, please keep your sister in your prayers."

Four heads bowed, and each prayed out of aching hearts for Alexi and for David.

When the dinner dishes were cleared, and the kitchen tidied, Eric and Kathy sat down together again.

"Eric, I want to go over there and confront her." Kathy's eyes were beseeching. "We've often asked her what's troubling her, but this is just too much. It's like she's giving us obvious signs, and we're not taking them up, not in a direct way."

Eric's brow furrowed again. "Kathy my love, we can't force her. We've invited her many times to confide in us. I just don't feel we can push her." His arm went around her shoulders as Kathy leaned in close to him. Her face was against his chest.

"I just feel we have to do something Eric." Kathy spoke haltingly.

"Honey," he replied after a pause, "maybe we should go see her, and just ask her about her new job. And tell her again how much we love her. That we're always there for her, especially if there's any way she needs our support."

"Could we Eric? Yes, we could at least do that, couldn't we?"

"Yes. We need to remember that David is her first line of support now. We need to be careful not to infringe on that. But we can let her know she's still our daughter, and we care about her."

David wasn't home when Eric and Kathy arrived. Alexi was in the kitchen.

"Hello, it's just us!" Kathy called, as she knocked, then opened the door.

"Hi Mum. Hello Dad. Come in!" Alexi willed a sparkle into her eyes, a smile to her face.

"We wanted to hear about your new job," Kathy said, as they all took a seat at the table.

"Well, I've only had three days," replied Alexi, managing a small laugh. "I'm still getting to know the ropes. But it's fun learning something new. And I like meeting the customers."

They chatted for a few minutes about Alexi's new experiences, laughing a little over her initial mistakes. There came a lull in the conversation. Kathy's head was bowed for a few moments, then she looked across the table to Alexi.

"Lexi, Lexi my treasure." Her voice quavered, and tears came to her eyes again. "You know how much we love you. If there's any way we can be a blessing, a help to you, you only have to ask."

Alexi said nothing. Tears came to her eyes too. Kathy pushed her chair back, and hurried around the table. Alexi rose to meet her. They threw their arms around each other. Eric joined them, and they moved to include him in their embrace.

Alexi was just a hair's breadth from breaking down completely, confiding to them all the agony. If David had been there to join with her, she would have. It seemed like a long time they stood holding each other.

Eventually, Alexi whispered, "Thank you Mum. Thank you, Dad. I appreciate that. I love you too."

As they drove home, it was clear to Eric and Kathy that Alexi had been on the edge of opening up to them. It cut their hearts afresh that she still resisted. But for the first time, she hadn't brushed off their concern. She hadn't said anything, but her tears had been a kind of admission. They were strangely comforted.

*

In the following days as Kathy brooded and prayed, she was reminded more often of the strange panic, the fear for Alexi's safety that came to her several times, all those years ago, about the time Alexi started school. She remembered that those fears were somehow linked with Auntie Aggie, and the foreshadowing Aggie had experienced following Alexi's birth. She'd seen a kind of vision of something dark and troubling, lying in her daughter's future. Kathy had never asked Aggie what she saw that day, but she was fairly sure there was nothing specific or detailed about it. She did know it was real, and that they were now living in it.

This realization brought more tears each day as Kathy prayed for Alexi and David. But it also brought some comfort. Somehow, she knew that there was hope, that whatever this chapter contained, it would have an ending.

*

The days lengthened into weeks, and still David and Alexi hadn't returned to the subject of their married intimacy. They did still find comfort in being close to each other. And so in bed together, they would hold each other, snuggling close. Gradually their intimacy increased, until finally their union was completed. Their lovemaking became a source of comfort to them, deepening the bond between them. At the same time, there was still a sense of reserve, a holding back from fully releasing their passion for each other. Alexi especially was never able to fully abandon herself to David, so her orgasm remained just out of reach.

The Barn remained a place of refuge for them both. Alexi went there more frequently, to sit, soaking up the cool, reverent atmosphere, finding some salve for her loss and grief. Aggie would see her come and go about every two weeks. David would accompany her less frequently. As Aggie watched them, she knew God was still active with them, gradually bringing them to a place where their wounds would be healed. Her prayers for them were encouraged.

For Alexi, the prompting to confide in Auntie Aggie persisted. It was strange. On the one hand, their connection with Auntie Aggie remained rather slight. They almost never spoke with her. On the other hand, their bond with her did have a feeling of depth, a depth that had been strengthened by the few words that had passed between the three of them at their wedding. And so for Alexi, whenever the burden of guilt seemed to press in on her, a quiet Voice, almost imperceptible, somewhere deep in her spirit would whisper, "Go talk to Auntie Aggie about it." The thought never made any more sense than it ever had, and it was slight enough to be brushed aside. So Alexi never sought her out.

At the end of May, just a few months after their first wedding anniversary, David and Alexi finished renovating the interior of their house. They were proud of their efforts, and were justly congratulated by friends and family. As though in celebration of their achievement, Alexi discovered her pregnancy. How different it was for them, being able to delight in their news. It brought a new lease of life for them. And of course, the tidings brought a massive lift to Kathy's spirit.

As with most events in her life, Alexi's feelings about the new life stirring within her were mixed. She was so glad they would have a child to care for. She was glad of the delight their respective parents felt at the prospect of becoming grandparents. But there was also the foreboding that she was an unworthy person to take on responsibility for a precious new life. So, she alternately exulted and fretted.

David's attention turned to bringing the exterior of their house up to standard, along with the lawns, driveways, paths and gardens. He still had about a year's work to do before all was in order. He hoped to have most of it completed before baby arrived.

*

Collin Campbell and Kelly Stephenson continued as fast friends. By now their friendship was definitely seen by all as a romance. But they were not rushing towards marriage. Colin had been a Christian for many years now, but he well remembered how the journey had been for him, growing out of the thoughtless, rebellious ways of his youth. Kelly had spent many years as a self-centered, cynical adult, so she especially wanted to make sure her new life in Jesus was well-established before committing herself to Colin. Finally, it was Colin who said to her, "Kelly, neither of us is perfect, and we never will be this side of heaven. Let's spend the rest of our lives growing together!"

The wedding date was set for late November. Naomi was delighted that Colin was to be her step-dad. She was part of the work force now, working as an apprentice auto electrician. It was an unusual choice for a girl, but Naomi didn't fit the usual molds. She didn't anticipate a career in auto electronics, but decided it would be useful work experience while she saved to go on to a university education. Colin already seemed a real father-figure to her.

Peter's friendship with Colin had grown, though the transition to thinking of him as step-father did not sit well. He was relieved that he and Colin could joke about the coming change. Kelly's daughter Debra was also back from Australia – she was living with her boyfriend in Levin, on the western side of the Tararua Range. It was about a two-hour drive for her to visit her mother, so she and Colin met only infrequently.

For Colin's part, he was delighted that his life would be joined with his firm friend Kelly, and that he would have at least some kind of fatherly role with her three children. He had never married, so he didn't have children of his own. He had no illusions about having all the formative influence of a father on these three young adults, but he felt he already loved them in a special way. He hoped and prayed that an affectionate friendship would grow with each of them.

Through their friendship with Naomi, David and Alexi found themselves being drawn also into the circle of Colin and Kelly's friendship. When November came around, they were among the well-wishers who celebrated the marriage of Mr. and Mrs. Colin Campbell.

*

David and Alexi's son Bryce was born almost two weeks after their second wedding anniversary. It was a normal birth, meaning that it was long, painful, and joyful for Alexi. And a long, anxious, joyful, and mind-blowing experience for David. What awe they felt as they watched Bryce cradled in Alexi's arms.

But Alexi also found another thought playing at the edge of her mind. A thought or a feeling? It was a hint of irritation, irritation at David being there at Bryce's birth. What business did he have watching the intimacy of her delivery, the pain, the flushed face, the pushing, trying to control her breathing? Alexi was startled and guilty as she recognized her thoughts. Of course David would be with her, supporting her. She loved him, admired him. He joined her in grateful amazement at the birth of their son. She shouldered the feeling aside, and turned to smile at David.

In the coming weeks, Alexi felt her whole attention being absorbed by her baby. The need for her to recover emotionally and physically, along with Bryce's demands for attention, seemed as much as she could cope with. She realized that David was dropping out of her focus. She managed to think at least a little of meals and laundry, but found she was leaving most household tasks to him. She was concerned at what was happening, and mentioned it to Kathy when she visited.

"It's natural honey, for most of your attention to be on your baby, at least for a little while. But it's good that you realize what's happening, and choose to direct some attention to David as well. He's doing a lot for you at present, but as you recover, you'll be able to take up more of the tasks yourself." Kathy smiled at her. "You do need to let him know that he's still number one."

Over the coming months, Alexi did recover, becoming more like the Alexi David had known before Bryce's birth. But it was not quite the same. Something was starting to slip.

It was mostly to do with the ongoing shame that lay at the bottom of their hearts. Like black, oily bilge water gradually rusting the steel structure of a ship. At first, they had found reassurance and encouragement from each other. Their closeness had helped them get through. But now the blackness was infecting even their marriage. It was almost imperceptible at first, and very gradual.

Up until now, lying close to David in bed was something Alexi looked forward to. But now it didn't feel the same. She knew that since their marriage, she'd not become a fully sexual wife, but up until now, sex had been nice, a close, bonding thing. Why was it beginning to feel like a chore? It wasn't long before David noticed the change in her. He was confused and hurt.

Both David and Alexi fought the growing sense of estrangement. They each prayed earnestly, and tried to mend things between them. But the arguments slowly became more frequent. Occasionally they talked of what was happening, but they didn't seem to be able to do anything that really made a difference.

There were just a few bright spots of encouragement in their lives. One of these was their visits to Colin and Kelly's house. Naomi would usually be there, and sometimes Peter. There seemed to be something solid and reassuring about the conversation and friendship in that house. They would come home feeling as though a little of the cloud had lightened.

*

263

Bryce was two and a half, and Alexi became pregnant again. They were managing to hold their marriage together – it wasn't as though they were constantly screaming at each other. It was more like colorless endurance, going from one day to the next, without much joy or enthusiasm.

Alexi hadn't been going to The Barn so frequently, though every few weeks she would seek solace there. The thought of a new child coming prompted her to seek out her refuge more frequently again. "Lord," she would pray, "why are we drifting apart? How can we bring another child into this? Please help us!"

She and David tried to keep their struggles out of Bryce's sight, but Alexi could see he was being affected by the tension between them.

*

David was present again when Alexi delivered their daughter Chloe. In the following weeks, Alexi fought with all her courage to keep from pushing David aside, as Chloe captured her attention. To her credit, she had some success – at least David was no more marginalized than he had been following Bryce's birth.

*

Somehow, Alexi and David kept going. Chloe was ten months old when it happened. It was Friday afternoon, the 5th of February, just nine days before their sixth wedding anniversary. Alexi wasn't sure what affected her that day, but suddenly she knew she couldn't go on another day. The Voice whispered to her again, "Go talk to Auntie Aggie." She went to the phone, and called her mother.

"Mum, something's come up. Can you mind the children for me until David gets home? Please?"

264

"Ah, yes, that will be fine. What's happened?" asked Kathy.

"Mum, I can't tell you about it right now. I'll be right over with the children. See you soon."

Kathy could hear the urgency in Alexi's voice. She had no idea what was happening, but she immediately called Eric at work.

"Eric, Alexi just called to ask me to mind the children. She didn't say what's happening, but she sounded distraught. Something's going on. Please pray."

"Sure Kathy," responded Eric. "Do you want me to come home?"

"No, I'll be alright. She's just dropping the children off. I don't know where she's going. She said until David gets home."

A few minutes later, Alexi arrived. Kathy was her usual welcoming self to the children – they were always happy to visit her. And she looked inquiringly at Alexi.

"Later Mum," was all Alexi said. "Thanks so much for looking after the children for me." And she was gone.

It was just a short drive from Te Whiti to Dalefield Road. This time Alexi meant to find Auntie Aggie. She parked the car, and walked first to The Barn. She would go in for just a few minutes, to calm herself a little. Then she meant to walk over to the cottage, and knock on the door.

Alexi opened the door of The Barn, and walked inside. Auntie Aggie sat at the table. A steaming teapot was before her, with two fine china cups on their saucers.

"Come in my dear," she said to Alexi. "I've been expecting you."

Chapter 27

A Long-deferred Conversation.

Alexi blinked. "What do you mean, you were expecting me? How did you know I would come today?"

"I've been praying for you all day, precious one. The Lord told me you would come about now."

"Precious one," muttered Alexi. "Precious one! You wouldn't call me precious if you knew who I really am."

Aggie smiled at her. "Would you like some tea? It's jasmine." She picked up the teapot, and began to pour the golden liquid into the two cups. Alexi stared at her. Suddenly, years of defenses crumpled. Alexi's lip quivered. She found herself kneeling on the floor, her elbows on a soft chair, her head in her hands, sobs shaking her whole body.

Aggie knelt on the floor beside her. Her hand stroked Alexi's back, a soft, crooning song flowing from her, with words Alexi didn't know. Gradually the sobbing quieted.

"Does David know where you are? Where the children are?" asked Auntie Aggie. Alexi shook her head. "I think you'd better call and tell him you're with me. The children are with your mother, right? Let him know that too. And ask him to come join us when he finishes work."

Alexi moved to the table, and picked up one of the cups. She took some soothing sips. Then, obediently, she walked to the phone extension on the wall, and dialed David's number. Thankfully, he was not out at one of the parks or gardens.

"David," began Alexi as he answered, "I'm at The Barn, with Auntie Aggie." She stopped, trying to corral her thoughts, find the words. "David, suddenly it got too much. I can't live with it all any more. I think I'm going to tell her. Everything."

David said nothing. Seconds passed. Alexi wondered if

266

their phone connection had failed. She was about to speak again, when David said, "Thank God Lexi! Thank God! Shall I come now?"

"Auntie Aggie said to join us when you finish work. Can you come here then? The children are with Mum."

"Can I get through the next two hours, until five o'clock?" responded David. "I suppose I can." Something like a sob escaped him. "Alexi, God bless you. God bless Aggie. God bless us. I don't know …. I'm not sure what this means for us, but I'm with you in this. I, I love you Lex." David hadn't told her that for a while, but he meant it with all his heart.

While Alexi was talking with David, Aggie pushed two of the soft, comfortable chairs closer together, and placed a small table between them, where she set their teacups. She sat in one of the chairs sipping her tea. Alexi took the other chair.

"Dear Lexi," Auntie Aggie said softly. "How burdened with pain you've been, for so long. How glad I am that you've come at last."

Alexi sat with bowed head. Auntie Aggie's words raised half-formed questions in her mind. But instead of pursuing them, she began to focus on how to begin her story. She raised her head, looking intently at Auntie Aggie.

"A few months before our wedding – it was in September – David and I had sex." Not the slightest flicker of surprise, shock, or judgement disturbed the grey eyes watching her. Just the same flow of love, filling the distance between them. Alexi was shaken. Her eyes dropped again as she continued.

"We didn't mean to. We, we hadn't planned it. I just got set off, and suddenly, I was all over him, and, and it happened. It was awful."

A small sigh escaped Aggie. A sympathetic click of her tongue. "You'd been troubled for a long time before September," she said. "Something was bothering you, almost from the beginning of your relationship with David."

"How did you know that?" Alexi wanted to know.

"You came up here often. After you left, I'd go sit in the seat where you'd been sitting, and pray for you. God doesn't show me everything – I'm not nearly wise enough for that. But he does trust me with some things. I didn't know what was troubling you, but I knew you were troubled, and I knew you sometimes thought of coming to talk to me about it."

Alexi's eyes opened wide, and her spine tingled a little. If only she'd come!

"So," Auntie Aggie continued, "was it about physical contact with David? Was that what was concerning you?"

"Yes!" Alexi replied. "Well, no! I mean we were just kissing, some cuddling – only what everyone seems to think is normal. We weren't …."

"But the kissing and cuddling were bothering you? And everyone seems to think that's normal, so you didn't know what to think. And then something happened that set you off, and bam! You fell in?"

Alexi nodded. "It was awful," she said again. "We were bumbling, hurried, not knowing what we were doing, just awful. And knowing we had betrayed ourselves was far more awful." Her eyes flashed a little as she looked up. "I was so angry! I didn't know it was possible to be so angry! I was furious at David for taking my virginity. And I was just as furious with myself, maybe even more furious, that I goaded him into it."

The summer's day outside was warm and drowsy. But the Barn, nestling near the cover of the bush, was cooler, quiet, still.

Alexi continued. "At first I thought I would have to change everything. I didn't want to just go ahead, dressed as a bride, as though nothing had happened. It felt false. Everyone thought we were just the ideal Christian couple. And especially the Youth Group kids – we taught them so much about being proud of their sexuality. And about carefully, gladly guarding it until they were married. What would it do to them if they found out we weren't keeping our own advice? And Naomi!" Her voice was rising in pitch, her cheeks becoming flushed. "Do you know how many hours I spent talking and praying with Naomi, guiding her away from being promiscuous? She had no idea of her own value, not until she came to Youth Group. What would I say to her?"

Auntie Aggie's head was nodding in sympathy. "Yes,

Lexi dear. It was hard for you. Very hard."

"So we decided to tough it out, just go on and pretend nothing had happened."

Alexi sat hunched in her chair. The gurgling of the stream could be heard in the quietness. The wind rustled the leaves outside, and every now and again a bird song would penetrate to where she sat.

Auntie Aggie wanted to say something, to soften the next part for Alexi... But she knew she must not. She sat waiting.

Alexi stood, moved restlessly to the table, then turned and came back to stand in front of Auntie Aggie. She was sure the love in those eyes would fade as she continued her confession. Unconsciously, she prepared herself for rejection.

"Well," she resumed at last, "there's more. Two weeks later, I missed my period. I got a pregnancy test. It confirmed I was pregnant."

She stared at Auntie Aggie, waiting for the shock, the withdrawal. It wasn't there. She plunged ahead.

"Now can you imagine how we felt! If just having sex was going to blow everything wide open, what would it do when my belly started swelling? Can you imagine that?" Alexi was almost shouting.

Auntie Aggie's face had become very solemn. But even now, no rejection, no accusation tempered the softness of her gaze.

Still Alexi stood in front of Auntie Aggie, her head drooping now to her chest. Her voice dropped to little more than a whisper.

"I got rid of it. I had an abortion."

Alexi's eyes were closed. She didn't want to see the condemnation.

Auntie Aggie rose to her feet. She stood facing Alexi. "I know, Alexi dear. I know."

Alexi's eyes snapped open. "You know? How could you know?

"You told me. When you showed David the pregnancy test card, you left it on the table for me."

Alexi could hardly have been more incredulous. "You've

known since the beginning? But you didn't .... At our wedding, you told us you loved us!"

"I do love you both. I love you very much. I've carried your secret every day. It's been almost as much agony for me as it's been for you." As she spoke, a slow, one-by-one march of tears began in the corners of her eyes, trickling down to her chin.

Alexi whirled, and began striding about the room. Her arms were crossed in front of her, hugging her chest. Finally, she stopped in front of Auntie Aggie again.

"You knew! You knew all along, and, and you didn't hate us?"

Alexi dropped to her knees again, crying, arms on the chair, head in her hands. Auntie Aggie knelt beside her again, with a hand on her head. Alexi reached up and drew the hand down into her own hands. She wept for a very long time, holding onto that hand as though she would never let it go. Aggie's tears continued to trickle too. One by one, one by one.

So they stayed until the sound of David's car was heard outside. Alexi rose to her feet. She flew to him as he came through the door, hugging him tight. His arms went around her.

"I told her. But David! She already knew! She's known all along! Remember when I showed you the pregnancy test? I accidentally left it behind. I came right back for it, and I thought she hadn't seen it. But she did! She's known all along! And, and it's like she kind of understands. She's not blaming us! David, I'm so, so glad I came here today."

Auntie Aggie was moving past them towards the door, intending to leave them alone for a while. But David reached out, and drew her into their embrace. Hugging Auntie Aggie? What an unthinkable idea! Yet, here they were, and it seemed the most natural thing they had done for a long while. Auntie Aggie seemed to think so too. Although the succession of tears still fell from her eyes, joy was in her face, like the first rays of the sun peeping over a hedgerow.

David lifted his face to look at her. "Thank you, thank you, thank you," he repeated over and over and over.

At length, Auntie Aggie stepped back. "Alright my dears, we have some logistics to attend to. And we have more to talk about yet, so I suggest you stay here the night. Lexi, I guess your mother won't object to looking after the children for the night. But she'll probably need to go to your house and get night clothes and such for them. Can she let herself in to get what she needs?"

Stay the night at Auntie Aggie's cottage? Wonder upon wonder!

"Yes," replied Alexi, "she knows where the key is hidden outside."

"I'll call your mum, and let her know where you are. I'm sure she'll be happy to keep the children with her." Aggie left David and Alexi to themselves, going back to her cottage to use the phone there.

Kathy was beginning to be concerned, so she jumped up quickly when her phone rang. She was surprised to hear Aggie's voice.

"Hello Kathy! Alexi and David are here with me. Kathy, I know you've been worried about them for a long, long time. And so have I – we've all been praying for them ever so much. Well, they've started talking about it all at last. The dam has broken. I know your mother's heart must be stabbed that they didn't come to you first. But they'll want to bring you and Eric up to date as soon as they can. Kathy, are you okay? This must be really unexpected for you!"

"Yes," answered Kathy slowly. "Yes, yes, we've been praying for this for so long. Oh, my heart is all of a whirl! I'm, I'm glad you're looking after them Aggie."

"I'm not sure how this is going to work," Aggie resumed, "I'll be in touch again tomorrow. But in the meantime, what they need most is some rest. I've invited them to stay with me for the night. Can you look after the children? Alexi said you can let yourself into their house if you need to go and get anything for them."

"Yes, yes, we can do that," Kathy responded. "And Aggie, thank you so much for taking care of them." She was crying now. "Oh, this is such blessed news! Thank you, thank you so much!"

Aggie returned to The Barn. "All is well," she told David

and Alexi, "your mum will look after the children overnight. Come and help me get a meal together for us, and make sure my guest room is ready for you."

The next hour was spent preparing a light meal, eating together, clearing and washing dishes. Then they were delighting in Auntie Aggie's beautiful guest room, discovering fragrant soaps and large soft towels, turning down bedcovers. Aggie realized with a pang of guilt, that her guest room hadn't been used in nearly thirty years, since before Ky's death.

They sat together in the lounge room as the daylight faded. David and Alexi were still pondering the kindness they were being shown, even though Auntie Aggie had known their terrible secret from the start.

"Time for some sound sleep now," she told them. "Tomorrow we can talk of what happens next, but first I think you'll sleep better than you have for – for how long? Years?"

And so, it was. David and Alexi cuddled up close, feeling the softness of their pillows, the cool touch of the sheets. They cried tears of relief, and gratitude, and apprehension for what might come next. A small glow of hope was rekindled in their hearts.

*

In the morning, they all sat at breakfast on Auntie Aggie's veranda. Afterwards, Alexi always remembered the fragrance of the clematis flowers, dancing bright blue among the dark green leaves.

"Well my dears," began Auntie Aggie as they finished eating, "the wound that has been killing you for so long, has been uncovered. It's time for healing to begin. There are a number of people you deceived, so you need to think about coming clean with them."

David and Alexi both knew that she spoke the truth, though so far, their thoughts hadn't moved ahead that far. Alexi especially wanted to resist confessing to anyone else. Auntie

Aggie had embraced them with love – would others be so loving? She drew a deep breath, before nodding in agreement.

"Pastor Scott was pastor at the time – he married you. So I think he is the first one we need to sit down with. Then he can join us in discussing what else needs to be done."

David and Alexi glanced at each other. Their hearts were heavy, yet hopeful. They had great respect for Pastor Scott. Again, they didn't speak, but nodded soberly.

Auntie Aggie continued. "Alexi, your parents know that the hurts are being broken open. I think we shouldn't keep them in suspense any longer. What say I see if they, and Pastor Scott, can join us here, say in about an hour's time?"

"Yes," responded Alexi. "And, and I need to confess to Hannah and Ted too."

"You do," Auntie Aggie agreed, "though maybe later? I thought they might be able to watch Bryce and Chloe while your Mum and Dad come here."

So, it was arranged. Pastor Scott was surprised, but he had long been concerned about the cloud over David and Alexi. How glad he was that at last they wanted to talk about it. Eric and Kathy were almost out the door before Aggie had finished inviting them. Hannah and Ted were a little reluctant at first to spend their Saturday looking after their nephew and niece, but when they understood it was about David and Alexi finally opening up, they were glad to help.

Aggie arranged six chairs in a circle in The Barn. Pastor Scott arrived just ahead of Eric and Kathy. Scott hadn't met David and Alexi for some time – he hugged and greeted them warmly. And of course, hugs from Eric and Kathy were tearful, joyful, prolonged. Soon they were seated in their circle.

Alexi took a deep breath, and began their story. Again, without putting blame on David, she described herself as being "set off", so that they ended up having sex. She described how devastated and ashamed they were, so that owning up seemed just too big an ordeal.

Kathy couldn't help breaking in. "Lexi, we wouldn't have condemned you! You could have come to us!"

"I know Mum," Alexi cried. "But it wasn't just you. If

we owned up, it meant everything changed. I wouldn't wear my white wedding dress. I know, that wasn't everything. It was huge for me, but I could have coped with things like that. But the thing was, we were on such a pedestal, everyone saw us as the great example of the young Christian couple. And we had tried to be! All our work with the young people! How let down would they be if they knew we didn't practice what we preached!"

Alexi paused for a moment before continuing. "So, we decided to push through without saying anything. It was selfish in a way, wanting to have the wedding and all, just as we were planning it. But really, we just couldn't face the letdown we would cause the kids."

Alexi paused again, and again, Kathy started to respond. But Alexi interrupted.

"Wait Mum! There's more."

Kathy sat back again, dread welling inside her. What more could there be?

Alexi stared at a spot on the floor, in the center of the circle. "Two weeks later, I found I was pregnant." Silence crashed about them all. Alexi raised her head again. "It was too much!" she cried aloud. "We couldn't take it!" Then, in a flat, broken voice, "I aborted the baby."

Eric and Kathy were frozen. She aborted her baby! Never, never, had Kathy imagined that her daughter would sit, broken before her, and she would sit immobilized, unable to go to her, to comfort her. But this! This! She aborted her baby! She aborted my grandbaby! The thought was unworthy, but it stabbed her heart anyway. Alexi sat, hunched over in her chair, head down. David moved closer to her, his arm over her shoulders.

Eventually, Eric stood, and moved to Alexi. He took her hands, and raised her to her feet. Then he moved around her, sliding into her chair. He gathered her to him, sitting her on his lap, pulling her head down on his shoulder.

"Lexi, my precious one. Lexi, I love you sweetheart." He crooned to her, as he had when she was a baby. She curled up in her Daddy's strong embrace. Mechanically, Kathy followed. She leaned over Alexi, kissing her head, murmuring, "Lexi, Lexi." But there was no flood of acceptance for her anguished daughter.

Her heart was just too stunned. They both knew it.

Soon, Alexi pulled herself up from her father's lap. She moved to stand before Pastor Scott. David rose, and stood beside her.

"Pastor, I deceived you. I lied to you. Not by what I said, but by what I didn't say. Can you forgive me?"

Scott Lampton's face was more serious than they had ever seen it. Eventually, he spoke. "You have both acted grievously. Grievously. But I see the depth of your sorrow. I hear your confession. God has forgiven you. I can do no less." His somber expression relaxed a little as he rose to his feet, and stretched his arms around them.

Shortly, everyone resumed their seats. They sat immersed in their own thoughts and prayers. Soon, Pastor Scott spoke again.

"David, Alexi, you have done right in making this confession. It opens the door for you to move on, to be restored. You know, The Book of James in the Bible tells us to confess our sins to each other, and pray for each other, so that we may be healed. David, Alexi, you confessed your sin long ago to God, and were forgiven. But it continued to hurt you, to grind you down. Now the day has come to confess to those who have been affected, to those who love you, so that we can join to pray for you, so that you can begin at last to be healed."

He paused, while the others present absorbed his words. Alexi especially was pondering. Forgiven. Healed.

"You know Pastor," she murmured, "over and over I've wondered - if God forgives my sin, why am I still so bowed down by it? That helps me understand."

He nodded and smiled at her. "For that reason, I would like to suggest we hold a small service of confession and restoration at the church. A memorial service, that marks the beginning of something new for the two of you. Not anything big – just the people who have been affected by this. We can talk about who you want to be there. The reason we have ceremonies is to mark new beginnings. This needs to be a new beginning for you two."

They all discussed the idea of a confession and renewal

service, and who would be invited to attend. They set Thursday evening as the best date. David said he would phone his parents, and see if they could come down for Thursday evening.

"Hannah and Ted need to come", said Alexi, "though I want to tell them personally first. And Naomi – I have to talk to her. She will be the hardest. She trusted me so much. I feel like I was more a hypocrite to her than to anyone."

"What about the rest of the youth group?" asked David. "We let them all down really."

"Yes," responded Pastor Scott, "but many of them have grown beyond youth group by now. The ones who were affected are not there anymore." He turned towards David. "David, so far Alexi has done most of the talking. I'm wondering what you have to say about all this. What part will you play in the service?"

"Pastor, you're right," responded David, "Alexi has done most of the talking so far. But I'm realizing that the responsibility is principally mine. I'm her husband. The buck stops with me. I have much to confess and repent of. You will definitely hear from me on Thursday evening."

He turned towards Alexi. "Lexi, you've been more than fair to me, the way you've described it all. But I pledge to you, that in the future, I will be a stronger man for you than I have ever been." His head bowed. "Lex, I'm so sorry for the way I've let you down." Alexi watched him in wonder, hope, gratitude. His gaze was filled with love and resolve.

Pastor Scott gave an approving nod.

"And with that in mind," David continued, "I think I would like to have the Youth Group there. I know that makes it much bigger, especially if they all come. And most of them don't know us now – they're new since we were part of the scene. But I have the feeling this could be quite powerful for the young people. What do you think Lex?"

Alexi considered. "I see what you mean David. It feels overpowering, but I think you're right. That means it should be announced at youth group tonight." She bowed her head. "Oh Lord, may our bitter path become someone else's inspiration."

"What about Colin and Kelly?" asked David. "They've become good friends to us. I'm sure they knew something was wrong, but they've never grilled us."

"Yes," agreed Alexi. "I would like to include them."

Soon afterwards, Auntie Aggie's guests began to disperse. David and Alexi wondered at the new bond that had developed with her, and thanked her many times over for her love and hospitality. They left with Eric and Kathy. David would collect the children and take them home, while Alexi would sit down with Hannah and Ted, and make her confession to them.

It was a sobering account for her sister and brother. They had always looked up to Alexi, and were shaken to hear her story. However, they were impressed by the humility of their big sister, coming to them to confess her wrongs, and ask their forgiveness. Soon they were hugging her, and crying together, as they told her they still loved her, and believed in her.

"Now for Naomi," thought Alexi, as she took her leave. "Lord help me!"

Colin and Kelly were pleased to see her, and a little surprised when she asked to talk with Naomi privately. Soon she and Naomi were sitting in the lounge room, with doors closed.

As Alexi sat, trying to collect her thoughts, she broke down. "Naomi, Naomi," she sobbed, "I'm sorry! I'm so sorry!"

Naomi was startled. "Lexi, what are you saying? What do you have to be sorry about?"

"I, I wasn't honest with you. I've always loved you so much, tried to help you, and pray for you, to be a good example to you. And then, something really bad happened. And I should have confessed to you that I messed up. But I just couldn't bring myself to let you down, when you had so much confidence in me."

Slowly, simply, Alexi told her story. When she got to admitting she aborted her baby, she broke down again. "I did a wicked thing. I thought of you, and all my words to you about being glad and proud to be a woman, keeping yourself against the time when you'd give yourself to the right man – oh Naomi, how hollow my words sounded."

Naomi sat staring at Alexi, her face expressionless.

"And when it came to the wedding," Alexi continued. "I went on pretending to be glad and carefree, like any young bride.

I pretended to you, as well as everyone else. I'm so ashamed."

A part of Naomi could see how distressed Alexi was, and wanted to forgive and console her. But she was deeply wounded. Her friend, the one she looked up to and trusted, had deceived her.

"Alexi, do you know how proud I was to be your bridesmaid? You're right, I did look up to you. I trusted you. And you were pretending?"

Alexi nodded miserably.

Naomi felt as though a large part of her world had just collapsed. "Thank you for coming to tell me," she said at last.

Alexi dropped to her knees. "Naomi, on Thursday night at the church there's to be a special little service. It's about David and me making confession to all the people we've let down. Naomi, please say you'll come! Please! Please come!"

Naomi nodded her head in a way that communicated neither agreement nor refusal.

"And Naomi, if you want to talk to your mum, or to Colin about all this, about how hurt you feel, that's okay."

On her way out, Alexi stopped to talk to Kelly and Colin. "I think you know that David and I have been living with a problem that's been eating us up for a long time. Something we haven't talked about. I'm sure you've noticed and been praying for us – thank you! Well, just today, we started talking about it. Pastor Scott's arranging a service Thursday night at the church, where we'll talk about, about what happened. We want you to be a part of that. Please come if you possibly can." Her voice slowed. "It affects Naomi. She feels betrayed. I … I'm so sorry."

Alexi turned and fled. She had known talking to Naomi would be hard. It was a thousand times harder than she thought it would be. She didn't feel ready to drive straight home. Instead, she continued up to Fourth Street, and stopped under the trees.

For a long time, Alexi sat with her head bowed over the steering wheel. "Lord," she prayed, "aborting my baby was by far my greatest sin. That's what has been stifling the life out of me. Out of us. And yet, and yet, deceiving Naomi, pretending to her, destroying her trust, that cuts my heart even more!" She paused. "Is that alright Lord? Do you understand?" A longer pause, and then, "Please Lord, please, don't let her faith be destroyed! Lord, don't let her give up on you, just because I was such a fool!"

Dusk was falling as she turned into her driveway.

Chapter 28

That You May be Healed.

David called his parents. His father answered. "Hello Dad. Look, something's come up. I know you and Mum have been concerned for me – and for Alexi. Ever since our marriage in fact. You've known there was something we weren't talking about. You've asked a few times what was wrong, and I brushed you off."

Terry wasn't quite sure where this was going. "Yes, David. Yes, I have felt brushed off several times."

"I'm sorry Dad. I appreciate your concern – we appreciate it. It's just …. Well, anyway, I want to be able to tell you about this face to face. We've been talking to Pastor Scott, and he's arranging a service on Thursday night, where it will all come out. Can you and Mum come down to be part of that? I'm sorry Dad, I know this sounds sudden and mysterious, and … I hope you can come – I want you both to be part of it."

"Just a minute David. Let me talk to Mum." Very soon he was back at the phone. "David, we've no idea what's going on. But evidently, you've had some sort of breakthrough. We're very grateful for that. We'll drive down on Wednesday. Can we stay with you and Alexi, and the children?"

"Of course, Dad. Thank you so much Dad, thank you!"

"Thank you, David, for giving us a part of this. Here's Mum." He handed the phone to Esther.

"David," she said through tears, "I love you very much. And Alexi. We don't know quite what's happening, but it sounds like the breakthrough we've prayed for."

"Yes, Mum, it is. Thank you for praying. And thank you for coming. Can't wait to see you both."

"Can't wait to see you all! Give our love to Alexi."
Esther hung up the phone, and turned to Terry. "What can have
been the trouble Terry? Thank God, it seems to be breaking
open."

*

Crawford Delaware was the pastor who succeeded Scott
Lampton as senior pastor at Carrington Church. That night, he
was speaking to the youth group.

"Many of you will know David and Alexi Manning, who
used to lead the youth group. They were married six years ago,
and resigned as youth leaders at that time. But since then, some of
us have been concerned about just how they're doing. It seemed
there was an issue troubling them that they weren't able to talk
about. Well, just this week, they did admit to a rather serious
matter. They talked to Pastor Scott, who has arranged a special
service on Thursday night, where they will confess the matter
that's been on their hearts, and we'll join in praying for them, and
affirming forgiveness for them."

The room was very quiet. Each one listened intently.

"David and Alexi feel especially that they betrayed the
youth of the church," Pastor Crawford continued. "Now probably
all of you here today, were not here when they were the leaders.
But you represent those who were here at that time. So they
would like you to be part of the service on Thursday night. They
believe that what they have to say will be important for each of
you to hear. So you're invited to join in the service." Pastor
Crawford scanned the faces before him. No-one had any
questions. "This is not easy for David and Alexi. Please be in
prayer for them. Thanks."

*

While Pastor Crawford was talking to the young people, Naomi was sitting with Kelly and Colin, recounting what Alexi had told her. She was devastated to know that the most solid friend she'd ever had, hadn't been honest with her. Kelly and Colin both showed grave concern as they listened, acknowledging how deeply hurtful this was for her. But at the same time, they weren't inclined to accuse Alexi. Naomi was grateful for their comforting love for her, ready to listen and console. Especially she valued Colin's secure, solid, masculine presence, disquieted, but not alarmed. Without it, the hammer blows to her faith and trust would have been more damaging still.

*

Terry and Esther Manning arrived late in the afternoon on Wednesday. They greeted Alexi and David warmly, and were delighted as always to see their grandchildren.

"Look at Chloe, crawling all over the place, and pulling herself up on the chairs!" Esther laughed. "She'll be running after Bryce before long!"

David helped them take their bags into the guest room. "Would you like to freshen up after your journey?" he asked. "Cup of tea or coffee?"

"I guess it won't be too long before dinner," Terry answered. "I think I'll pass."

"Yes, I'm fine for now, thank you," agreed Esther.

"Well, Mum, Dad, I don't want to plunge you straight into this the moment you walk in the door. But I know you're anxious to hear what's up, and I don't want to spend time dancing around the obvious. Why don't we go into the lounge room now? Lexi will look after the children."

Terry and Esther exchanged a glance. "Okay, let's go," Terry responded.

For the next twenty minutes, Alexi could hear a low murmur of voices from the lounge as she moved about the kitchen. "What are they thinking? What will they think of me? Of

282

us?" Her heart was heavy as she went about her dinner preparation.

Finally, the door opened. They came back into the kitchen. Alexi eyes remained fixed on the dishes she was handling. "Are they angry? Thinking their son deserves better?"

Esther's face was wet with tears. She came straight to Alexi, and threw her arms around her. "Oh Alexi! Alexi! You poor, precious girl! How you've suffered!"

They stood hugged together, both weeping. Terry joined them. Esther noticed Bryce watching them anxiously.

"Bryce honey, it's alright. Mum and Gran and Pops are all kind of sad and glad at the same time. Do you want to come join us?" She reached out to draw him in.

David watched from the doorway, as his wife was affirmed and comforted. Gratitude swelled up in him.

*

On Thursday evening, Pastor Scott turned on the lights near the front of the sanctuary. Further back, the room was in darkness. David and Alexi, Terry and Esther, arrived at ten minutes before seven. Auntie Aggie was at their house, minding the children. Eric and Kathy came in next, with Hannah and Ted. There were hugs all round, though Alexi felt the wall of reserve still separating her from her mother. Colin and Kelly arrived, with Naomi.

Alexi hurried to Naomi, and whispered, "Thank you! Thank you!" Naomi gave the faintest of smiles in response.

Pastor Crawford came in, with twenty-five of the Youth Group.

Pastor Scott stood, noting that all seemed to be present. He prayed for the presence of God to be deeply felt by each one. Then he turned to David and Alexi.

"I'll go first," said Alexi, stepping up to stand beside the communion table. She took a deep breath, then began to describe how happy she and David had been with each other, until the night when, so unexpectedly, their restraint had cracked. Her voice was soft, but it carried easily to the three occupied rows of pews.

"How distraught we were," her voice pleaded with them all. "How angry with ourselves! We should have owned up. But we'd worked so hard with so many of the young people, building up their pride in themselves, protecting them from falling into sexual activity before the time was right. And here we were, smashing our own credibility. We couldn't face it. We started pretending that all was well, that nothing had changed."

Alexi paused for a long moment before continuing. "We hated pretending so much. But we began to get used to it. We thought, somehow, all would be well." She was still speaking slowly, softly. "Then, we discovered I was pregnant." A murmur ran along the rows of young people. "If it was shameful already, how could we cope with being pregnant?"

Suddenly, Alexi dropped to her knees. Her head was thrown back. "I killed my baby! I killed my baby!" Her voice rose into the high dimness, splintering off the wooden scrollwork. Now she leaned forward, her head on the floor, sobbing, sobbing.

A strangled cry came from the front row. Kathy leapt for her daughter, throwing herself down beside her, her own keening cries joining the echoes. "Lexi! Lexi! My love, Lexi my love!" All Kathy's reserve evaporated as she joined Alexi in her grief.

Naomi rose to her feet, her face wet with tears. Conflict raged within her. Compassion welled up as she watched Alexi's grief, but her own heart was still so raw, so freshly broken. Dumbly she moved to stand on the far side of Alexi, her hand on her head.

For several minutes Kathy and Alexi remained huddled on the floor. At length they stood, and hugged each other for more long moments. Naomi still stood beside them. As Kathy released Alexi, drawing back a little, Naomi moved hesitantly to offer her own hug. Her heart was still a maelstrom of love and pain, but she offered what she could.

"Thank you for asking me to join you." Naomi murmured the words, then disengaged, and moved back to her seat.

Now David came to stand with Alexi, holding her as she regained some composure. Someone brought her a glass of water. David returned to his seat, as Alexi concluded her confession.

"Aborting my baby was terrible. I've lived with that every day since. But there's one other thing that distresses me almost as much. It's the way I pretended. At least up to the wedding. I was dismayed at how easily I could call up the bright, bubbly, bride, all full of lightness and fun. How I hated myself for that. Please." She looked around the faces before her. "Please forgive me!"

Alexi stood with head bowed. Pastor Scott joined her, putting his arm across her shoulders. Tears marked his face too.

"Father," he prayed, "we have heard the confession of your daughter Alexi. We declare in the name of Jesus that she is forgiven. We declare in the name of Jesus that for her, the healing journey has begun."

Everyone began crowding around Alexi, blessing her, hugging her. The youth group members were deeply sobered. They came to her, many of them with tears overflowing, thanking her, telling her how blessed they were.

As everyone resumed their seats, Pastor Scott called on David. "Come and share your part of this story David."

David moved to take Alexi's place. "Lexi has told you of the heavy guilt that has been weighing us down, beginning in September of eighty-six. I have to tell you that none of this would have happened if I had shown the strength Alexi needed to see in me." He looked along the rows, before continuing.

"It began when I never thought to question the standard of romantic behavior that everyone seems to think is normal. That is, that young couples will cuddle some, kiss some, and not much more than that before they marry. That is what we did. And I didn't know any better. I didn't even know enough to think about it, or discuss it with Lexi. And I never knew until it was too late, how deeply that behavior affected her. Not that we kissed so very passionately. But it was enough to set her on edge. And I never knew that, because I never asked. I never even had the leadership to ask her about her thoughts. And she found it hard to tell me, because, as I said, what we were doing everyone seems to think is so 'normal'".

David stopped, and looked along the rows of young people. "I may sound quaint, but I tell you all. Save kissing for when you are married! It is intimate, arousing behavior! Don't do it until you are within the safety of your married nest!"

He threw a quick, loving smile to Alexi, before continuing. "Even so, all may have been well if I had not made another stupid mistake. It was almost by accident. I hadn't planned it. But one night I let my hand rest on Alexi's breast. I had a passing thought that we were close to being married, so why not? Again, I had no idea the effect it would have on her. She's been very generous in describing our blunder. Actually, the responsibility is mine. I was the one who disrespected her, who stupidly triggered us."

Again, his gaze went to the rows of youth. "Hear me! Leave all intimate behavior for the safety of marriage. That is where it belongs!"

All eyes were on David, in close attention. "I was weak again when we found Alexi was pregnant. The thought of abortion came up somehow. It horrified both of us. But on the other hand, revealing our weakness would blow everything so wide open. All our work with the youth, our future as leaders with any credibility. All those we had counselled and prayed with so earnestly. It seemed we had two equally impossible alternatives. So we left it hanging. Again, I didn't understand what was happening with Alexi. She felt incredibly alone, abandoned. How different it would have been if I had made strong choices at that point, declared that we would reveal our guilt, and come through somehow. It would have been hell. But nothing like the hell of aborting our baby, and betraying our friends."

David turned to face Alexi. He had been close to tears while he was speaking. Now they welled over, running down his cheeks. "Alexi, I have failed to be the man you needed me to be. I disrespected you. I abandoned you." He dropped to his knees. "Alexi, can you forgive me?"

She rose, and came to stand in front of him. "I forgive you my husband. I love you. Come, let's start over."

Again, Pastor Scott came to stand beside them. Again, he

prayed, declaring them absolved from their guilt, free to begin rebuilding. Again, all gathered around them, blessing them, thanking them.

*

When David and Alexi, Terry and Esther arrived home, Auntie Aggie was waiting for them.

"Alright my dear ones, already I see the light returning to your eyes, your shoulders are straighter. My heart is so joyful. But tonight, it's late. I will go now. And tomorrow you'll probably spend time with your families. So, Saturday morning Alexi, please come to me! Let us talk, and share your joy!"

Alexi hugged her tightly. Already, hugging Auntie Aggie felt like something she'd always done.

Chapter 29

Names New and Restored.

Terry and Esther, Eric and Kathy, were more than grateful that David and Alexi had broken out of their lonely despair. The grief and sadness left its deep mark on all of them, but on Friday morning, as Terry and Esther were farewelled back to Auckland, there was laughter, tears and hugs all round.

On Saturday morning, Alexi was impatient to keep her appointment with Auntie Aggie. Kathy was more delighted than ever to watch the children for her, telling her to take her time. She parked her car beside The Barn, and was about to enter, when Aggie appeared at the door of the cottage.

"Come, my dear," she called. "I have fresh scones, with raspberry jam."

Alexi gave a little giggle, and ran to join her. They sat at the kitchen table, with tea and scones before them. But the tea became cold, and the scones were neglected as they chatted, their full hearts bubbling over.

Aggie had been praying for them throughout the service on Thursday, and she had felt much of it in her spirit. But she wanted to hear Alexi share all that had happened.

"The young ones were clearly very moved," Alexi told her. "They thanked us over and over for sharing our blunders, and all the sorrow that resulted. They were so kind!"

Aggie's eyes glowed. She was warmed by the gladness flowing from Alexi.

"But guess what Aggie!" Alexi was unaware she had dropped the 'Auntie.' "David was so strong! I was so proud of him! He took responsibility, said that as my husband the buck stopped with him! He said that he disrespected me by touching my breast that night. And about the kissing – he never thought for himself about that, or asked me what I thought about it. He apologized to me – in front of everyone! Already it's different! I feel safer with him, more protected than I've ever felt before!"

Her eyes shone, even as fresh tears filled them. Aggie moved around the table, and they stood hugged together, tears flowing from them both. A few moments later, Aggie gave a start, pulling back from Alexi.

"Lexi!" she cried. "Lexi! Look at me! I'm crying! I'm really crying! I'm bawling like a baby!"

She knelt on the floor, face raised, lifted up with amazement. Her hands passed over her face, feeling its wetness.

"All my life, all my life, as long as I can remember, I've never really cried. Even when Ky died." Her voice was filled with wonder. "My tears were always stop-and-start, one by one. Never a flow like this! Now, look at me! My face is a mess!"

For a long time she knelt, silent, lost in her thoughts. Alexi could see the joy and wonder in her face, and didn't interrupt. Eventually, Aggie spoke again, her voice barely above a whisper.

"Lexi, it's strange isn't it, that I should be so filled with joy that I can cry, really cry? Something's happening to me! I believe it's to do with privately carrying your grief for so long, and now sharing your joy that the pain is breaking up. And it's happening for me too! All the hurts, going back as long as I can remember." Her voice trailed off, her gaze meeting Alexi's. Something of the wonder stirring in her heart was communicated to Alexi – her heart too felt strangely stirred.

"I never knew, I never realized." Aggie seemed to be speaking to herself, though she knew Alexi was there, listening. "I never knew how much I walled myself off. I can see it now, an old mossy stone wall, built with layers of dressed stones, about four feet high. Built in a square, right around my heart. But it's breaking up!" Her voice rose above a whisper, speaking now directly to Alexi. "I see cracks right through it, and the stones are sliding off, falling to the ground!"

Alexi had come to Aggie in gladness that her own pain was breaking up. Now her gladness was doubled as she found their roles reversed – she was supporting Aggie, as much older barriers around her heart cracked and began to tumble.

Aggie stood up. "Alexi my dear," she said, "let's make a fresh pot of tea! Or would you rather have coffee?" Gaiety came back into her voice and her face. She smiled brightly at Alexi.

They sat with fresh cups of tea before them. "Aggie," began Alexi. She was becoming dimly aware that she was using Aggie's name without the customary 'Auntie.' But it seemed to no longer matter. She brushed the thought aside. "Aggie, do you know that as well as your tears, your smile is breaking out in a new way? Not that you ever looked exactly grumpy. But now you're smiling all over your face!"

"Am I? I am too! Oh, my Lord, what new things are you doing for me! How grateful I am! Thank you that my friend Alexi is here to share this with me."

Their eyes met again across the table. Spontaneously they rose, and danced together around the room, giggling as they circled.

"Goodness," laughed Aggie five minutes later as they plopped back into their chairs, "how long is it since I did anything like that?"

"I think the new you started to break out quite a while ago," observed Alexi. "Way back at our wedding, you told us we were welcome at The Barn. Of course, we'd made ourselves welcome without ever asking!" she added mischievously. "And then when you had us stay the night with you a week ago. That was so special! Besides the privilege of staying at your house, it felt like a whole new friendship with you was opening up."

Warm gratitude filled Aggie's face. "Thank you, Lexi. Do you have any idea how happy I was to welcome you? It did my heart so much good to have you stay. I felt guilty when I realized my guest room hadn't been used since before Ky died. And not too often before that! And I feel so guilty to realize how much I've closed myself off."

Aggie's face became sober again as she thought of the unsuspected defenses around her heart. "That wall was growing before my memories begin," she said. "It started with my birthmark. That seemed to wall me off from other people. They mocked me. And the bullying through school. When Ky and I couldn't have children, that added a couple of courses of stones. When Mum died I was overwhelmed, but then Ky died not too long after! Oh, layers of long, heavy stones weighing me down!" She closed her eyes, then spoke again. "But now! Lexi, the lightness that's beginning to seep into me! I just can't describe it! Lexi, thank you, thank you for coming to confess your despair to me. Do you see how being admitted to your heart is blessing me, way beyond anything I could have imagined?"

They sat in silence, hands clasped across the table.

*

As Alexi drove to Te Whiti to pick up her children, long buried gladness swirled in her heart. She'd forgotten it was possible to feel such lightness. The contrast with the heaviness she had lived with so long was enough to bring tears pricking behind her eyes again. When she came into the kitchen at Shepperd's Rest, Kathy saw immediately the new peace in her face. It was enough to have her run to her daughter again, flinging her arms around her.

"Lexi, my heart is breaking with happiness to see the dark clouds leaving you! Oh, I love you so much!"

*

David and Alexi began growing closer again. It would take time for years of irritation with each other to be turned around, but they were each deeply grateful for the new wind blowing through their home. Each day, their appreciation for each other grew. A new sense of love welled up, reminding them of the days before their world crashed. Alexi noticed that David was taking care to sound out her thoughts and feelings on a whole range of issues. Evidently his words had been sincere – he didn't want to overlook anything that was important to her, as he had in the past. In response, she felt a new sense of security in his love. He really did want to look out for her. It was early days, and they would likely need some help along the way, but for now, they were enjoying a rekindled friendship.

As the weeks passed, their lovemaking became once again a time of comfort and connection, something they looked forward to. Alexi was still not able to fully abandon herself to David, but even so, it was nice.

Since their marriage, they had gotten into a pattern of few social contacts. Apart from Kelly and Colin, they rarely visited anyone. The habit didn't change immediately; first they needed time to settle into a new security with each other. So the changes taking place were not immediately obvious to the Carrington Church community. But to close friends, and family, David and Alexi looked like a new couple. Pastor Crawford called on them several times, and was encouraged by what he saw.

It was different for Aggie. Everyone noticed that something new was happening with her. Suddenly, her smile was full of brightness and welcome. She began inviting people to The Barn, and visiting friends in their own homes. From being a respected but peripheral figure, Aggie took on a new kind of energy. Before, she would give her small, soft smile, and walk on by – now, she became engaged with people, pausing to chat and laugh.

*

One afternoon, Alexi was at The Barn. Aggie was busy baking when she arrived, so she lay Bryce and Chloe on Aggie's bed for a nap, then returned to sit at the kitchen table. Soon she rose, and went to help roll out some dough. The two women chatted brightly, but Aggie noticed Alexi seemed to have something on her mind. She hazarded a guess.

"How's life for you and David?" she asked. "Still falling

in love all over again?"

Alexi smiled, a little hesitantly. "David's trying really hard," she said. "He's taking time to be with the children, being firm with them when they need it, and playing with them. They love it when he's around." She sprinkled more flour onto the dough she was rolling. "And with me, well I know he's trying to be nice. But sometimes, he just doesn't seem to get the way I'm feeling. Oh, I don't know, maybe it's just me."

She gave Aggie a wry smile. Aggie nodded, encouraging her to continue. "For a while it seemed we were getting off to a really good start. But now ... He'll say something, and then it seems I take him the wrong way, and I get a little snappy back to him, so he gets hurt, and ..." She sighed. "I think I'm having a hard time really trusting him again. And it's not fair – I was just as much at fault as he was."

Aggie looked at her thoughtfully. "Lexi, you told me that first disastrous time you came together, that it was awful. Is it still, well, awful?"

Auntie Aggie was so knowing and wise. Alexi had a fleeting thought that she could probably ask any question she liked without seeming intrusive.

"No, no, it's nice," she replied quickly. "Those times, and just lying cuddled up together, those are the best times. Although, even then, there's still something in me that holds back. David notices it I'm sure. I think he gets a little frustrated. I've never come fully to ... you know, to ..."

"Never reached your climax?" Aggie used the word for her.

Alexi nodded, eyes fixed on her task with the rolling pin.

"You know, there was a marriage counsellor ... let's see, what was his name?" Aggie searched her memory. "Dr. Wakeman, that's it. Ky went to him a couple of times before we were married. Ky wanted to find out how much he didn't know, that he needed to know! He thought Dr. Wakeman was really helpful. Good ideas on how couples understand each other, build their friendship, communicate with each other. He was good on the bedroom stuff too."

Alexi looked up. That sounded promising.

293

"Of course, it was a long time ago," added Auntie Aggie. "He used to be in Upper Hutt. Maybe he's moved on or retired."

At home that evening with David, Alexi cautiously opened the topic. "David, we're doing so much better than we were. So much better. And yet, we still seem to end up getting under each other's skin. It's probably me more than you – I just don't know how to do better. Auntie Aggie was telling me today about this marriage counsellor Ky went to before they were married. Ky thought he was very helpful. Do you think it would help us to find someone like that? I want us to be able to move on from the little spats we have."

David sat, considering. "It's a pretty deep hole we're digging ourselves out of," he answered. "It wouldn't hurt I guess." He paused. "It does sound scary. I'd be scared that someone would be telling me what to do or say, when they don't really know me, don't understand me. But anyway, let's give it a try. I'll see if I can find this Dr. Wakeman.

It turned out that Dr. Wakeman had retired. He was living in a snug retirement house in the hills north of Martinborough. And yes, he was open to still seeing the occasional client at his home. David made an appointment.

Over the next few months, Ky's recommendation, as handed on through Aggie, proved accurate. Dr. Wakeman was able to show them gentler, more attentive ways of listening to each other, building their trust in each other. After a few weeks, they started working as well on the intimacy issue. As Alexi learned to relax, releasing any sense of demand, letting her enjoyment slowly build, so her sense of arousal gradually returned.

Auntie Aggie visited Alexi's house now, almost as often as Alexi came up to The Barn. Alexi gave her occasional updates on their progress with Dr. Wakeman. On a morning late in June, with the leaves outside covered in frost, Alexi shyly gave her news.

"Well, my dear friend, a while ago I told you I was a woman without a climax. Today, I can tell you that has changed."

Auntie Aggie gave a knowing smile. "That is wonderful Lexi! Let me give you a hug" Even after knowing the new Aggie for many weeks now, it still felt a little incongruous to Alexi, thinking of reserved, constrained Auntie Aggie as she had been, who way back then, had never-the-less experienced the delight with her husband Ky that Alexi was just discovering with David. Alexi shook her head, wondering at the strange complexity of her friend.

They went on to talk about the worship and Bible study time coming up on Friday. For about a month, a diverse group had been meeting at The Barn each Friday evening. They called it Bible study, and of course they did have their Bibles at hand, but mostly, it was informal, usually beginning with some well-loved songs, before lapsing into a prayer time that was mostly individual, yet within a corporate sense of experiencing the Lord's presence together. Eric and Kathy were part of the group, along with Hannah and Ted. Colin and Kelly joined in too, and Colin's mother Zoe. Zoe was into her seventies now, yet still healthy and active. She lived still in her own house, though there were plans afoot to build a second dwelling on Colin and Kelly's property where she could live. It was more to reduce her isolation than because she needed physical care.

David and Alexi brought the children each Friday. They each had a small bed placed a little further back in The Barn, away from the light, where they could sleep undisturbed. Even for the adults, the only illumination was from the fire, flickering and glowing from the fireplace.

That Friday, as Alexi watched David, guitar chords flowing from his fingers, the firelight chasing shadows around him, her heart swelled with gratitude for the renewal they were finding - individually, as a couple, and as a family. "Thank you, Lord," she breathed. "Even after … after everything, you're still picking up the pieces of my life again! Thank you, Lord."

*

Another three weeks passed. Now the days became really wintry and cold. The Friday evening group was glad of

295

both the light and the warmth of the fire. That evening, David and Alexi had an announcement. "We're pregnant!" The rest of the group crowded around them, all delighted, congratulating them. Eric and Kathy's joy soared of course, but even more so knowing the renewal of the home to which the little one would come.

Alexi managed to pull Aggie aside long enough to whisper, "I think it was the night when I ... You know, I told you ..."

"Oh, yes, when you reached your ... Oh, yes, how special!" They shared a conspiratorial giggle.

As usual, they sang for some twenty minutes, feeling the Holy Spirit move and settle among them. Then quietness gathered them in, punctuated by cracks and sighings from the fire. Aggie was sitting on the edge of the group, over near where the children lay sleeping. Presently, she heard a familiar Voice.

"Dearest, it's several months now since I gave you back your tears and your smile. Are you glad of them?"

"Oh, yes Lord! Thank you!"

"Yes. You are using them well. That stone wall around your heart is all but gone."

A pause. Then, "Dearest, tonight you heard that Alexi is with child again. She is carrying a son."

"A son? Lord! You're telling me their secrets? David and Alexi don't know that!"

"The secret is safe with you. I have a reason for telling you. Dear One, knowing she is carrying a son, do you envy her?"

Aggie took her time. Finally, she said, "Lord, that is tough. I did so want children. At least a son for Ky. It was so hard when I didn't conceive. So, yes, maybe a little. But no, not really. I'm glad, glad for them, for all you're doing for them. Yes, I am!" She could almost feel the embrace of the Lord's arms around her.

"Beautiful Daughter, Alexi also told you there was joy at his making. Do you envy her for that?"

Again, Aggie's words came slowly. "Lord, you know how much I miss Ky! What a gift he was to me. You know I sometimes long to feel his arms around me again! But no, I don't envy Alexi. Thank you, thank you for restoring that delight to her!"

"Well-spoken Dearest. Now it's time to take back your name. Cup your hands in front of you."

"Hands cupped?" Without realizing it, Aggie spoke aloud. She pushed her chair back a little as she held her hands in front of her. It was enough for the others in the room to notice. They watched to see what was happening.

Aggie leaned forward, peering into her hands. Something was forming there. A large pearl, quickly growing to fill her cupped hands. As it grew, a pale blue radiance glowed through it and around it. As Aggie watched, a word appeared, dark blue flowing script across the top of the pearl. "Agnes."

The others watching couldn't see what was in her hands, but they could see the blue glow showing through her fingers.

She spoke aloud again. "It's beautiful, marvelous!" Then, "It's my name! The Lord is saying I'm to take back my name, Agnes. It's the same as Ky saw! A pearl, a beautiful pearl, with my name written across it! Agnes!"

"Yes, Agnes. No more Aggie," the Lord spoke in her heart again. "You are Agnes, or perhaps for the children, Miss Agnes. I know you will wear your name well."

Nobody wanted to leave. They crowded around Agnes, embracing her, affirming her name. So Auntie Aggie disappeared from Carrington Church. In her place was a wise, friendly, woman of God whom everyone knew as Agnes.

That night, as she fell asleep, Agnes felt herself to be more closely held in the Lord's loving embrace than ever before.

*

The next Friday evening, everyone was still buoyed by the experience they had shared with Agnes. Following last Friday, it seemed that this night could only be an anticlimax. But no, the Lord had a fresh revelation for them. This time he spoke to Alexi and David.

They had settled again into their time of personal listening prayer. All seemed as normal for about half an hour, when Alexi spoke.

"The Lord is giving me a picture. There's something very clear, very real about this one. I'm sitting beside a creek. It's a spring morning. I can hear the bees in the flowers, and there are tuis and bellbirds. Oh, I know where it is. It's the Totara Creek, just above Totara Flats Hut. The track is winding down past the creek, towards the hut. It's so pretty."

She paused for a few minutes. The others watched her, sensing the presence of the Lord.

"There's someone coming up the track. Coming from the hut. It's someone with long black hair. A man. And there's a child walking with him, holding his hand. It's a girl, a little girl, about six, skipping along holding his hand. It's Jesus' hand! Yes, Jesus is walking towards me, with this beautiful little girl."

Alexi's eyes were closed, her cheeks a little flushed. She was evidently seeing this scene very clearly.

"They're getting closer to me. Jesus has stopped, but the child is walking slowly on towards me. She's stopped in front of me, looking at me with big, curious eyes. She looks like, like me. No, she looks like David."

Suddenly she leapt to her feet, eyes wide, turning towards David. "David, it's our daughter! Jesus is showing me our daughter! Oh, she's beautiful!"

Alexi dropped to her knees, bending forward with head to the floor. "Precious, precious girl!" she murmured. Then her head came up again. "David, her name, she says we never gave her a name! What's her name?"

Their eyes locked for a long moment. Then they burst out in unison, "Agnes Joy! Her name is Agnes Joy!"

Alexi's eyes closed again, head in her hands. "Agnes Joy, dear one. Your name is Agnes Joy." After a moment, she spoke again. "She's going back towards Jesus, skipping, saying her name. She's carrying a soft toy in her hand. She's reached Jesus. He catches her up, holding her. They're laughing together. Now, he's put her down. They're coming on up the track. They're walking by me. She's still skipping and laughing. Jesus is turning his head towards me, he's smiling at me! They've gone on by, disappearing round the bend in the track."

298

For the second time in two weeks, the group in The Barn felt overwhelmed by the Lord's kindness. Alexi especially, as she clung to David, was murmuring, "Thank you Lord, thank you! Why are you so kind to me?"

*

Agnes felt a tiny tremor under her feet. She looked up, listening. The mountains stirred, a small quiver sighing through their roots. They were silent again.

*

Two weeks later, Alexi called at The Barn to show Agnes a baby blanket she had begun knitting in preparation for their new arrival. She had plenty of time, but it was a pretty pattern she had noticed, so she was making an early start. They were in Agnes' bedroom, where Bryce and Chloe had fun rolling back and forth on Agnes' bed.

Agnes and Alexi were still talking about the special vision she had of the daughter she had never seen, and the opportunity to name her.

"Agnes, I remember when we talked with you at our wedding, you said you still have Bagley, the teddy I gave you when I was just little. Mum told me that sad things had happened to you, so I wanted you to have him, so you wouldn't be so sad."

"I've always kept Bagley Lexi. You were so sweet to give him to me, and I've kept him, sitting up right over there in that chair. Except ...."

But Alexi was continuing. "Agnes, I just realized this morning. You know I said that Agnes Joy was carrying a soft toy? Well, that's what it was! It was Bagley! I suddenly remembered what it looked like, the toy she was carrying! It was my old teddy!"

299

Alexi stopped. Agnes was looking at her wide-eyed. "Lexi, I was just going to tell you! It's so strange. That teddy has always sat, tucked into that chair over there in the corner. But he's gone! I know I haven't moved him. But for the last two weeks, he's been missing!"

Now both of them were incredulous, staring at each other.

"Enoch …. disappeared …… because God took him away. Do you suppose …....." murmured Alexi.

"I don't know," said Agnes, "but I guess the Lord knows I don't need Bagley anymore."

About the Author.

Gordon grew up on the North Island of New Zealand. During his last year of High School, his family moved to Masterton, close by the Tararua Range. It was there that he became familiar with its peaks, trails and hiking huts, and also the beautiful Wairarapa District.

In 1968, Gordon was married to Tricia, the love of his life. There have been many strands to his life, including school teacher, computer consultant, cab driver, missionary, …. The latter began when Gordon and Tricia joined Youth with a Mission, working in Primary Health Care and Counseling. They were based in Hawaii for several years, moving out from there to minister in Asia and South America.

After returning to home base in New Zealand, God called them a few years later to move to the US, where Gordon completed his qualification in Marriage and Family Therapy. They live in Connecticut, not far from their daughter and grandson, though at a much greater leap to their son in Melbourne Australia.